Therapist Gold

Treating Fear Based Trauma and Attachment Trauma

Gordon Emmerson & Christiane Essing

Copyright Gordon Emmerson 2025

Old Golden Point Press

Blackwood, Victoria:

Australia

ISBN-10: 9924995-7-0

ISBN-13: 978-0-9924995-7-0

Contents

List of Illustrations

List of Tables

Foreword

Once again Gordon Emmerson surprises us with his new work.

As a scientifically and psychotherapeutically active colleague, he has succeeded in gaining Christiane Essing, co-founder of the German Resource Therapy Center, one of the most internationally experienced Resource Therapy (RT) trainers and therapists, as co-author for his latest project. As a result of their profound knowledge and expertise, the two have succeeded in presenting a book that is the product of the rich experience of both authors.

I met Gordon Emmerson at the Parts Conference in Heidelberg in 2011. He introduced us to a new psychotherapeutic system, which he called Resource Therapy. He asked for a volunteer for a demonstration, so I was able to experience his work personally.

Trained in depth psychology, Gestalt and Ego State Therapy, I was fascinated by the clear structure and organization of his method. Emmerson was a student of Watkins, the founder of Ego State Therapy. This may be the reason why different approaches entered into a fruitful liaison in Emmerson's development of Resource Therapy: On the one hand, his precise scientific way of thinking and, on the other hand, his contact with psychodynamic theory and therapy.

Ego States were first mentioned by Freud's colleague Paul Federn (Federn, 1952), whose student was Eduardo Weiss, who eventually trained John Watkins.

In the prologue to his book "Resource Therapy, the complete guide with case examples & transcripts", Emmerson writes, "Resource Therapy (RT) is a new, brief Psychodynamic Therapy. It provides detail and clear regiments to respond to the causal factors that result in pathology." (Emmerson, 2014)

The author continues, "The psychodynamic movement had succeeded in creating a theoretical understanding of the causes of pathology but failed to find ways to address these causes in order to eliminate the symptoms."

Emmerson states, "The cause of psychological distress was left unresolved, while the therapeutic focus was on attending to the symptoms.

Foreword

What is needed is:

1) A theory of personality that accurately recognizes the cause of psychological stress, and

2) A clear intervention strategy to enable therapists to locate and to resolve these causes.

When the causes of pathology are resolved the symptoms related to that pathology are also resolved. It is important to understand the precise parts of the personality that relate to specific types of pathological symptoms.

In this book, Emmerson and Essing go into more detail about precisely this approach to resolve fear-based and attachment-based trauma. They represent two of the most common pathologies of the RT model: Vaded with Fear and Vaded with Rejection. In the usual clear presentation, you will be guided from the process of making an exact diagnosis and its possible pitfalls to the RT-specific interventions, and you will be given the opportunity to gain a deeper insight into the differentiated diagnostic and therapeutic process by means of detailed and diverse case examples.

The most important basic features of the RT personality theory and the 8 pathologies are deepened, expanded and considered in different contexts. The ICD diagnoses are linked to the two pathologies Vaded with Fear and Vaded with Rejection, the various forms of expression of anxiety and psychological traumatization are discussed and explained in the context of RT-specific diagnostics and therapy.

The structured layout, clear tables and detailed illustrations make reading easier and promote understanding the approach. With this book, the two authors have succeeded in adding an essential work to the literature on Resource Therapy. Reading the book, you can feel that it is an important personal concern for both of them to share their profound knowledge with others for the benefit of patients. They deserve our thanks and recognition for this!

This book is helpful for RT-experienced therapists as well as therapists familiarizing themselves with RT. It provides both extensive input and a reference option at their disposal, offering valuable guidance and support. It is to be hoped that the fruitful collaboration between the two authors will be continued and supplemented in a similar form in the treatment of other RT pathologies.

I am sure Paul Federn would be delighted and proud of his great-grandchildren's generation.

Dr. Karlheinz Erbe, Bamberg, March 2025

    Neurologist, Psychiatrist

    Child and Adolescent Psychiatrist

    Vice President: Resource Therapy International

Preface

Fear Based Trauma and Attachment Trauma

This book explains and provides interventions for two major areas of therapy:

1) **Fear Based Trauma** is the underlying cause for anxiety disorders, panic attacks, phobias, PTSD, agoraphobia, baseless physical fears, and other fear related disorders.

2) **Attachment Trauma** is the underlying cause for feelings of inadequacy (I'm not good enough), the need to please, over-competitiveness, fear to stay in a relationship, and for all eating disorders. Both fear-based trauma and attachment trauma are the core reasons for addictions, Obsessive Compulsive Disorder (OCD) and most unwanted behaviors, as these behaviors are a form of self-medication to avoid the anxieties of these traumas.

These two problem areas make up a major portion of client presentations. They are areas where clients are often less responsive to treatment.

Resource Therapy

The personality has different parts or states. One state may be confident, and another state may feel more fragile. One state may gamble, and another state may hate gambling. When healthy, these different parts are our resources.

Resource Therapy (RT) is a therapy with the purpose to help resources move from sometimes working against each other to working together, from sometimes feeling overwhelmed to feeling supported and appreciated, from sometimes being pathological to being healthy. It is a highly focused intervention that provides a way for therapists to work directly with the part of the personality that can benefit from change.

Resource Therapy is a modern, brief psychodynamic approach that offers structured methods to directly address the root causes of psychological distress. Traditional psychodynamic therapies, led by Freud, recognized that early life trauma contributes to later psychological issues. However, they lacked effective techniques to resolve these issues, leading to the rise of approaches like Cognitive Behavioral Therapy (CBT), which focused more on symptom management than resolving underlying trauma.

RT builds on the psychodynamic understanding of trauma but introduces precise interventions that aim to heal the origins of pathology, not just its symptoms. It emphasizes the need for a clear theoretical understanding of pathology and targeting interventions.

RT views the personality as made up of different "Resources" or parts. When these parts become pathological, they cause distress:

- **Vaded States** hold negative emotions.
- **Retro States** perform unwanted behaviors.
- **Conflicted States** are in opposition with other parts.
- **Dissonant States** functionally hold the conscious when another state would be preferred.

Resource Therapy offers clear diagnostic tools and techniques for accessing and resolving these states, leading to symptom relief and the restoration of healthy personality functioning. RT is applicable to the complete range of conditions, including OCD, depression, addictions, eating disorders, and PTSD.

States that are Vaded

The term **Vaded** refers to a state that is holding a pathological level of emotion. It has been (in)vaded with a level of emotion that the client cannot process, and this unprocessed emotion can cause issues for the client later. A state with Fear Based Trauma is Vaded with Fear and a state holding Attachment-Based Trauma is Vaded with Rejection.

This book details how to find the cause of these pathologies and how to resolve the negative feelings associated with them. It is grounded in a broad-based personality theory and includes a diagnostic classification with eight pathologies covering the spectrum of psychological disorders. A clear and direct way to resolve the causes of Fear Based Trauma and Attachment Trauma is detailed. Finding the exact causes for the symptoms and attending to them directly brings positive change.

Acknowledgements

Christiane Essing

Firstly, I would like to express my gratitude to Professor Gordon Emmerson for developing Resource Therapy, for introducing it to the professional world, and for his unwavering dedication to promote it worldwide. It was during a congress in Heidelberg that I had the privilege of learning about RT. This encounter has had a life-changing impact on both my personal and professional life.

I also thank Dr. Karlheinz Erbe and his wife Margareta Viering, who have committed themselves selflessly to helping others. They got the ball rolling, and together we founded the Resource Therapy Center Germany (Ressourcen-Therapie Zentrum Deutschland).

I'm also incredibly grateful to my awesome family, my husband Bernd, our son Simon and his partner Anna Lena, who have been so supportive and understanding during my frequent absences while I was busy writing. The extent of the hours devoted to being co-author of a book was initially surely underestimated.

I would also like to thank my clients. It is through them that I get to witness the beauty of RT every day: How respectful, powerful, and effective it is, and at the same time its great inherent naturalness and logic. Learning from working with my clients' parts is what made my contribution to this book possible in the first place.

Last but not least, with a wink, I would like to thank "THERAPIST", "DEDICATED", "CREATIVE", "GIVING", "CURIOUS" and all other parts of me that were involved for their active and helpful participation in this process.

Gordon Emmerson

I want to thank my son, Daniel, for his rock-solid support through all endeavors I attempt, and my friend, Delwyn Goodrick, for her final read of the document and for her steadfast support.

Acknowledgements

I also want to thank my co-author, Christiane Essing, for her brilliant understanding and incisively clear communication of the Resource Therapy process. My deepfelt appreciation and gratitude goes to her.

Introduction: What is Therapist Gold?

All client problems have a cause. Finding and resolving that cause is the goal. While clients sometimes report knowing the cause of their problem, they will often later conclude their initial reasoning was mistaken. It is locating and processing the root of the client's issues that is 'Therapist Gold'.

How a client presents

Clients come to therapy with different types of issues. Not all problems have to do with issues buried from experiences in their past, but some do. Not all problems are a reaction to former trauma, but many are. When an unresolved state is responsible for a negative emotional reaction it is important for the state that carries that anxiety to gain a feeling of peace and appreciation. Then, when it comes into the Conscious again it will hold these more positive feelings instead of anxieties or feelings of insufficiencies.

When clients feel an emotion that doesn't match what is happening around them it most likely comes from a part that is carrying unresolved feelings from the past.

I (Gordon) worked with a woman who had such a fear of spiders she could not even be close to a picture of a spider. Intellectually, she understood that the picture could not hurt her, but emotionally she experienced a high level of fear, and she had to get away from the picture. In a single session we found the cause of this fear, resolved it and later that evening she was able to catch a spider she found in her house and carry it outside and set it free.

If a wild dog is coming at you growling and baring its teeth, or if you get so close to the edge of a cliff that there is a danger that you might slip and fall, then fear is your friend. It helps keep you safe. But, if you are afraid of a picture of a spider, fear is not your friend. That fear comes from an unresolved event in the past.

There is a reason for everything. If your car doesn't start, there is a reason. If there is an explosion, there is a reason. If a client has an emotion that seems like it came from nowhere, there is a reason. Therapist Gold is finding this reason. Therapist Gold is finding the origin of the problem and resolving it.

Then, when done properly, the negative feeling is gone. The part that held the negative feeling then feels connected and safe.

Client's description of the problem

Clients may describe negative events they have experienced, and they may present a negative event as the cause of their problem. But not all negative experiences cause pathology. We need a method to connect today's negative emotion to the precise unresolved event it relates to. When we find the exact causal event, we avoid superfluous work, and we ensure the best opportunity for change. There is little benefit in working through events with clients that have nothing to do with the symptoms of their presenting concern.

The therapist

Therapists invest a lot of energy in finding the right way to help their clients, but often they don't know which interventions will resolve the cause for their client's presenting concern. Finding the cause and knowing exactly what to do when the cause is evident can result in more effectiveness, direction and lightness in the therapeutic process.

Addressing the client's problem in the way described in this book is a gentle and highly powerful therapeutic procedure and can result in getting to the root cause much faster than expected, often within minutes. It is recommended for the therapist to gain some personal experience as a client with this method to be better aware of its power and depth.

Working with highly emotional clients

Many therapists, when the client gets highly emotional during a session, will back off and return to stabilizing the client, fearing the client could be overwhelmed or re-traumatized. This is a lost opportunity to help the frightened state that has assumed the Conscious. At this time, when we can see the emotional state, we have the exact state that needs help in the Conscious. Bringing a traumatized state into the Conscious and 'backing off' can be re-traumatizing, and it can make the state feel its problems are too big to be helped. Processing the state's negative feelings and help it feel empowered and supported is de-traumatizing.

Diagnosing the pathological state into the right category and finding the cause is the best way to help the pathological state and de-traumatize the client. It is a very gentle way for the client to be freed of fear or a negative core self-belief.

Fear Based Trauma: Vaded with Fear

A person is traumatized when he or she experiences an overwhelming event which cannot be integrated and processed. Fear Based Trauma occurs, when the overwhelming event causes the person to fear for their life or their physical safety.

Since children don't have enough understanding of life and fewer coping abilities, they are much more prone to being traumatized than adults. Little things can traumatize, or, in other words, "vade" little people. Often an event that can traumatize a child does not appear traumatizing at all to an adult. Parents may not realize that an experience was too overwhelming for the child. They may not even be aware it happened.

Clients, at first, will not be able to identify what could have had such a great impact to cause a psychological disorder later.

A State Vaded with Fear is almost always vaded in childhood and the client is often not aware of the event that caused the traumatization. Therefore, a special technique is needed to find this event. This technique is called "Bridging" and will be explained in detail later in the book.

If an event results in Fear Based Trauma during adulthood, clients know exactly when their fear started. The unwanted symptoms would not have been present prior to the traumatizing event. Usually these are "big events" that would be difficult to process for most people, like a war, an accident, a natural catastrophe, or aggravated assault. In this case, therapists can process the trauma directly, without having to bridge.

How do we know if a client has a State Vaded with Fear? A State Vaded with Fear will, when conscious, be physically afraid. A State Vaded with Fear can cause pathologies such as those listed in Table 1.

Introduction: What is Therapist Gold?

Table 1: Sample of Pathologies related to Vaded with Fear

Pathology	Relation to "Vaded with Fear
Anxiety Disorders	**Vaded with Fear** represents a heightened state of anxiety, where the individual is overwhelmed by irrational fears. In Resource Therapy, this state is addressed by identifying the parts that hold this fear and helping the client access more resourceful, calm, and grounded states to overcome it.
Borderline Personality Disorder	The fear of abandonment and emotional instability in borderline personality disorder can be linked to a **Vaded with Fear** state. Resource Therapy works with the parts of the self that feel fear-driven and unstable, helping to access internal resources for emotional regulation.
Obsessive-Compulsive Disorder (OCD)	OCD is often driven by obsessive thoughts rooted in fear (e.g., fear of contamination or harm). **Vaded with Fear** states in Resource Therapy may be addressed by working with the parts that hold these irrational fears and obsessions, while activating internal resources that provide relief and control, reducing compulsive behaviors.
Post-Traumatic Stress Disorder (PTSD)	PTSD involves recurring, intense fear and anxiety linked to traumatic events. For a **Vaded with Fear** state, in Resource Therapy we would work to resolve the fearful part stuck in the trauma and work to bring in healing resources to process the trauma, manage the fear, and restore stability and safety.
Dissociative Identity Disorder (DID)	DID involves fragmented personalities, often due to trauma and overwhelming fear. The **Vaded with Fear** states represent the fearful, dissociated parts. Resource Therapy aims to access these parts fostering healthier, more cohesive states of self, reducing the fear and confusion that come from fragmented identities.

For the complete list of associated pathologies see Table 13: Vaded with Fear Pathologies, on page 369.

20

Attachment Trauma: Vaded with Rejection

Attachment Trauma occurs when the overwhelming event causes a person to feel rejected to such an extent that the resulting feelings of inadequacy, loneliness, disorientation or worthlessness are too much to integrate and process. The state is frozen from then on in its negative core beliefs and low self-worth.

A State Vaded with Rejection was almost always vaded in childhood. It is extremely rare for this not to be the case. Clients may think they know when their childhood issues started, but they are usually wrong. The overwhelming event that caused the traumatization is called the "Initial Sensitizing Event" (ISE) (Bosewell, 1987).

"Initial," because we are looking for the first time the state experienced these overwhelming feelings. There might have been many similar experiences during the client's childhood, but to resolve the cause, we need to go to the root. In order to get to the root, the Bridging technique needs to be applied so that we can gain access to the emotional memory, as the client will not be able to remember intellectually what caused the injury. The unresolved emotions will lead the way to the Initial Sensitizing Event, and afterward, the client will understand the connection between the ISE and the adult feelings.

How do we know if a client has a State Vaded with Rejection?

A State Vaded with Rejection will feel 'not good enough'. It may feel unlovable. The client may have a strong need for approval, may feel horrible when not approved of, and may feel great when approval is there. There may be a feeling of never really being loved, "I am told I am loved, but I'm not really loved because I am a fake." The client may be afraid to start something new because of a fear of not being good enough, or of being found out.

There may be a need to compete, not to enjoy the competition but 'to be good enough', to have either clothes, car, house, or a body that can bring approval. Vaded with Rejection can result in shopping addiction, eating disorders, or narcissism. Vaded with Rejection can result in these clients seeing others on a hierarchy, either above or below themselves. They may gain or lose self-worth according to how they see themselves on that hierarchy.

Introduction: What is Therapist Gold?

A State Vaded with Rejection can cause many pathologies, such as those listed in Table 2.

Table 2: Sample of Pathologies related to Vaded with Rejection

Condition	Relation to "Vaded with Rejection" in Resource Therapy
Anorexia Nervosa	**Vaded with Rejection** in anorexia nervosa may manifest as intense feelings of being rejected and controlled, leading to anorexia. In Resource Therapy, this state would be addressed by working with the internal parts that feel rejected or inadequate, and replacing those beliefs with more resourceful, nurturing states that promote self-acceptance and healing.
Attachment Disorder	Attachment disorders often arise from early experiences of rejection or abandonment. **Vaded with Rejection** in Resource Therapy would involve working with the parts that carry the pain of these early rejections, helping to heal the attachment wounds and establish healthier, more secure attachment patterns by accessing inner resources that offer safety, trust, and connection.
Low Self-Worth	**Vaded with Rejection** is a direct contributor to low self-worth, where individuals feel unworthy or unlovable. In Resource Therapy, the focus is on identifying the parts that hold these rejection-based feelings and replacing them.
Suicidality	Suicidal thoughts may arise from feelings of deep rejection, hopelessness, and not being valued. **Vaded with Rejection** in Resource Therapy involves working with the parts of the self that feel rejected or hopeless and helping to access internal resources of hope, self-worth, and the will to live, focusing on restoring a sense of belonging and value.

For the complete list of associated pathologies see Table 14: Vaded with Rejection Pathologies, page 377.

Unit 1: THEORY

How can we fix what we don't understand?

The psyche is composed of parts. One part may gamble while other parts may regret gambling. One part may be cognitive, discerning, and intellectual, and another part may be petty and reactive. Some parts can hold feelings of anxiety while others do not. In therapy it is most beneficial to work directly with the part that needs change.

Understanding how parts relate with each other in the psyche is key to knowing how to foster positive change. This unit defines both

1) how parts are organized within the psyche and

2) the issues that can arise when parts become less functional.

There are eight ways that parts can become less functional, non-normal. While this book relates to only two pathological types, Vaded with Fear and Vaded with Rejection, it is helpful for the reader to gain a contextual understanding of how these two pathologies are placed into the complete array of pathological types. Therefore, each of the eight types of pathologies will be defined, and two of those eight, Vaded with Fear and Vaded with Rejection, will be the central focus.

Chapter 1: Core Terms

Core terms related to Resource States

1. **Resource States:** All states within the psyche are referred to as Resource States. These are the essential blocks of the personality. Conscious, Surface, and Underlying refers to the position in the Psyche a Resource State may be in at a point in time. Any state may move between these three positions.

2. **Conscious State**

   o   The single state that is active in the Conscious at any given moment.

   o   This state is responsible for experiencing, feeling, and making decisions.

3. **Surface States**

   o   States that are near the Conscious but are not currently holding it.

   o   These states observe and advise, often offering guidance to the state in the Conscious.

4. **Underlying States**

   o   Dissociated states that are not in the Conscious or observing.

   o   These states are further removed but can be accessed when needed or triggered.

5. **Introjects**

   o   Internalized representations of external figures that each state may hold.

   o   Introjects (internalized impressions) can influence the perception and behaviour of Resource States.

Interaction Dynamics

The interplay between Resource States is driven by their activity and position (Conscious, Surface, or Underlying) and the influence of their Introjects. This dynamic defines the overall structure and functionality of the psyche and offers a fascinating lens through which to understand therapeutic processes and internal experiences.

Resource States

We each are composed of a varying number of parts which are called Resources, or Resource States because they have skills that were formed in childhood when we repeated a behavior over and over again.

Especially in early childhood, each time a behavior is repeated, neural axon and dendrite growth occurs training synaptic connections among the neurons. Over time this set of neurons becomes very good at its behavior and when we need to repeat that behavior, we automatically fire up that set of trained neurons to best complete that particular behavior.

If you learn to play the violin, over time you get better and better at it, and you are best at it when you get into your violin playing Resource State. You may also have a trained 'nurturing state', a trained 'assertive state', and so on. We have lots of states and we each have different states because we have different histories.

Most of our states are healthy and helpful, but sometimes states become traumatized, conflicted, or misused and this can result in psychological issues. Our personalities are a mosaic of our states, with no one state being the core. There are some states that are used more than others, and some may not be used anymore.

Conscious, Surface, and Underlying States

Resource therapy theory explains every psychological disorder. There are psychological disorders that are not based on organics, where a person may be born with, or develop an organic disorder or a chemical imbalance. But beyond that, every psychological disorder relates to what's happening with our states now, and to what happened to them in the past. Table 3 illustrates the locations within the psyche a Resource State may occupy at a point in time.

Table 3: Positions Resource States may take

Resource States

Conscious State:
(= the one state in
  the Conscious)

⇨ Only one state possible
⇨ The awareness of self
⇨ Experiencing and deciding

Surface States:

⇨ Zero to several states possible
⇨ Observing and advising
⇨ Communicating with the
  Conscious State

Underlying States:
(= subconscious)

⇨ Several states possible
⇨ Dissociated from the Conscious

A state can be the one state in the Conscious that is experiencing and deciding, it can be a Surface State, observing and advising, or it can be in an underlying position, often referred to as "the subconscious". So, the terms Conscious, Surface and Underlying define a position a state can be in at a point in time. Our states move from one position to another within our personalities.

The Conscious State

At any time that we are awake and aware we have one state in the conscious. This state is called the Conscious State. It is the state that is experiencing what is happening and that makes the final decision on what is done. It will later have the best memory of what happened, and its memory will hold the most feeling about what it experienced.

The state that is conscious may hold the Conscious for hours or for only a few seconds. Imagine being on a basketball team. When you are in the game, hopefully you have your sporting state conscious, the state that has practiced playing and can focus intently on the game. If you are taken out of the game and you sit on the bench with other players, you will most likely change Resource States. You may change to a more social state or to a state that can watch intently from your current location. You might even go into a coaching state.

Surface States

We also have Surface States. These states are observing what is happening. They will also have a memory of what happened, as long as they were surface during the occurrence. A Surface State can speak to the Conscious State and advise it or criticize it.

When you sit down to rest, the state that was tired and sits down is the Conscious State. A Surface State may feel there is work to be done, so it may say to the resting, Conscious State 'You should be doing your work.' A different Surface State may have a third opinion.

When I go to buy a car, I welcome the input from my Surface State that is concerned about how much money I have, from the Surface State that knows what lightens my heart, from the Surface State that knows about mechanics, and from the Surface State that is concerned about the environment.

Underlying States

Underlying States are dissociated from the conscious mind and are not aware of what is happening in the present moment; thus, they will have no memory of it. Just like the smell of a fire may wake you from an unconscious State, Underlying States that are traumatized may become conscious when events remind them of their traumatic event. Likewise, Underlying States that are not traumatized may be roused when the topic of their specialty becomes cognizant. Given the opportunity to go skiing, the state that is experienced at skiing may become the Conscious State.

A Surface State may become disinterested or bored and move into an underlying position at any time. Sometimes, one state can force another state into an underlying position. By forcing another state into an underlying position, the person will no longer be able to hear the voice or the advice of that state. The gambler may not always hear the advice of the state that is concerned about the budget, or while binging the binging state may force other states into an underlying position and the person will temporarily no longer hear the rational concerns about diet. This is the dynamic that occurs with addictions and OCD.

An Underlying State can move directly from an underlying position into the conscious. When this happens the person will suddenly have no memory of what just happened. You may have just read two paragraphs in a book and suddenly have no memory of what you just read. You may leave your couch position from watching TV and walk to the fridge and open the door, then think, 'What am I doing here. I must have wanted something, but I don't know what I wanted.' You may return to the couch, sit down and re-enter your TV watching state and then remember what you wanted. A person can suddenly become overcome with negative feelings when a Vaded Underlying State enters the Conscious.

So, our one Conscious State may be conscious from a few seconds to a few hours, our Surface States can move to the Conscious or to an underlying position, and our Underlying States may move to a surface or conscious position, see Figure 1.

Figure 1: Movement of States

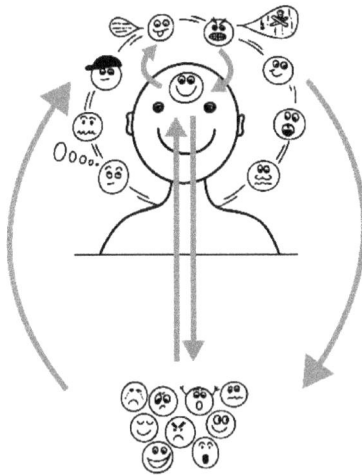

A state may move between being Conscious, Surface, and Underlying.

When someone has an experience they are experiencing it from the state that is conscious at that moment. Later, when a different state enters the Conscious and recalls what happened, the same depth of feelings will not be felt. But when the state that was conscious during the experience comes back into the Conscious it brings with it its more profound feelings. If it has unresolved feelings, if it was traumatized, whatever feelings it's holding, it brings those with it into the Conscious.

So, when a state is traumatized, even in childhood, and when it comes back, when something wakes it up, it brings those feelings of trauma into the

Conscious. That is what is happening with phobia or PTSD and several other pathologies.

Usually, we have a few of the same states that are commonly surface, states that we use a lot. Sometimes there is a state that we had used a lot and then stopped using it very often, or at all. It will assume an underlying position. Hopefully, we will have kept using some of our childhood, fun-loving and useful states from childhood into adulthood.

Occasionally we may smell or see something that brings back feelings and memories from long ago. That is a state that has been underlying for a long time, coming into the Conscious.

Position of Resource States during hypnosis

Hypnosis is where there are relatively few Surface States. The Surface States sink into underlying positions.

In a light or medium state of hypnosis, there will be one or two Surface States that are observing. And often people will report "I was watching. I can remember what was going on." And after the person comes out of hypnosis, they usually have the memory of what was happening. So, in a light to medium state of hypnosis there are some Surface States that are observing.

If the person goes into a deep state of hypnosis, all of those Surface States sink below the surface and become underlying, and then there will be no memory of what happened during the hypnosis, other than with the state that actually experienced it, the state that was conscious during the procedure.

That's all hypnosis is. It's just a focusing into one state, where there's relatively few Surface States, and the level of hypnotic depth is merely defined by how many Surface States there are, how surface they are. The more they sink below the surface, the deeper the state of hypnosis.

What DID informs us about states:

Further proof of our separate states is DID (multiple personality). DID, Dissociative Identity Disorder, is a coping skill learned in a chronically abused childhood, to be able to experience life from states that were underlying during the abuse. Since they were dissociated from the Conscious during the abuse they can provide a respite from trauma.

Over time and with chronic abuse that happens day in and day out for months or years, it's not unusual for the abused child to develop a coping skill for the next day, "I don't want to think about it. I don't want to think about it, I don't want to think about it." And, by practicing not thinking about it, there is an atrophying of the synaptic connections between the state they are in the next day, and the state that experienced what happened the night before.

So, this atrophying of communication links between states causes multiple personality. And there's different levels of that where sometimes a person can have no memory of the previous state whatsoever. And sometimes there is some memory. Sometimes there are some states that share memories, and sometimes there are not. Sometimes a state 'Mary' will remember everything that another state, 'Jane', did during the time Jane was in the Conscious, but the Jane state doesn't remember anything that Mary does.

The only difference between the alters of a person with DID and the Resource States of someone without DID is the level of memory they share. Because alters share little or no memory with other parts they must also develop more autonomy, thus they can appear as separate personalities.

Introjects

In Resource Therapy, an Introject is an internalized impression of a person, an animal or an inanimate, like a mountain, a fire, or an item. Each Resource State holds its own Introjects. For example, a child state may hold an Introject of 'Dad' as being a disciplinarian, but an adult state of the same client may hold an Introject of Dad as being a gentle helper. When this client is speaking from the child state its feelings will be evident, as will the feelings of the adult state when it is holding the Conscious.

Introjects are important in therapy for several reasons. When a child state holds an Introject of something physically threatening, a person, a flood, or an animal, the trauma that is felt is fueled by the impression it holds. Part of the resolution is to ensure that the child state learns the frightening event is no longer happening and thereby the power of the Introject to scare is removed.

Chapter 1: Core Terms

When a state is traumatized, it has been traumatized by someone or something. The Vaded State holds an internal impression of the Introject (the perpetrator, the animal or a thing like a fire, flood, or car crash). Negative Introjects are the ones that are keeping the state in its traumatized condition. For the traumatized state, the Introject is still feared or still rejecting and it is still holding the power. The aim in therapy is to empower the Vaded State and to disempower the negative Introject.

Not only do Introjects play an important role in traumatizing a state, but they also play a role in de-traumatizing a Vaded State. Introjects are more often positive than negative. Introjects of loved ones are positive and they can help states feel more positive and more empowered. A client can focus on the internal impression of a loved person, a loved animal, or a loved place. The Introject a client holds of a hot bath, or a sunny beach may be used to assist in relaxation.

A child state that felt rejection from an Introject of a parent can learn it was the parent who was not good at being unconditionally loving at that time. This removes the feeling that 'I am unlovable', as the knowledge that 'the parent was unable to share unconditional love' removes the blame from the child. For this cathartic change in understanding to occur, it is imperative that the child state be holding the Conscious. In other words, this is not an intellectual process that can be resolved mentally. It must be resolved emotionally. The steps for this transformation are a major offering of this book.

Takeaways from Chapter 1: Core Terms

Chapter 1 introduces key concepts of **Resource Therapy**, which views the human psyche as composed of multiple distinct **Resource States**—individual parts or modes of being that develop through repeated behaviors and experiences, especially in childhood. Neurons that fire together, wire together. Hebbian Theory is a concept proposed by Donald Hebb in 1949, stating that neuronal connections can be remodeled by experience (Hebb, 1949). These states are not just metaphorical but neurologically grounded and can shift positions within the psyche.

Core Concepts:

1. **Resource States**:
   These are the fundamental parts of our personality. Each one holds certain skills, traits, or emotional patterns and can be healthy or traumatized. They're created through repeated behaviors and learning.

2. **Positions of Resource States**:

   o **Conscious State**: The state currently active and experiencing life, making decisions, and forming memories.

   o **Surface States**: Close to consciousness, these observe and advise but are not in control.

   o **Underlying States**: Dissociated or inactive states, often inaccessible unless triggered (e.g., by trauma or specific cues).

States can **move fluidly** between these positions.

3. **Function and Movement of States**:

   o Our behavior and feelings change based on which state is conscious.

   o Surface and Underlying states can influence or take over the Conscious.

- o Transitions can be abrupt and may explain phenomena like forgetfulness, sudden mood changes, or compulsions (e.g., in addiction or PTSD).

- o Hypnosis involves shifting most Surface States into Underlying positions, leaving mainly one focused state Conscious.

4. **Introjects:**

- o Internal representations of external people, animals, or things.

- o Each Resource State holds its own Introjects, which influence feelings and behavior.

- o **Negative Introjects** (e.g., a feared abuser) can keep a state traumatized.

- o **Positive Introjects** (e.g., a loving parent, pet, or safe place) can help healing.

- o Therapy aims to **empower Vaded (traumatized) States** and **neutralize negative Introjects**.

5. **Dissociative Identity Disorder (DID):**

- o Seen as an extreme form of state separation caused by chronic trauma.

- o States (alters) may not share memory, leading to the experience of separate personalities.

- o In non-DID individuals, Resource States usually share more memory and function more cooperatively.

Key Point:

Rather than having a single core personality, we are a **mosaic of states**, each with its own perspective, memories, and emotional tone. Understanding and working with these Resource States, especially the traumatized or hidden ones, offers a powerful therapeutic model for emotional healing and self-integration.

Chapter 2: The Eight Pathologies

Resource Therapy not only provides a complete and thorough personality theory, but it also has its own diagnostic classification with eight pathological conditions a Resource State can be in, see Table 4. These eight pathologies cover **all existing psychological disorders** except for organically caused disorders. In other words, a therapist who has learned to RT diagnose can offer treatment for **every** concern a client presents within the psychological spectrum, whether that's fear-based disorders, OCD, eating disorders, self-harming behavior, addictions, suicidal ideation or any other presentation. In Appendix 5: Pathologies by Diagnoses you will find a list of the most common pathologies and the corresponding Resource Therapy diagnosis related to each.

The majority of our states are normal and healthy. However, there are eight pathological conditions states can suffer from, 4 of which are emotional (Vaded), 2 are behavioral (Retro), 1 when states are conflicted with each other (Conflicted), and 1 when the wrong state is holding the Conscious (Dissonant):

1. **Vaded States:** A client may complain about unwanted emotions. These are specified into four different types of emotions:
    - fear
    - feelings of rejection
    - confusion and
    - disappointment.

2. **Retro States:** A client may complain about unwanted behavior. The states that carry out unwanted behavior are called Retro States, as the client has decided that their previous behavior is no longer wanted. There are two types of Retro States.
    - Retro Original: Unwanted behavior originally learned during childhood to help the child get something, and
    - Retro Avoiding: Unwanted escape behavior that has been learned to help the client avoid negative feelings.

3. **Conflicted States:** When a client complains about an inner division, conflicting endeavours, or ambivalences the client may have two states that compete to win the client's time. When neither of these conflicted states are Vaded or Retro they are called Conflicted States. Conflicted States do not like or respect each other.

4. **Dissonant States:** A client may complain about not being able to function fully, feeling frustration in coping abilities or with a task. This presenting concern points to a Dissonant State. A Dissonant State is merely a normal state that is holding the Conscious at the wrong time. A tennis player may not play well when in a state that really wants to win because it is not the state that normally plays tennis.

See Table 4 to gain a better understanding of how therapists determine the conditions of states.

Table 4: Resource State Conditions

Resource State Conditions		
Normal	⇨ A healthy state, it acts in accordance to the person's values and wishes ⇨ Congruent	Normal
Vaded	⇨ The state displays unwanted emotions	Fear Rejection Confusion Disappointment
Retro	⇨ The State displays unwanted behavior	Retro Original Retro Avoiding
Conflicted	⇨ Two (or more) states are conflicted to the point of anxiety	Conflicted
Dissonant	⇨ The wrong state for the situation is in the conscious	Dissonant

See Table 5 to gain an initial understanding of how diagnoses are made.

Table 5: Resource Therapy Diagnosis Flowchart

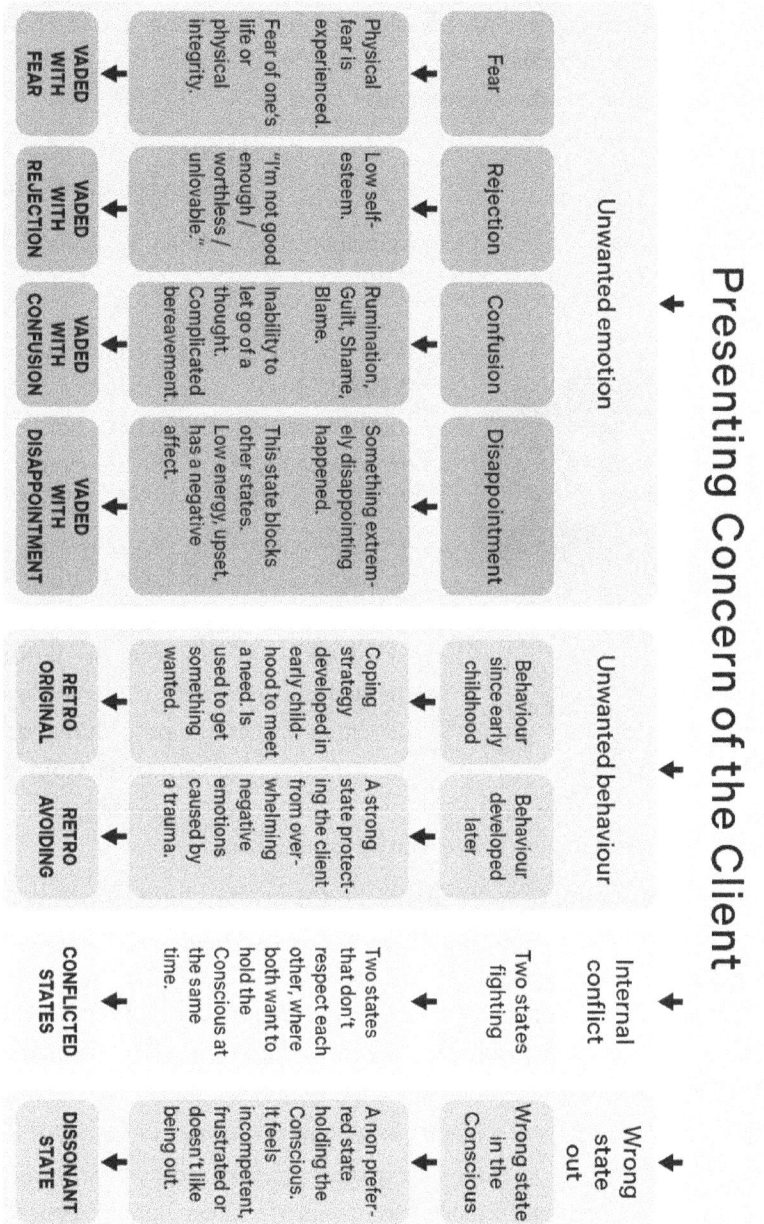

Presenting Concern of the Client

Category	Sub-type	Description	Diagnosis
Unwanted emotion	Fear	Physical fear is experienced. Fear of one's life or physical integrity.	VADED WITH FEAR
	Rejection	Low self-esteem. "I'm not good enough / worthless / unlovable."	VADED WITH REJECTION
	Confusion	Rumination, Guilt, Shame, Blame. Inability to let go of a thought. Complicated bereavement.	VADED WITH CONFUSION
	Disappointment	Something extremely disappointing happened. This state blocks other states. Low energy, upset, has a negative affect.	VADED WITH DISAPPOINTMENT
Unwanted behaviour	Behaviour since early childhood	Coping strategy developed in early childhood to meet a need. Is used to get something wanted.	RETRO ORIGINAL
	Behaviour developed later	A strong state protecting the client from overwhelming negative emotions caused by a trauma.	RETRO AVOIDING
Internal conflict	Two states fighting	Two states that don't respect each other, where both want to hold the Conscious at the same time.	CONFLICTED STATES
Wrong state out	Wrong state in the Conscious	A non-preferred state holding the Conscious. It feels incompetent, frustrated or doesn't like being out.	DISSONANT STATE

Pathologies that are a focus of this book

This overview covers Fear Based Trauma and Rejection Based Trauma, followed by treatment actions in the next unit. Understanding these pathologies will help before learning their treatments.

1. Fear Based Trauma:

Definition and cause of States Vaded with Fear

Figure 2: Vaded with Fear

Fear Based Trauma occurs when an individual experiences an overwhelmingly frightening and deeply impactful event which cannot be integrated. The event is interpreted as potentially life-threatening or as a threat to physical or psychological safety. Some examples of Fear Based Trauma are accidents, acts of war or terrorism, natural disasters, near drowning events, emergency medical procedures, assault or violence. You can suffer from shock trauma from experiencing these sorts of events or just witnessing them. For children much less dramatic events can be traumatizing.

Since we always have one state in the Conscious, during a traumatizing event there is a state in the Conscious which experiences the traumatizing event, while other states may be in an underlying position and not experiencing it. Surface States will observe the event, but they will not directly feel the experience. The state experiencing the situation feels overwhelmed with physical fear and is unresolved: It is "Vaded with Fear".

From this moment on, when it comes into the Conscious again, it cannot be there in its former resourceful way. It comes to the Conscious with the fear and terror it's holding, and the client re-experiences that state's physical fear every single time this state is in the Conscious. When a frightening event occurs, which happens usually during childhood, and it is not processed or discussed, it can result in the child, or more precisely, the child's state that was conscious when the event occurred, holding onto the fear. This fear state can continue into adulthood, often with the client being unaware of where the feeling is coming from.

However, with therapy, this state can be brought into the Conscious and it can learn that the past is no longer happening. It can achieve a sense of connection and safety and let go of the negative emotions that were not understood.

In Resource Therapy we learn how to bring the traumatized state to the Conscious within minutes, so we can work with this state directly and help it feel safe immediately. By this it will be de-traumatized.

The pathology "Vaded with Fear" refers to physical fear. If the client doesn't experience physical fear but a fear of not being good enough, of failing or of not being lovable, this fear is caused by a different pathology: A State Vaded with Rejection.

Example of origin for Fear based Trauma

A young girl was on a walk in a grove of tall trees. She accidentally stopped walking in a place where she was standing on a large ant's nest. When she noticed the ants, they were swarming around her. While not badly hurt, she was terrified. She did not tell her parents and did not have a chance to feel supported or did not have a chance to process the event.

The event where a state becomes vaded is called the Initial Sensitizing Event (ISE) (Boswell, 1987).

Example of pathology

Later in life when she saw a spider the terror of the 'ants' event would return to her Conscious. She became unable to even look at a picture of a spider without feeling terrified. She had no idea why she had a spider phobia. The emotional terror of her experience with the ants had been somehow later in life transferred to spiders. The state that had experienced the 'ants' event, and that was still holding this fear, was now triggered by spiders and came to the Conscious with the same fear it felt during the scary event many years ago.

Associated pathologies

If a client experiences the feelings of a State Vaded with Fear directly with the state holding the conscious the resulting pathologies include, Panic Attack, Phobias, PTSD's, many anxieties, and physical fear. If the feelings of a State Vaded with Fear are being avoided, it can result in pathologies like Addiction, OCD, Self-harming behavior and pathological gambling.

Diagnosing a State Vaded with Fear

The single feeling that characterizes a State Vaded with Fear is the feeling of physical fear that does not match the current setting. For example, if a person feels fear seeing a poisonous spider crawling on their arm a level of fear is normal, but if a person looks at a picture of a spider, a feeling of panic is not expected. The fear that keeps us from the edge of a cliff is normal and healthy, but the fear that keeps us from leaving the house into a safe community is pathological.

Treatment

When trauma occurs, the state "freezes" in this experience. For the Vaded State the traumatic situation is still happening, it's still dangerous. It is overwhelmed with the feelings of fear, and anytime this state enters the Conscious, the person will feel that fear. We need to update the State Vaded with Fear by letting it experience, during the intervention, that the trauma is NOT happening anymore, and that it is safe now. It is the change in experience that moves a State Vaded with Fear back into a normal condition.

Continuing to merely talk with the state the client is in when coming to therapy will not help a State Vaded with Fear. Talking with a reporting state that knows about the Vaded State does not lessen the fear the Vaded State holds. It is necessary to bring the Vaded State into the Conscious and help it learn it is now safe and supported. The steps to help these states are a focus of this book.

Once the state is no longer holding the fear it will no longer come into the Conscious with that fear. It can instead come into the Conscious with its former resourceful abilities.

2. Attachment Trauma:

Definition and cause of Vaded with Rejection

Figure 3: Vaded with Rejection

Attachment Trauma arises when you don't feel that you get the love, care, attention, understanding or unconditional acceptance you need during childhood. It can stem from overwhelming events like the death of a caregiver, but it can also stem from less dramatic but painful experiences like a lack of affection from emotionally distant parents. Examples are childhood neglect, absent caregivers, growing up around addiction or violence, cold and controlling caregivers or overly ambitious caregivers who expect the child to excel.

It can also result from a frightening experience from controlled crying, or from the change in attention received after the birth of a new sibling. A child can have a State Vaded with Rejection even when loving parents are trying their best to rear their children. It is possible for one child to get traumatized while another child with the same experience might not.

The state that is experiencing an overwhelmingly rejective event will be left feeling rejected, feeling not good enough, feeling unloved, feeling wrong, or feeling abandoned.

If the state is unresolved, meaning that it has not gained any help to integrate the overwhelming experience, the client re-experiences rejection-related feelings every time this state comes into the Conscious, often being completely unaware about why those feelings are present.

Experiences that can possibly vade a state with rejection could be a harsh scolding of a parent or caregiver, being alone in a situation in which orientation or support is needed, exposure to criticism and high expectations, parentification, or a teacher who causes the child to feel embarrassed.

Also, feeling rejected is an interpretation. A child may feel rejected when a parent does 'controlled crying', or it may feel abandoned by a parent who is busy working. It may also feel rejected when its emotions are not acknowledged. Typical sentences of parents are "You don't need to be afraid," or "Don't be such a drama-queen." They indicate that the parents have low understanding for the emotions the child is experiencing. Therefore, the child learns that its feelings are wrong. Which may lead to a belief structure of "I am wrong."

Our culture has generally moved from extended family/community child rearing to often a two or one parent home. It is challenging to ensure the child feels unconditionally loved.

Where occasionally a state may become Vaded with Fear in adulthood, Vaded with Rejection almost exclusively happens during childhood. Vaded with Rejection is the cause of attachment disorders.

Example of origin

Vaded with Rejection is very common. Parents can do the very best they can and still a child can have states that have been Vaded with Rejection.

Example   1
A three-year-old girl is excited about getting a new baby sister. Then this three-year-old begins to miss the time mother previously spent with her. Her mother is now very busy taking care of the immense demands of the new baby. The three-year-old then does something to get her mother's attention, the mother lashes out toward the child. With the built-up feelings of rejection that the child already holds, the reaction of the upset mother feels overwhelming to the three-year-old. The state that is admonished becomes vaded.

Example   2
A parent was not ready for children. This parent may have their own issues and tells their child, "I should never have had you." The parent may show a lack of love and a lack of wanting the child. When a child is feeling fragile a parent saying "I should have never had you" can move a normal state into being Vaded with Rejection.

Example of pathology

A client may present with the impression that friends are not supportive enough. The client may feel that 'no matter how hard they try' it is not good enough. This client may be overly sensitive to others' opinions. This client feels 'not good enough'.

Generally, a client having a State Vaded with Rejection can have a feeling of having to work hard to be accepted. When this person does well and gets praise, they can feel very positive, but if there is doubt about approval this person can feel terrible. There can be a deep sense of failure. There can be a feeling of being unlovable, a feeling of being fake, and if a person says, "I love you," that does not really count because they don't really love who I really am, because I am a fake and unlovable.

Associated pathologies

A State Vaded with Rejection can bring about addictions and eating disorders, can bring about feelings of incompetence, and can bring about fear of not being good enough at work or not being good enough to start a new job. It can cause a fear of relationships. A person may suffer from over-shopping in an attempt to "become better."

It may lead an individual to grapple with forming secure attachments in adulthood. The child part that was frustrated in not receiving love continues to feel incomplete regardless of adult relationships. Even when the adult receives love, this child part continues to feel the rejection from childhood. As an adult the person may even consider ending a relationship upon hearing their partner express love, as the declaration may not translate to overcoming the overwhelming feelings of being unloved. The fight for love is over, but the feeling of being unloved is still present, because with Vaded with Rejection, it is the child part that needs love more than an adult part. Despite significant efforts to experience love, the sense of love may remain incomplete.

Vaded with Rejection is associated with insecure fear, rather than physical fear.

Treatment

Like with the pathology Vaded with Fear, the person with a State Vaded with Rejection can only become free of this feeling when the state that holds the negative feeling is worked with directly. The therapist can talk for years to other states about the feeling, but the client will hold that underlying feeling until the state (or states) that holds this unlovable feeling is worked with directly. The treatment will focus on helping the Vaded State understand that while it is lovable, the rejecting person (parent, caregiver, teacher, friend, or anyone else) had not been able to treat the child the way a child deserves and needs to be treated. This will assist the state to let go of the dysfunctional core belief of "I am not good enough." During the treatment, the Vaded State will also experience what it is like to be loved and accepted unconditionally and will feel loved, worthy and relieved at the end of the session. It will be de-traumatized.

Pathologies that are not a focus of this book

It is useful to understand the range of pathologies clients may present with for two reasons.

1) The therapist will need to be able to diagnose the client's issue into a type of pathology to select the most appropriate intervention. By understanding the range of pathologies therapists will be more adapt at recognizing when a state has a fear or rejection-based pathology, and when a client has a different type of issue that requires a vastly different intervention.

2) Gaining an understanding of the complexity of issues that clients may suffer from gives the therapist a greater understanding of the nature of the psyche. This is beneficial in maintaining a sense of direction in therapy. It is not a good feeling to feel lost during a client presentation.

Therefore, the six remaining pathologies that are not fully presented in this book will be briefly noted. While most client presentations are either fear based, or rejection based, should the reader want more information on how to process clients with these other types of presentations that information can be found in Resource Therapy (Emmerson, 2014).

3. Guilt, Blame and other Ruminations:

Definition and cause of Vaded with Confusion

Figure 4: Vaded with Confusion

Guilt, shame, blame, confusion and complicated bereavement are usually not seen as trauma-related, but they are. This person, or rather, the state of the person that was conscious at the difficult experience, is overwhelmed with an inability to understand: It is Vaded with Confusion. This can cause a person to ruminate about a problem in a relationship, a guilt, a blame, a loss, or any important topic without being able to settle with it. They cannot stop thinking about something they did, or that someone else did, or failed to do. The main symptoms are an uncomfortable rumination or an inability to let something go.

These states are usually Vaded with Confusion in adulthood, although it can happen in childhood.

Example of origin

Here are some examples of events that clients have reported, leaving them with a State Vaded with Confusion.

Example 1

A client found out after the death of her sister that she had previously had an affair with my client's husband. She had thought her sister was her best friend, her confidant, and she could not understand how she could have an affair with her husband. My client could not stop thinking about it, could not sleep, and reported she could not go an hour in any day without it being a concern.

Example 2

A client reported an ongoing guilt over sexually abusing her brother when they were children.

Example 3

A client lost her sister in a car crash when a drunk driver pulled into her lane. My client could not stop thinking about how unfair it was that the drunken driver was living, and her innocent sister was dead.

Example 4

A client ruminated about the affair her ex-husband had when they were married. She felt if she stopped blaming him that would mean that he got away with it.

Example 5

A client ruminated about the loss of a job. The feeling was that it was age discrimination and there was continued fretting about being discriminated against in getting a new job.

Example of pathology

Examples of pathology for Vaded with Confusion are listed above with the examples of origin. The common denominator of Vaded with Confusion is rumination. It may be rumination about an event or the rumination of guilt or blame.

Associated pathologies

Clients with a State Vaded with Confusion may report sleeplessness, an inability to focus or concentrate, or an inability to move forward in life because of a feeling of being held back by past events. Complicated bereavement may be caused by a State Vaded with Confusion, as the heavy feelings this state is experiencing can interfere with the healthy grieving process.

Treatment

RT-based empty chair work greatly assists clients with a State Vaded with Confusion. This empty chair protocol is unique to Resource Therapy and is distinctly different from Gestalt work or other protocols. The key to this treatment is not to fix the problem, but to help the client gain an understanding of the overall context. This is done when the client is encouraged to speak to the person that causes the rumination or confusion in an empty chair, expressing feelings, worries, questions and thoughts thoroughly. The client then moves to the empty chair and speaks back as the person that caused the rumination. The experience in the other person's chair is cathartic, as it allows the client (or, more precisely: The State Vaded with Confusion) to feel and speak from the perspective of the problematic person. It is also possible to do this when the problematic person is deceased. When the client returns to their chair, they bring with them a better understanding of the context of the issue they had felt confused about.

The Resource Therapy steps in this process are important to follow but are not a focus of this book (see Resource Therapy, (2014).

4. Depression:

Definition and cause of Vaded with Disappointment

Figure 5: Vaded with Disappointment

A State Vaded with Disappointment forcefully holds positive states below the surface, in an underlying position. Depression can be caused organically (non-psychologically) or by a state that is Vaded with Disappointment. It's a state that has lost something that was profoundly important, and it has become so sorrowful because of that loss that it blocks other states from positive feelings and positive activities. The loss can be the result of a death of a person or an animal that was important, the loss of a job, of health, of youth, or any other profoundly important aspect of living.

The blocking of other states can be a bounded group of states, such as states associated with a relationship, or the blocking can be a global blocking of all other states that might otherwise enjoy positivity.

Example of origin

Example 1

A woman discovers her partner had an affair. She is profoundly sad and disappointed. She no longer feels like being intimate with him, she no longer feels like traveling with him, she no longer feels like having a pleasant conversation with him. This is an example of a bounded group of states that have been blocked. She is still able to focus on work and her friends.

Example 2

A man loses his wife to cancer. She was profoundly central to his life. He no longer feels like doing anything that would give him joy. Everything feels meaningless. This is an example of global blocking.

Example of pathology

When the blocking of positive states is global, depression is the result. A state may be Vaded with Disappointment at any time in life, although most client presentations relate to those vaded in adulthood, see Table 6. Depression may also have a physical origin due to chemical imbalances. Depression due to chemical imbalances may be best treated with medication.

Associated pathologies

Pathologies associated with a State Vaded with Disappointment are depression, or loss of interest and energy for some aspects of life.

The disappointed state has lost its mission, its meaning in life. It needs to feel understood, and it is important for it to gain a feeling it can still contribute to the client's life - possibly in a different way.

Change needs energy, so at first the treatment will focus on activating the client to do something regularly again that they have enjoyed in the past. For this to work, permission needs to be granted from the disappointed state for positive Resource States which can enjoy something like going for a walk or reading a book to return to the Conscious. To gain this permission, the disappointed state needs to be negotiated with so it will allow the positive Resource States to become active again. The next step is to find the purpose the Disappointed State had before it became so disappointed and to negotiate a way it can resume its former function in spite of its profound loss. When the disappointed state has found an alternative way of being meaningful and of contributing its skills, it might still feel sadness about its loss, but it will stop blocking other states from enjoying positive activities. It will be able to integrate the disappointing event and is not vaded anymore.

Table 6: Time of life when states are Vaded

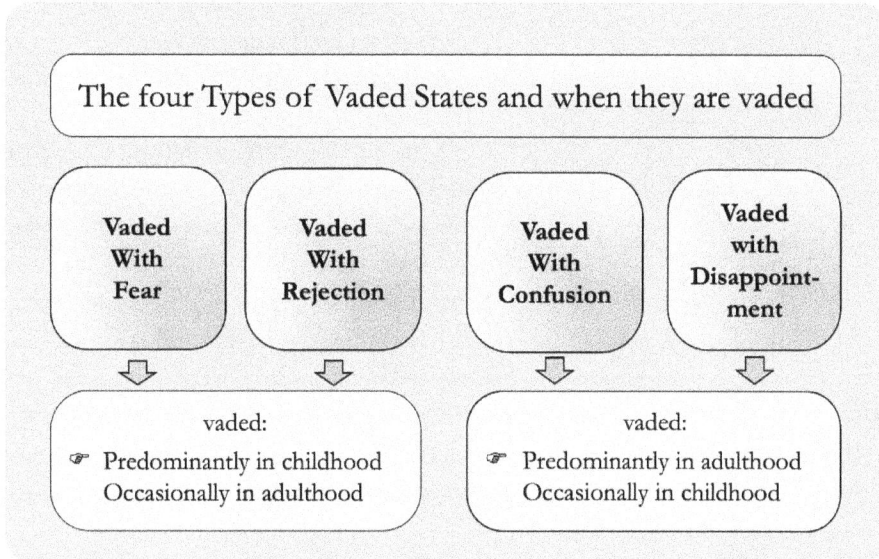

The four Types of Vaded States and when they are vaded

Vaded With Fear	Vaded With Rejection	Vaded With Confusion	Vaded with Disappoint-ment

vaded:
☞ Predominantly in childhood
Occasionally in adulthood

vaded:
☞ Predominantly in adulthood
Occasionally in childhood

Each of these states represents a different emotional response influenced by life experiences at various stages. Understanding when they are most commonly vaded can provide insight into the therapeutic focus.

5. Unwanted behaviors learned in childhood:

Definition and cause of Retro Original

Figure 6: Retro Original

Children develop coping abilities which are useful in childhood but can lead to unwanted behavior later in life. This is why this coping behavior is called 'Retro Behavior.' Whether Retro Original or Retro Avoiding, Retro Behavior is behavior that we did that had some positive return, and then later we decide we no longer want that behavior, for example, being rageful. As a child a tantrum may give us what we want, but as an adult we may not want to go into rage.

The State that is in the Conscious conducting the unwanted behavior is called a "Retro State". It believes it is helping the person by conducting the behavior, while other states of the same person dislike the behavior and bring the person to therapy, so that he or she can cease the behavior.

Example of origin

Our Resource States come from the coping skills we learned in childhood. A Resource State is formed by doing a coping skill over and over again in childhood when the brain is high in neuroplasticity. This creates a physical neural pathway made of axon and dendrite trained synaptic connections that we can easily return to when we need those skills. These skills may be in play in learning violin, in nurturing, or even in tantrums.

It may have been helpful for a child in a violent environment to be unseen and to develop the coping skill of withdrawing. Later in life, in a safe relationship, this behavior may be disturbing to the person or to the people around them.

It may have been a good strategy as a child to have a temper tantrum at the cash desk in order to get the candy bar, but later in life rageful behavior might not be wanted anymore.

Examples of pathology

Some examples of Retro Original behavior are withdrawal, rage, pouting, and passive aggressive behavior. In childhood, these behaviors may have helped the child cope or get what was wanted, but in adulthood these behaviors may no longer be wanted.

A client became rageful in a bar and continued beating a man until his friends pulled him off. He came to therapy because he was no longer at peace with his out-of-control rage. Out of control rage is most normally the result of a state that is Retro Original, while out of control anger is most normally the result of a state that is Retro Avoiding (protecting the person from the feelings of a State Vaded with Fear or Vaded with Rejection).

Treatment

To help a client cease an unwanted behavior it is essential to negotiate directly with the personality part that is conducting the behavior. This is called "Retro State Negotiation". In this negotiation the Retro State is first of all praised and appreciated for its efforts to help (but not for its behavior per se) and then it gets support in learning positive replacement behaviors which allow it to remain important and helpful without conducting the unwanted behavior. As a consequence, the Retro State can still accomplish its mission in a way that is beneficial to the client and can let go of the Retro behavior for good.

6. Unwanted escape or avoiding behaviors including Addictions:

Definition and cause of Retro Avoiding

Trauma leaves traces. A traumatized person can suffer from recurrent, negative feelings associated with the traumatic event, without even understanding what the distressing event was. One thing that can provide relief from the unresolved feelings of a negative event is for a stronger state to take over the Conscious and fill it with a focus that forces the traumatized Vaded State out of the Conscious.

Figure 7: Retro Avoiding

Avoiding behavior that keeps the mind focused on something different can temporarily save the client from the negative feelings. A Retro Avoiding State takes over the Conscious just as a Vaded State starts to enter the conscious and forces the Vaded State out of the Conscious.

The state that is conducting avoiding behavior to avoid negative feelings is called a "Retro Avoiding State". It's aware that the person needs protection from negative emotions, and it takes over control to offer this protection, even though other states often dislike or even loathe the behavior. It's capable of shutting any other state down so it can maintain its avoiding behavior.

Retro Avoiding States are strong states that can dominate the Conscious, forcing other states (that might normally moderate behavior) into an underlying position. When a state is in an underlying position it is not watching what is happening and it cannot communicate with the Conscious state.

This is the reason why the person with issues like gambling, alcoholism, workaholism, or anorexia can't change their behavior as long as the Retro Avoiding State is in control, even though some of their other states would deeply desire to do so.

Example of origin

A client has a State Vaded with Fear. When it comes into the Conscious the client experiences unwanted feelings. The client may feel this state near the Conscious and feel anxiety. This client visits a casino and enjoys the lights, the high focus on winning or losing and the activity. While in the casino the client feels free of the fear and free of the anxiety of the fear coming out. Another trip to the casino proves equally effective in providing an anxiety-free period of time. This is how addictive behavior emerges.

Example of pathology

The client becomes addicted to gambling. That underlying anxiety is a driver to force the client back to gambling. Gambling becomes a self-medication for the anxiety.

In the same way, the client may find a drug that blocks the anxiety state from the Conscious. That drug becomes the 'drug of choice' because it results in a self-medication that helps the client feel so much better than feeling the anxiety.

Associated pathologies

A Retro Avoiding State is a savior state that feels like it is helping to save the client from anxiety or feelings of panic. It is a strong state. The behaviors it uses to save the client may be any psychological addiction, a drug, self-harming behavior, an eating disorder, OCD behavior, or even things like workaholism, shopping addiction, or gardening addiction. The Retro Avoiding State can even take over the conscious immediately before the trauma feelings are experienced.

Treatment

Retro Avoiding Behavior is a coping strategy of the psyche caused by trauma. Before the state that is conducting the behavior can change its behavior, the underlying trauma that is causing it needs to be resolved. Resource Therapy provides techniques which enable the therapist to pinpoint the traumatic event (or events) that caused the unwanted behavior – the root, the gold. So, first the underlying trauma needs to be resolved. The treatment for resolving the underlying trauma (which could be a State Vaded with Fear or a State Vaded with Rejection) will be detailed in the treatment unit of this book.

In a second step, the Retro Avoiding State needs to be negotiated with directly, praising and appreciating it for its efforts to help (even if the way this state helped was negative). The negotiation leads to the state having positive ways to help in the future.

Retro State negotiation is detailed in Resource Therapy, (2014).

7. Inner Conflict between states:

Definition and cause of Conflicted States

Figure 8: Conflicted States

Inner conflict stems from two (or more) states within the personality that want something different. This can result in procrastination, chronic fatigue, sleep disturbance or cognitive dissonance. These states are otherwise normal, meaning healthy: They are not traumatized, not deeply confused or disappointed and not the wrong states for the situation. The only pathology they hold is, that they are in conflict, usually over which one will be able to hold the Conscious. One may want to rest, and one may want work to be done. They both want to hold the Conscious at the same time.

Sometimes states can also be conflicted over a major decision. Conflicted States have a lack of positive understanding and communication with each other.

Conflicted States do not respect each other, and do not communicate directly with one another in a positive way. They do not like each other.

When states are not conflicted, they can communicate together to come to the best decision. For example, you might consider what you want to do with your weekend, hearing ideas from different states. You may be aware of the discussion of ideas in your head. But when states are conflicted, they create a level of anxiety as they struggle against each other. A work state may not respect a state that wants to rest. It may send the message that the state that wants to rest is lazy, as the rest state struggles against it.

Conflicted states differ from Vaded States. A Vaded State feels overwhelmed with negative feelings. It is often not liked by other states, but it is not conflicted with them. It just feels overwhelmed and other states do not like that. Both of the states that are conflicted with each other do not like each other.

Conflicted states are different from Retro States (states that do behavior the client does not like). Most states do not like the retro behavior of Retro States, but the Retro States are just doing what they feel is their role. They have no feelings about the other states. Both of the states that are conflicted with each other do not respect each other.

If States are Vaded or Retro they should not be treated as conflicted with a Conflicted State intervention. There are specific interventions designed to help states that are Vaded or Retro.

Example of origin

A state, such as a work state, is focused on what it needs to do, and it may not be understanding of other states. When it attempts to fulfill its purpose, it is interrupted by another state or states. It is frustrated by this conflict, and because it does not have a respectful association with the other state there is no compromise.

Example of pathology

A person comes home from work and feels tired and in need of rest. The person flips on the TV. A voice is heard in the head, "You lazy slob. You have work that needs to be done. Get off the couch and get to work." The state on the couch is frustrated by the voice and tries to avoid it or shut it off.

Here one healthy state wants to help the person with rest and rejuvenation. Another healthy state wants to get work done. They are in conflict. They do not respect each other. While they send messages to each other they do not have positive, collaborative communication.

Associated pathologies

Other examples of Conflicted States include 'a state that wants to sleep, and a state that wants to think', 'a state that wants to leave a relationship and a state that wants to stay', or 'a state that wants to play and a state that wants to get work done'.

Treatment

A changing chairs activity is helpful for Conflicted States to begin to understand each other and begin to communicate more positively. Each state is encouraged to express itself to the other, then the client changes chairs and responds from the other state. It is the therapist's role to help each state to learn to respect the other state and to help the two states to communicate positively with each other to collaborate in the future over time and decision making.

8. Having the wrong personality part out:

Definition and cause of Dissonant States

Figure 9: Dissonant States

A Dissonant State is a healthy state except it is in the Conscious at the wrong time. When a state is dissonant, the client will feel 'in the wrong skin', will feel frustrated with a lack of comfort or a lack of ability.

Normally, when we begin an activity the state that is our best state for that activity automatically enters the Conscious. A tennis player, when stepping on the court automatically enters the state that enjoys playing tennis, the state that is best at playing tennis.

Example of origin

Occasionally a state that is not the best state for the activity enters the Conscious. This is usually a state that feels compelled to help, but it is unable to function appropriately.

Example of pathology

For example, a tennis player may really want to win. The state that really wants to win, really wants to do a good job, may hold the Conscious when the player steps onto the court. This is not the state that enjoys playing, not the states that can naturally play with abandon and creativity.

Associated pathologies

A student may be able to write good papers, but when attempting to write a thesis may have writer's block. Here again, the state that really wants to do a good job, a state that is aware of the gravity of a good thesis enters the Conscious. This is not a writing state.

A person at a party may not really have wanted to go, and while at the party the person may stay in the state that resents being there. The better state to have in the Conscious would be a state that could have as good a time as possible with the people at the party.

Treatment

The key to affecting change is to talk directly with the state that is pathological. Resource Therapy provides a special technique to ensure that the state that needs to be worked with is in the Conscious. This action is called "Vivify Specific." So, when the Dissonant State is in the Conscious and has been spoken with, a better Resource State for the frustrating situation is found. If the Dissonant State is "just" dissonant and does not hold any other pathology, it will gladly agree to the preferred Resource State to take over the Conscious in the future. It is relieved that it can step back.

Treatment for dissonant states is quite easy and straightforward.

RT Actions:

We have explored the eight categories used to diagnose client issues. Depending on the diagnosis, a defined series of interventions can help move the pathological state to a state of normality. These are the technical procedures (Actions) that may be learned and applied in the appropriate sequence depending on the presenting concern. See RT Actions, page 365, and RT Actions for each Diagnosis, page 367365.

How States Vaded with Fear and States Vaded with Rejection can manifest as symptoms

Now that we have a better understanding of how Retro Avoiding States interact with States Vaded with Fear or Rejection we are ready to look at the two different ways these two trauma-based states can manifest.

A State Vaded with Fear or a State Vaded with Rejection can manifest as symptoms in two different ways. Either the client will experience the negative feelings of the traumatized state in the Conscious or will avoid those negative feelings with a focused behavior, with a Retro Avoiding State in the Conscious.

When a State Vaded with Fear is holding the Conscious, it will result in anxiety disorders such as phobias, PTSD, or panic attacks, but if it is held out of the Conscious by a Retro Avoiding State, the client will **avoid** the negative feelings, which will result in pathologies like Addictions, OCD, Eating Disorders or self-harming disorders.

When the state is Vaded with Rejection, the client may either experience feelings of being worthless, not good enough or unlovable, or may avoid these feelings by focused avoiding behaviors resulting in pathologies such as Eating Disorders, Shopping Addictions, or Perfectionism, see Table 7.

Table 7: How States manifest when Vaded with Fear or Rejection

Pathology	When Vaded Conscious (Traumatized state is the Resource State that is Conscious)	When Vaded Avoided (Traumatized state is kept out of the Conscious by avoiding behavior)
Vaded with Fear can cause	Phobias, PTSD, Panic, Situational Fear General fear, anxiety, panic	Addictions, Drug Taking, OCD, Withdrawal, Anger Avoidant or reactive behaviors
Vaded with Rejection can cause	Striving for overachievement or withdrawing from meaningful relationships or tasks	Addictive behavior, eating disorders, perfectionistic behavior, workaholism and other avoiding behaviors

This concept is actually very simple. The feelings are with the state. If the Vaded State is in the Conscious, then the feelings are in the Conscious and feelings-based pathologies will be the result. If a Retro Avoiding State creates a behavior to keep the Vaded State out of the Conscious, then avoiding behaviors will be the result.

Example of origin

Vaded with Rejection is very common. Parents can do the very best they can and still a child can have states that have been Vaded with Rejection.

Example   1

A three-year-old girl is excited about getting a new baby sister. Then this three-year-old begins to miss the time mother previously spent with her. Her mother is now very busy taking care of the immense demands of the new baby. The three-year-old then does something to get her mother's attention, the mother lashes out toward the child. With the built-up feelings of rejection that the child already holds, the reaction of the upset mother feels overwhelming to the three-year-old. The state that is admonished becomes vaded.

Example   2

A parent was not ready for children. This parent may have their own issues and tells their child, "I should never have had you." The parent may show a lack of love and a lack of wanting the child. When a child is feeling fragile a parent saying "I should have never had you" can move a normal state into being Vaded with Rejection.

Example of pathology

A client may present with the impression that friends are not supportive enough. The client may feel that 'no matter how hard they try' it is not good enough. This client may be overly sensitive to others' opinions. This client feels 'not good enough'.

Generally, a client having a State Vaded with Fear can have a feeling of having to work hard to be accepted. When this person does well and gets praise, they can feel very positive, but if there is doubt about approval this person can feel terrible. There can be a deep sense of failure. There can be a feeling of being unlovable, a feeling of being fake, and if a person says, "I love you," that does not really count because they don't really love who I really am, because I am a fake and unlovable.

Associated pathologies

A State Vaded with Rejection can bring about addictions and eating disorders, can bring about feelings of incompetence, and can bring about fear of not being good enough at work or not being good enough to start a new job. It can cause a fear of relationships. A person may suffer from over-shopping in an attempt to "become better."

It may lead an individual to grapple with forming secure attachments in adulthood. The child part that was frustrated in not receiving love continues to feel incomplete regardless of adult relationships. Even when the adult receives love, this child part continues to feel the rejection from childhood. As an adult the person may even consider ending a relationship upon hearing their partner express love, as the declaration may not translate to overcoming the overwhelming feelings of being unloved. The fight for love is over, but the feeling of being unloved is still present, because with Vaded with Rejection, it is the child part that needs love more than an adult part. Despite significant efforts to experience love, the sense of love may remain incomplete.

Vaded with Rejection is associated with insecure fear, rather than physical fear.

Treatment

Like with the pathology Vaded with Fear, the person with a State Vaded with Rejection can only become free of this feeling when the state that holds the negative feeling is worked with directly. The therapist can talk for years to other states about the feeling, but the client will hold that underlying feeling until the state (or states) that holds this unlovable feeling is worked with directly. The treatment will focus on helping the Vaded State understand that while it is lovable, the rejecting person (parent, caregiver, teacher, friend, or anyone else) had not been able to treat the child the way a child deserves and needs to be treated.

This will assist the state to let go of the dysfunctional core belief of "I am not good enough." During the treatment, the Vaded State will also experience what it is like to be loved and accepted unconditionally and will feel loved, worthy and relieved at the end of the session. It will be de-traumatized.

Takeaways from Chapter 2: The Eight Pathologies

Resource Therapy (RT) offers a personality theory and diagnostic framework with eight pathological conditions that cover all psychological disorders except those with organic causes. These pathologies allow therapists to diagnose and treat a wide range of client issues, such as fear and attachment-based disorders, OCD, eating disorders, addictions, and more. The pathological conditions are divided into four categories: Vaded (emotional), Retro (behavioral), Conflicted (inner conflict), and Dissonant (wrong state in consciousness).

The Eight Pathologies

Two Pathologies in Focus in this book

1. **Fear-Based Trauma (Vaded with Fear)**:

   o **Cause**: Overwhelming, frightening events (e.g., accidents, violence).

   o **Symptoms**: Phobias, PTSD, panic attacks when the state is conscious; addictions or OCD when avoided.

   o **Treatment**: Bring the traumatized state to consciousness, help it feel safe, and process the event to resolve the fear.

   o **Example**: A girl terrified by ants develops a spider phobia later in life.

2. **Attachment Trauma (Vaded with Rejection)**:

   o **Cause**: Lack of perceived love or acceptance in childhood (e.g., neglect, harsh criticism).

   o **Symptoms**: Feelings of worthlessness or unlovability; may lead to eating disorders or perfectionism when avoided

   o **Treatment**: Help the state feel loved and accepted, resolving the belief of being "not good enough."

   o **Example**: A child feeling rejected after a new sibling's arrival struggles with self-worth as an adult.

Other Pathologies (Brief Overview)

3. **Vaded with Confusion**: Rumination or inability to let go (e.g., guilt, blame). Treated with RT's empty chair technique to gain understanding.

4. **Vaded with Disappointment**: A deeply disappointed state that blocks positive states, causing depression. Treatment negotiates with the state to allow positive activities.

5. **Retro Original**: Childhood coping behaviors now unwanted (e.g., tantrums). Treated by negotiating new behaviors.

6. **Retro Avoiding**: Escape behaviors (e.g. addictions) to avoid traumatic feelings. Requires resolving underlying trauma first, then negotiation.

7. **Conflicted States**: Competing states causing indecision or procrastination. Treated with a changing chairs activity to foster mutual respect.

8. **Dissonant States**: Wrong state for the task (e.g., poor performance). Treated by replacing with the appropriate state.

Diagnosis and Treatment

- RT diagnoses pathological states based on client complaints (unwanted emotions, unwanted behaviors, conflicts, or poor performance). See Flowchart on page 37.

- Treatment involves specific RT actions (Appendix 2) to address the pathological state directly, moving it to a normal condition.

- Vaded states manifest either as direct feelings (e.g., anxiety, worthlessness) or avoidance behaviors (e.g., addictions, perfectionism), depending on whether the state is conscious or suppressed by a Retro Avoiding state (Table 7).

This framework equips therapists to pinpoint and treat the root of psychological issues efficiently by working directly with the affected personality states.

Unit 2: PRACTICE

Introduction to the Core Processes

This section is the cornerstone of the book, detailing the steps to identify and address the root causes of Fear-Based Trauma (States Vaded with Fear) and Attachment Trauma (States Vaded with Rejection). By following these steps, states can be guided back to a 'Normal Condition', without pathology and able to contribute to the personality in a healthy way.

Reading Recommendations:

- **First Read:** Provides a broad understanding of the process.

- **Further Study:** Enables the reader to refer to the steps while working with clients.

- **Practical Application:** A deeper understanding will develop after working with a few clients using these techniques, eliminating the need for step-by-step references.

Chapter 3: Resolving Fear Based Trauma

Pathology: Vaded with Fear

The way this section is organized:

- First, the steps to move a State Vaded with Fear back into a normal condition will be listed, along with the page numbers where each is discussed. This is so you can quickly see the resolution process.
- The techniques will be explained in more detail.
- Finally, several transcripts of clients are provided so you can see how the steps flow together, and so you can see how clients react to each step. There will be bracketed illustrative comments within these transcripts.

Steps to resolve Fear Based Trauma:

1. **Diagnosis: (page 73)**

   - The process begins with diagnosing a state as 'Vaded with Fear'. This occurs when a client reports experiencing physical fear in an inappropriate situation.

2. **Getting the state feeling fear into the Conscious: (page 75)**

   (the Vivify Specific Action)

   - Once the therapist identifies the client has 'fear-based trauma,' the next step is to bring the Vaded State into the Conscious. Only this vaded, traumatized state can lead the therapist to the trauma's cause.

3. **Bridging to the Initial Sensitizing Event (ISE): (page 80)**

   (the Bridging Action)

   - With the Vaded State in the Conscious, the therapist can bridge to the ISE using the feelings of the Vaded State.

4. **Resolving the Trauma: (page 88)**

   - The Vaded State holds the false belief that the traumatic event is still occurring. By bringing the event's image into the Conscious, this illusion can be broken.

   4.1 Addressing the Provoking Introject: (page 88) – **(The Expression Action)** - To dismantle this illusion, the Vaded State, while in the Conscious, is asked to speak to the provoking Introject. This could be a person, animal, or inanimate object like a storm or fire. To ease this process, it is good to help the client imagine the Introject in a more manageable form, such as a tiny person, or a candle if the Introject is a fire. Shrinking the Introject is a good way to make it easier for the client to speak to the Introject (page 162). The act of speaking to the Introject dispels the illusion of the ongoing past event, proving it has no power.

   4.2 Removal of the Provoking Introject: (page 93) – **(The Removal Action)** - The state then gains the power to decide that the provoking Introject is no longer needed within their inner space, termed as 'Removal'. This transforms the state from vaded to more positive.

5. **Creating a feeling of positivity for the state:** (page 96)

   (the Relief Action)

   - A nurturing state is introduced to the previously Vaded State to provide support and connection. It's crucial that the previously Vaded State has already realized its own power before this step, understanding that the provoking Introject holds no power. Permission is sought from the previously

Vaded State to allow another state to assist in the future, thereby lessening its sense of responsibility.

6. **Finding a better State to face current problem:** (page 102)

(the Find Resource Action)

- A more mature state is recruited to handle the current issue, as a child state (even if no longer vaded) may not be best suited for adult concerns.

6.1 Young state thanks the future acting state: (page 103) - **Gratitude and Assurance** - The previously Vaded State expresses gratitude to the adult helping state, reinforcing that it no longer bears responsibility, while also motivating the adult state through appreciation.

7. **Ensuring the intervention was helpful:** (page 105)

(the Imagery Check Action)

- The original image of the problem is reintroduced, demonstrating that the helper state can now manage the issue effectively, without trauma.

8. **Debrief with the Client:** (page 108)

- Finally, the client is invited to ask any questions they may have.

Table 8 summarizes the Resource Therapy Actions to resolve a State Vaded with Fear.

Table 8: Actions to resolve a State Vaded with Fear

Steps to Resolve Fear-Based Trauma:	RT-Action:
Find what the client is ready to change	Diagnosis
Get the pathological state into the Conscious	Vivify Specific
Get to the Initial Sensitizing Event (ISE) by bridging	Bridging
Shrink and express to provoking Introject	Expression
Removal of the provoking Introject	Removal
Find a nurturing state	Relief
Find a better state to face current problems	Find Resource
Check the efficacy of the therapeutic intervention	Imagery Check

Why does trauma linger?

Trauma is the experience of extreme stress that overwhelms a person's ability to cope. But what causes a person, or more precisely, the person's state that was conscious during the traumatizing event, to **stay** in that traumatized condition?

If no appropriate crisis intervention or support is available to help the person to integrate the overwhelming experience, it will be cemented into the traumatized state's perception. For the Vaded State it's not something that happened sometime in the past and is now over, but it is the current imprint of that fear, pain, horror, helplessness or deep loneliness living inside it. It's stuck in the belief, that the negative event is still happening.

We need to find the root of the problem. The root is the traumatizing event that is causing the client to carry these negative feelings. It's the Initial Sensitizing Event (ISE), **the very FIRST overwhelming experience the pathological state has suffered.**

Other negative experiences will have followed, because each time this state enters the Conscious it will hold its negative feelings, but we need to find the first one, the ISE. It is the negative feelings at the ISE that continue to fuel the feelings of trauma. It is this event that the Vaded State feels is still happening.

It is the root of the physical fear problems that cause issues like Phobias, Panic Attacks, PTSD, Nightmares and Sleep Terror, generalized Anxiety Disorders, Self-Harming Behavior, Addictions, DID, Workaholism and OCD.

Step 1) Diagnosis

A different course of action is needed for each of the eight pathologies. The first step is always to diagnose the presenting concern of the client into the appropriate pathology. Only then can the correct steps be taken. To be able to diagnose precisely, RT therapists ask the client, "What are you ready to change today?" The answer to this question will point to the exact pathological state that needs change. A traumatic event, like for example, a traumatic childbirth, cannot be diagnosed without knowing what change the client is aiming for, as it may have caused a State Vaded with Fear, Rejection, Confusion or Disappointment.

If the client presents with, for example, Phobia, Panic Attacks or Generalized Anxiety Disorders, the diagnosis is "Vaded with Fear". For a list of Vaded with Fear associated disorders see Appendix 3: Pathologies linked to Vaded with Fear.

Here are some statements that point to a State Vaded with Fear:

- I'm afraid to leave my house.
- I can't get on a plane.
- I'm afraid to even look at a picture of a spider.
- There are too many people around me at the shopping centre.
- I don't like driving ever since the accident.
- Some people scare me.
- I often feel physical fear.

Chapter 3: Resolving Fear Based Trauma

When someone experiences fear in a safe environment, a feeling that doesn't fit the situation, we know that a Vaded State has been triggered. It is stuck in its fear with the belief that the world is dangerous. A series of therapeutic steps will enable the Vaded State to let go of the illusion that the past is still happening and that the Introject is still holding power. They need to be followed in sequence to de-traumatize the state.

Locating the causal state

Step 2) Getting the state feeling fear into the Conscious

(The Vivify Specific Action)

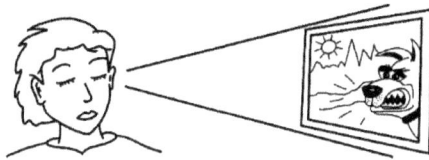

Figure 10: The Vivify Specific Action

Only the state that experienced the traumatizing event can lead us to the traumatizing event. The process of bringing the right state (the traumatized state) into the Conscious is called "Vivify Specific," because we need to re-vivify a recent specific event in which the client experienced the unwanted feeling of fear. It must be a specific event, as any generalizing is a mental process, and we need to bring the emotional state into the Conscious, not an intellectual state. When the client is re-experiencing these feelings of fear, it means that the Vaded State is holding the Conscious, and we can then work with it.

Conceptual Understanding

The Vaded State must be conscious to lead us to the event that vaded it. The Vaded State acts as our guide, someone who has been there before. However, it can't simply tell us what vaded it, but it can lead us there if we focus on the feelings.

When clients are asked why they are having an unwanted feeling, they often provide their best guess, which is frequently incorrect. For instance, a client who has experienced sexual abuse may attribute almost any negative feeling to that abuse. While sometimes true, often the negative emotion is connected to something else. Our goal is to identify and process what is necessary to help clients with their unwanted emotions.

To achieve this, we need to guide the client away from thoughts and intellectual attributions and instead focus on a specific recent situation where the unwanted feelings were experienced. By having the client re-experience this specific situation through imagery, the corresponding unwanted negative feelings are re-activated. The client can feel that fear now, allowing the Vaded State to move from a subconscious position into the Conscious, where it can be addressed immediately.

There is one exception to this process: When the client is already emotional and experiencing the fear. In this case, the Vaded State is already Conscious and can be worked with directly (explained below). Ensuring the Vaded State is conscious is the first step in reaching the Initial Sensitizing Event (ISE).

Often, clients will report the issue, but the Vaded State is not in the Conscious. One state will be discussing another state, often complaining about the Vaded State, saying things like, "I want this fear to go away!" Usually, an intellectual state is describing an emotional state.

When the vaded emotional state is not already in the Conscious, we need to use the Vivify Specific Action to bring the Vaded State into the Conscious so it can lead us to the root of the problem—the ISE.

Instructions for getting the right State into the Conscious (Vivify Specific)

a) Gain an understanding of which state is needed in the Conscious:

- To process fear-based trauma, we need the traumatized state in the Conscious, the state that is FEELING the fear.

b) Find one specific time this fear was experienced:

- Ask the client: "When was the last time you felt this way? I need to know one precise time you have felt that fear, one point in time."

c) Re-experience the situation in imagination:

- With the client's eyes closed, have them re-imagine the situation in their mind. Switch to present tense language and take verbatim notes:

  o "Now allow your eyes to close so you can really focus on this and describe the situation in the present tense, as if you were there now. What time of day is it? Is it light or dark? Are you standing or sitting? Who is there? What is the impression on this other person's face?"

d) Notice when the Vaded State is in the Conscious:

- Continue until you observe signs that the Vaded State is in the Conscious. These signs may include changes in voice, fear, tears, discomfort, changes in breathing, muscle tonus, etc. Another indication is when the client appears to be feeling the corresponding emotions, rather than just talking about an event.

Once the Vaded State is in the Conscious and displaying a level of the unwanted emotion, the next step can be taken: Finding the moment of the first traumatization. This process is known as "Bridging."

Important points in Vivify Specific Action

Find a specific point in time:

- Ensure the client describes a specific point in time. If the client generalizes about an experience, it means an intellectual state is holding the Conscious, which is not what we want. For example, if the client says, "It happens when I am talking with someone who I feel is above me," they are generalizing. This indicates the client is speaking from a non-vaded, thinking state, about when the Vaded State is often out. We need to communicate directly with the Vaded State to find the root of the problem.

Wording:

- Never ask the client to 'think' during Vivify Specific, as an intellectual state will enter the Conscious to answer your question. Focus on feelings and experiences.

Use present tense language:

- As soon as you locate 'one specific event', switch to and maintain present-tense language throughout the process. Instead of saying, "In this situation, who was there?", say, "You are in the living room now. Who is there? What is the expression on his face?" Insist that the client speaks in present-tense language.

Not too long and not too short:

- If you continue vivifying the situation after the Vaded State is already in the Conscious, there is a risk of losing the state. Conversely, if you move too quickly and the state is not yet in the Conscious, finding the first moment of traumatization will not be possible.

Core Feelings:

- Watch for statements of core feelings. When the client expresses core feelings like, "I feel scared," "I'm horrified," or uses sentences that point to core feelings like, "I want to run," "My heart is racing," "I want to get out of here," it indicates the Vaded State is in the Conscious, and you can proceed to the next step. You should write these core feelings down so you can repeat them to keep the Vaded State in the conscious.

Outline of the Steps of the Vivify Specific Action:

a. *Identify the Needed Resource State:*

- Understand which specific Resource State needs to be brought into consciousness.

b. *Ensure Specificity:*

- Be persistent in having the client pinpoint a specific time when this Resource State was previously conscious.

c. *Vivify the Time:*

- Encourage the client to vividly describe the specific moment, including details such as what was worn, the time of day, lighting. who was present, their expressions, the temperature, and any other relevant details.

d. *Use Present Tense Language:*

- Once the client starts describing the specific moment, begin using present tense language to help bring the desired state to the surface.

e. *Document Details:*

- Take detailed, verbatim notes of what the client says.

f. *Ensure the Desired State is Conscious:*

- Continue the process until it is clear that the desired Resource State is fully conscious.

Examples

Examples of Getting the right state into the Conscious may be found on the following pages, 181, 193, 212, 238, 255, 269, 288, 307, 323, and 323.

Step 3) Getting to the Initial Sensitizing Event

(The Bridging Action)

Purpose

Bridging is the process that brings the Vaded State from feeling upset in the present backward in time to the first situation in which the state experienced such an overwhelming amount of fear that it could not integrate this experience. It is the emotion the Vaded State experiences, when Conscious, that is the Bridge, Therefore it is important for the client to hold that emotion throughout the bridging process to locate the ISE. Once this Initial Sensitizing Event is found, its upset feelings can be resolved.

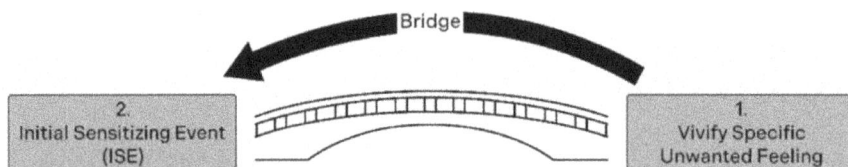

Figure 11: Bridging with Fear Emotion

Conceptual understanding

Often, when big things happen in childhood, our parents (or someone else) help us feel better. Even though it might have been upsetting or scary, we feel understood and relieved. When this occurs, no state becomes Vaded with Fear or Rejection. It is when the child does not get that sense of support and understanding that a state may become vaded.

There are many reasons a child state may not get support and understanding. Sometimes the child is embarrassed or afraid and therefore does not tell anyone. Sometimes the child is feeling rejection from the person they would normally get support from. Sometimes the child is told not to tell. Or it is simply not aware, for example, that being abused is not 'normal' or not something it 'deserved'.

It is the unprocessed feelings of this child state that linger as a Vaded State. The Vaded State is left with the heavy feelings of fear. It is overwhelmed with the bad feeling, and when it comes into the Conscious it brings that unresolved negative feeling with it.

The client usually cannot intellectually know what exactly the traumatizing event was that is causing the pathology. How is it possible to find the ISE if the client cannot know? Thankfully, we have two types of memory: The intellectual memory and the feeling memory, called Sensory Experience Memory (SEM, Emmerson 2017). When an event occurs, the state that was conscious during that event will have both the intellectual memory and the Sensory Experience Memory (SEM) of the event. A person telling about what happened a couple of hours ago may be quite emotional when telling about it. But, over time, there is a separation between the intellectual and the Sensory Experience Memory. This is how a person will feel the emotions of an event that happened long ago (the SEM), without those emotions being connected to the intellectual memory.

The Sensory Experience Memory (SEM, the feeling memory) is held by that traumatized childhood state, and when something happens later in life the feelings of that Vaded State can come into the Conscious and this feels overwhelming. Due to the separation of the intellectual memory and the feeling memory, the adult will often not know where these feelings are coming from.

Bridging uses this feeling memory to take the client to the Initial Sensitizing Event, the event when the state became vaded. This re-unites the SEM with the intellectual memory and provides an opportunity for the childhood state to finally get the processing it needs, to finally understand it is not happening now, to finally feel support and understanding.

The Vaded State is an emotional state. An intellectual state is not emotional, and, while it can be very useful, it is not helpful in locating the ISE. The way to find the ISE is to first make sure the Vaded State is holding the Conscious (see the section directly above), and while holding that state in the Conscious, use it to guide you to where it was vaded. Sorry, but you cannot just ask it, "When did these feelings start?". Any time you ask an intellectual question you are inviting a different state into the Conscious, and you are stopping the bridging process.

Therefore, all questions must be about feelings and experiences. The feeling (Vaded) State will be able to answer these questions while staying in the Conscious.

There is one exception when we don't need to bridge. We know that most states were vaded in childhood, but a state may become vaded with fear in adulthood. It would take a major event to traumatize an adult state, like a car crash, a robbery or a war experience and the person would remember that well. The client will report everything being normal before that event, then there will be a big change following the event. For example, after a car crash the client may no longer be able to drive, or following a frightening incident the client may no longer be able to leave the house.

When this happens, no Bridging is necessary. The therapist can go directly to processing the event (see the next section, Relieving the trauma, page 88). If a state is vaded in adulthood it will be crystal clear when it happened, otherwise the state was vaded in childhood.

Instructions for getting to the ISE: Bridging

The best way to learn Bridging is to carefully read these instructions, then look at several of the examples. You can refer to these instructions to get a better conceptual understanding of what is important in the process.

Important Steps for Bridging to the ISE When the Vaded State is in the Conscious

a) Hold the State in the Conscious:

- It is necessary to keep the state in the Conscious throughout the Bridging process.

b) Identify the current body location:

- After Vivify Specific, ask for the current body location of the feeling being experienced with the Vaded State in the Conscious.

c) Determine the age of the Vaded State:

- Using the feeling and its physical localization, determine the age of the Vaded State (the age it feels will be the age it was at the ISE).

d) Funnel the Vaded State into the ISE:

- Once the age is identified, funnel the Vaded State into the Initial Sensitizing Event (ISE).

Note:

Bridging is not difficult if you avoid common mistakes. It requires learning and practice to effectively carry out this process.

a) Holding the Vaded State in the Conscious

It is important to hold the Vaded State in the Conscious through the Bridging process and through the processing work at the ISE. If you lose the Vaded State, Bridging doesn't work. You might end up at the wrong ISE, or find no ISE at all, or the whole process may get interrupted. So, to help hold the Vaded State in the Conscious, keep repeating the core feelings it has told you in Vivify Specific. This is very important. When a state hears its feelings repeated, it keeps listening and communicating. It continues to hold the Conscious.

Below, in the examples, you will find the times that the core feeling of the Vaded State was repeated during the process. These repeats are shaded.

To ensure the Vaded State stays in the Conscious and to avoid activating a different state than the Vaded State, it is necessary to be aware of the following pitfalls:

Remember that the Vaded State is most normally a child state. You should think of speaking to a child when talking with it. If you ask an adult-question or a why-question, you will lose the Vaded State.

Don't ask a question that would require thinking or that another state would have to answer. Don't ask a question where generalizations would have to be made, because a thinking state would have to answer this. Don't use words like "think", "think back", "think about", "remember" or "know". They will activate a state that is good at thinking and remembering.

You should never ask a client, "When was the first time you felt these feelings?" An intellectual state will think about this question and attempt to answer it and will usually be wrong. For example, a person who has panic attacks will report the first panic attack they remember, but that is not the ISE. That is merely the first time they remember these feelings being a problem.

b) Finding the body location of the core feeling

In the first step, in Vivify Specific, we have brought the Vaded State into the Conscious and have learned the negative feelings it is holding. These are the feelings that will lead us to the ISE. Now we want to find out where in the body this feeling is located by asking the Vaded State, "Where in the body are you feeling this right now?" Usually, it is in the chest or stomach, but it can be in other body locations. This will be followed by a series of sensory questions, like, "How big is that area? Is it the size of a golf ball, tennis ball, or football? Is it dark or light in there? Is it hard to move or easy to move in there? Is there a color?" Remember to continue repeating the feeling of the Vaded State in every question, e.g., "In that dark area, where it feels like "no matter what I say I'm in trouble," is it thick or thin, is it hard to move or easy?"

Even though questions about the color or the texture of a feeling might appear strange, they are important. They help to keep the Vaded State in the Conscious, "feeling" and "experiencing." Getting a sensory description of the area where the feelings are felt, better grounds the client into the Vaded State and prepares the client for the next step, which is, to find out the age of the Vaded State with all those overwhelming feelings. It will be the age it was during the first traumatizing situation, the ISE.

c) Getting the age of the Vaded State

When it is apparent that the client is well into the experience of the Vaded State, and when you have a good understanding of the description of the area where the feelings are felt, say something like, "Just sit above that (e.g.) dark, reddish area, you are a child, and just let your child feet dangle back and forth in that dark, reddish, 'no matter what I say I'm in trouble' area. Notice those dangling feet. How old are they?"

Notice here, we are not asking the state to think. A Vaded State is not a thinking state. It is a feeling state. I am asking the state to report its feelings. A Vaded State will feel the age it was at the ISE. Children are accustomed to dangling their feet. Their feet do not reach the floor when they sit in a chair. Therefore, using the imagery of dangling child feet inside the reported area of the body, the age that is felt is the age the client was at the ISE.

Funneling the state into the ISE

Once you have a childhood age for the Vaded State, it is usually quick to funnel the state into the image of the ISE. "Being 5, feeling unheard and in trouble, are you inside a building or outside in the open air? Are you alone or are you with someone else? These questions usually result in the client talking about exactly where they are. As long as the client is still holding the same emotions that were reported as problematic, this is the ISE.

You will know you are at the ISE when the Vaded State is able to describe where it is, and what is happening. The state should be showing the same emotion or feelings that the client reported as problematic.

The last part of Bridging is to get a name for the state at the ISE. "What can I call you?" You can give suggestions that fit the state at the ISE, like AFRAID, ALONE, LOST, but the state should choose or at least give an okay for the name.

Outline of the Steps for the Bridging Action

a. Ensure the client is in the Vaded State:

- Confirm the client is in the Vaded State by observation.

b. Hold the client in that State:

- Maintain the client in the Vaded State by constantly restating its feelings.

c. Locate the body part holding the feeling:

- Identify where in the body the feeling is being held.

d. Determine the age of the Vaded State:

- Find out the age the Vaded State feels, possibly by asking about dangling feet or saying, "The voice I am hearing sounds like a child's voice, not an adult voice. How old is this voice?"

e. Funnel the State into the ISE:

- Use the identified age to guide the state into the Initial Sensitizing Event (ISE).

f. Name the Vaded State at the ISE:

- Assign a name to the Vaded State at the ISE (e.g., "SCARED", "HELPLESS", "EXPOSED" or "PANIC"). This name is often negative, but it can be changed later.

Important in the Bridging Action:

<u>Keeping the Vaded State in the Conscious</u>

- Don't risk losing the state by activating an intellectual state. Avoid words like "think," "remember," and "know."

- Don't ask questions that need to be answered by an intellectual state, like for example "Has it always been like this in your family?" The client will have to think about the past and a thinking state will answer. The Vaded State will not be in the Conscious anymore.

- Don't linger or take too long. While Bridging, or even after reaching the ISE, if you leave long pauses or if you ask too many questions the Vaded State may become bored and another state may take the Conscious.

- Work swiftly and don't wait until the client has finished crying.

- Don't switch into past-tense language. Present-tense language helps make the scene real to the client.

Bridging is not a long process. You should know the purpose for each step so you can move on once you have met that purpose. Bridging is a process that takes some practice, and you will get better at it as you practice.

When observing a therapist Bridging who understands the process, it can look somewhat magical. It may be good to read and re-read the examples, as you continue to practice the steps in Bridging. It is a skill well worth learning.

What to expect at the ISE of a State Vaded with Fear

At the ISE of a State Vaded with Fear you will encounter scenes or situations that scared the child or that were interpreted as life-threatening, such as: In the living-room with a violent parent, alone in the dark, getting lost, being threatened or hurt by, e.g., an older brother or a bully, observing others getting hurt, being in an accident, nearly drowning in the sea, or being bitten by a dog.

Examples

Examples of Bridging may be found on the following pages, 216, following pages, 182, 193, 216, 241, 256, 270, 291, 308, 325, 343, and 356.

Step 4) Resolving the Trauma

Processing the trauma is de-traumatizing the Vaded State so it is no longer vaded. It is no longer holding or feeling the trauma. Therefore, if this state enters the Conscious in the future the client will not feel negative feelings.

Following Bridging, when we get the Vaded State to the ISE, the trauma that was not processed previously can now be processed. We do not want the state to be carrying traumatic feelings that can come to the surface. At the ISE, the state will at first believe the past is still happening. It will believe the bully still has power and can hurt, or that the accident is still happening. The following steps help the state become empowered over the provoking Introject and help it realize that the situation is not happening anymore. The provoking Introject is the person who the client was afraid of, or the scene it was afraid of, such as an earthquake, a fire, or an accident.

Step 4.1) Addressing the provoking Introject:

(The Expression Action)

Expression disempowers the Introject and empowers the Vaded State. Expression is the most important step in the process of bringing the Vaded with Fear state to a normal, healthy condition.

Purpose of Expression

Figure 12: The Expression Action

Since the Vaded State is stuck in its traumatic experience, we need to help it realize that the past is not happening anymore and that the Introject (provoking Introject) is just an illusion that holds no power.

By giving the Vaded State the opportunity to shrink the Introject (whether that's a person or an inanimate like a fire or an ocean) down to the size of a pea, it can experience that it **owns** the Introject, that it can **change** its appearance and that it can **express** anything it wants to say safely. Becoming conscious of this fact, the Vaded State immediately feels empowered and safer.

Conceptual understanding for Fear Trauma

Vaded States feel and believe that the past is happening right now. They believe the bully still has power or that the floodwater is still rising. They experience the feelings of the past because they believe it is current. If you bridge to an ISE where there was severe trauma the client may show a lot of fear because the Vaded State is stuck in that illusion. In reality the client is sitting in the therapy room and there's nothing to fear there.

The client's mature states know the past is past, but the States Vaded with Fear or Rejection do not. That is why it is imperative to work directly with the Vaded State, not with an older more mature state. If the state you are speaking with sounds reflective and mature, then you are not speaking with the right state.

Expression is a step that proves to the Vaded State that the past is **not** still happening. When you say, "We know the bully is not really here as we are sitting in the therapy room. Let us just shrink him down to 1 cm tall with a squeaky little voice but be careful not to step on him because you want to be able to tell him what you want to say." This is a better way to help the Vaded State to feel empowered than by just saying, "You have more power than he does" as that statement is often not believed. But by explaining to the Vaded State that it needs to be careful not to step on the provoking Introject, it feels more empowered.

Saying, "This is not happening now, so you can say anything you want," helps the state understand it is safe now. It would not be able to speak if it thought it would be in trouble, so when it speaks to the provoking Introject, and nothing happens, it is proof that now it is in a safe place. The illusion that the past is happening has been broken. It only needs to say a few words to break this illusion, like for example, "Go away! You scare me!".

This is an important step in working with both Vaded with Fear and Vaded with Rejection states, but it is of primary importance to working with the Vaded with Fear states. The Vaded State learns that it has the freedom to speak because it is only speaking to a memory fragment.

The Expression step does not need to be long. It is not necessary for the state to say everything it feels, it is only necessary that it shows it is able to speak to the provoking Introject.

When the State Vaded with Fear describes what is happening at the ISE there is either another person there that makes it feel scared, an animal, or it can be a scary inanimate like an accident or a flood. It is important that the state speaks directly to the provoking Introject.

When the Vaded State is hesitant to say something to the Introject, it's good to ask if it's okay for you (the therapist) to speak first. This is a double bind, by giving two possible outcomes, in essence saying, "I can speak before you or you can speak first". Either choice results in the Vaded State speaking. If the Vaded State prefers you to say something first to the provoking Introject, you can say something like, "Look at you. You are tiny with a squeaky little voice. You are not even here. Look at that expression on your tiny face. That is sort of funny. (Then to the Vaded State) Now you tell him. Tell him how he makes you feel. You can tell him anything because he is not really here. Tell him out loud so I can hear you". (Note: The client defines the gender of the provoking person.)

While it is important that the Vaded State says something – it doesn't have to be much.

When the provoking Introject is not a person:

Sometimes a state can be Vaded with Fear when another person is not involved. For example, a dangerous animal may cause overwhelming fear, and so can a flood, a fire, a body of water, and many other things. When fear is the result of something other than a person it is still helpful for the Expression action to be used. By speaking to the fire, or the wild animal there is a demonstration of awareness that the past is past. This proves that the client does not need to avoid the provoking Introject. The client can face, and speak to, the provoking Introject.

Instructions for "Expression"

a) Empower the Vaded State and create safety:

- Let the Vaded State know that the event is not happening right now.

- Reassure the Vaded State that the Introject is not really here.

- Shrink the image of the Introject to something like one inch (2 cm) tall with a squeaky little voice.

- Ask the Vaded State to be careful not to step on the Introject.

b) Ensure Expression:

- Make sure the Vaded State expresses what it wants to say to the Introject.

When the Introject is not a person:

- Shrink the fire, the ocean, the dog, the accident, or the car similarly and have the Vaded State express to it.

Important in the Expression Action:

Sequence of steps

- Remember the sequence of the steps. Expression is the first thing we need to do when we have found the ISE, followed by the next step, Removal.

Length of action

- This action is very short. It's enough, if the state says something like, "Go away!"

Wording

- Remember the wording. Saying for example, "Let's shrink him down to 1 cm tall..." gives the Vaded State the feeling that we're in this together. This may make it easier for the Vaded State to do what we ask it to do than if we said, "Shrink him down to 1 cm tall."

As the words we use can make things more difficult or smoother in the whole process of resolving trauma, you will find examples with clients on the pages below.

Chapter 3: Resolving Fear Based Trauma

Examples

Examples of Expression may be found on the following pages, 185, 198, 221, 247, 260, 275, 296, 313, 330, 346, and 358.

Step 4.2) Removal of provoking Introject

(The Removal Action):

Removal provides more empowerment for the Vaded State by allowing it to decide whom or what it wants in its space.

Figure 13: The Removal Action

Purpose for Removal

The purpose of Removal is to empower the Vaded State and to help it feel safe. In this step we ask the Vaded State if it wants the provoking Introject to remain in its space, or if it wants the provoking Introject to leave. It is an especially important step for States Vaded with Fear, as it can be quite liberating for the state to send the person, animal or thing that has previously been feared out of its space.

States Vaded with Fear will almost certainly want the provoking Introject to be removed, and States Vaded with Rejection may or may not choose for the provoking Introject (rejecting person) to be removed.

Conceptual understanding

After the state has proved it has the power to speak to the provoking Introject in the expression step, it can decide if it wants the provoking Introject in its space, or if it wants the space clear. This is very empowering regardless of what is chosen.

Removal is a step that works only following the empowerment step of Expression. Expression shows the Vaded State that the past is over, and it can safely voice its desires. With this power the provoking Introject can now be removed from the space of the Vaded State. Without Expression, the Vaded State would still hold the belief that the provoking Introject is current and has more power than it does.

Each state holds its own Introject. A child state may have an Introject of Dad as a loud and scary Dad, whereas an adult state may have an Introject of Dad as an ageing helpless and fragile Dad. Removal only removes the Introject from the space of the state you are speaking with. Other states can and will have that person as an Introject in their space.

Interestingly, each state owns its Introjects, although it is not aware of that. A state that fears a bully from the past owns, and is empowering, the Introject of that bully. The bully is not in the therapy room, only the image of the bully that is held by the Vaded State. The Vaded State is fearing what it, itself, owns and what it empowers. Resource Therapy helps the state realize its power over the previously feared Introject.

Instructions for "Removal"

The step of Removal is fast. It is merely saying something like, "What you told the bully was really good. Do you want him to stay in your space, or do you want him to leave? It's totally up to you. It's your space and you can have what you want." If the client says, "No, I don't want him here," (which is most likely when working with a State Vaded with Fear) you can say, "Okay, that's good. Let's just clear the space, swoosh. He is gone. You can have lots of light if you want it. It's your space so you can have it any way you want."

Important in this action:

Don't linger

- When a State Vaded with Fear is at the ISE, it feels fear, sometimes great fear. We want to only spend the time with each step that we need to fulfill the purpose the step has. When we bridge, we want to get the age of the Vaded State and get to the ISE. At the ISE, we only want to get the name of the Vaded State, and we want to find out who or what the feared Introject is. For Expression, we only need to know who or what to shrink and have the Vaded State express to that. And in Removal we only want to offer the option of keeping the image of the Introject, or removing it, so that the Vaded State realizes that it's holding all the power. If you take too much time going through these steps the client may get bored and another state may take over the Conscious.

Examples:

Examples of Removal may be found on the following pages, 185, 224, 228, 249, 262, 279, 299, 315, 332, and 350.

Step 5) Creating a feeling of positivity for the state

(The Relief Action)

After helping clients process the negative feelings they have taken on and carried, we want them to again feel positive. We want the Resource State that had felt overwhelmed to be able to return to its positive role. The steps above result in the Vaded State to no longer be vaded. The ISE has been located, and the state has become empowered, but the following steps help the state feel really good about itself, and they help prepare the client for dealing with the same issue in the future by locating a strong state to help.

Figure 14: The Relief Action

A previously vaded child state should not be expected to deal with difficult adult dilemmas. Therefore, it is good to find the best state the client has, to deal with difficult settings.

Relief

The Relief action helps the previously Vaded State to feel protected, safe and nurtured.

Purpose of Relief

States Vaded with Fear have felt bad for a long time, since the ISE. The empowerment phase above is to help them understand that the past is not still happening, and that there is nothing for them to fear.

We don't want to just leave them alone and unconnected, even though they no longer feel overwhelmed. We want them to feel positive and supported.

The purpose of the Relief action is to help previously Vaded States to feel positive about themselves, to help them feel connected, safe and loved.

In Relief, a nurturing part of the client is found to come to the previously Vaded State and give it love and support. This feels good to both states. It feels good to receive love and support, and it feels good to give love and support.

Conceptual understanding of the Relief Action

A state holding an overwhelmingly negative feeling, will bring that feeling to the surface when it comes into the Conscious. A state that feels love and support will likewise bring that feeling into the client's awareness when it comes into the Conscious.

We want all our states to feel positive about themselves and to feel positive connections to other states. Relief is an important step to promote a feeling of positivity.

The Relief Action is helpful to both states that were Vaded with Fear and Vaded with Rejection. It helps the state that was Vaded with Fear feel safe and supported and it helps the state that was Vaded with Rejection feel loved, and lovable.

The Relief Action should not precede the Expression because we want the state to become empowered first, rather than to just hide behind a nurturing state still feeling that there is something there that is bad. Once it has claimed its own power with Expression and Removal, Relief is the icing on the cake, where it is enabled to also feel nurtured and positive.

Instructions for "Relief"

a.	Find a helping, nurturing state.
b.	Get a name for the helping state.
c.	Instruct the helping state.
d.	Ask the previously Vaded State how it feels now with the helping state by its side.
e.	Find a new name for the previously Vaded State.
f.	Gain permission from the previously Vaded State for another state to act in the future.

Examples:

Examples of Relief may be found on the following pages, 186, 200, 225, 245, 262, 279, 298, 316, 333, and 348.

a.   A Find a helping, nurturing state

The first part of the Relief Action is to find a helping adult state that can give love and support to the previously Vaded State.

The best way to find a helping adult state is to call the client by name and ask the client how she would help a person in the situation of the Vaded State at the ISE. "Kylie, if there was a 5-year-old child, someone you knew and cared about, like your child or a little sister, and that 5-year-old is alone in a room after having experienced a bad time, Kylie, how would you help that child? What would you do?" By phrasing the question like this, you practically always get the state out who really wants to help the child state.

This is better than saying, "I would like to speak with a part that is nurturing. Just say, 'I'm here', when you are ready to speak." because some clients have a hard time locating a nurturing state. Externalizing the person that needs help ("someone you know and care about") makes it easier for the client to access a nurturing state.

b.   Get a name for the helping state

As soon as the answer to "How would you help" is given, say, "What can I call you, part?"

c.   Instruct the helping state

Then we merely instruct it to go to the child state and do what it said it would do. For example, if the state named itself HELPER:

> "HELPER, thank you for being there. HELPER, I want you to go to 'FRIGHTENED' right now. HELPER, the more things you do, the stronger you become, and you can do many things all at once. So, you will always be able to be there with 'FRIGHTENED'. Go to

'FRIGHTENED' right now and put your arm around her and let her know you will always be there for her."

d. Ask the previously Vaded State how it feels now with the helping state by its side

'FRIGHTENED', how does that feel? Can you give 'HELPER' a bit of a hug also, because that will make both of you feel good. (Answer) That's great.

e. Find a new name for the previously Vaded State

Now that you have HELPER there with you, you don't really feel FRIGHTENED anymore, do you? (Answer) What would you like to be called now, that better reflects the way you feel now?" (Answer) "That's a beautiful name. From now on I'll call you 'new name'."

Purpose for getting a new name

A Vaded State feels bad. A State Vaded with Fear feels overwhelmed. Therefore, it will most often give itself a negative name such as 'PANIC'.

Following resolution, when the state is feeling safe and loved, it is good to get a new name for the state that reflects its new feelings.

Conceptual understanding for getting a new name

The name a state chooses reflects how it feels about itself. A bully may call a person a negative nickname and that does not feel good to the person. It makes the person not feel good about themselves. We want states to feel good about themselves.

A state will not accept a positive sounding name when it feels negative. Imagine feeling beaten down and humiliated and then someone asks you if you would like to be called 'HAPPY'. You would not. But, following empowerment and loving support, and a loving hug from a helping state, the previously Vaded State is ready to get a positive name it can have for now and for the future.

When it is time for a state to choose a new, more positive name, it's nice to confirm that the chosen name is good, "That's a beautiful name. From now on I'll call you 'NEW NAME'.

To get a better indication of context and different phrasing it is probably best to review the examples below.

Examples

Examples for getting a new name for the resolved state may be found on the following pages, 228, 250, 263, 281, 300, 318, 335, and 351.

f.   Permission for another state to act in the future:

"Now that you are feeling much better and have a helping part there with you, is it okay with you if a more mature state takes care of the adult stuff on the outside, and you can stay comfortably where you are?"

Purpose for permission for another state to act in the future

The previously Vaded State is asked if it is okay if a more mature state handles difficult situations in the future. The purpose of this is to help the child state to feel less responsibility and to help other states to become aware that an opening to help is available.

Conceptual understanding

It is not unusual for two or more Surface States to want to be out at the same time. States like to hold the Conscious, especially when they feel they have the skills that the occasion demands.

Imagine being in a committee room with several people. One person has held a position for years. The other people in the room may not seriously consider taking on that position if they feel it is already assigned.

Similarly, for example, each time the client had intimate relations a Vaded State that feared intimacy may have taken over the Conscious. A more mature, sensitive part that enjoys connection and physicality may have wanted to be in the Conscious in the past during these times of intimacy, but the Vaded State that felt overwhelmed took over the Conscious with its fears and negative feelings, so the more mature, healthy part could not be in the Conscious to enjoy the moment.

Following the resolution of the Vaded State, it no longer is driven into the Conscious with its unresolved feelings. By asking it if it is okay with it if a more mature state handles future times of physical intimacy, it opens the door for a more appropriate state to hold the Conscious during those times. It is like a person in the boardroom saying, "I no longer want that position." Other people will be able to consider if it is right for them.

This step is short and easy. It merely rests on the therapist saying something like this. "You are a great, sensitive part. You are wonderful. You can feel deeply. Is it okay with you if you only come out when it is really safe, and we will find a more mature part to handle the adult things on the outside?"

You can also add, "Sensitive parts are great. You might help the adult see beauty in a night sky, or in a safe hug. But it may be better if more mature parts handle the difficult times. Is that okay with you?"

Examples

Examples of permission may be found on the following pages, 251, 264, 301, 319, 335, and 352.

Important in the Relief-Action:

Make sure to address the client by name when asking how he would help a child he loved and cared for. This ensures that the best state of the mosaic of all his states will answer the question.

Step 6 Finding a better State to face current problem

(The Find Resource Action)

Figure 15: The Find Resource Action

Purpose

Find Resource is an RT action to find the best Resource for a particular need. It is used often in Resource Therapy, but in the context of helping states that have been Vaded with Fear or Rejection, it is used to find the best state to handle the situation that previously brought a Vaded State into the Conscious.

Conceptual understanding

It is always good to have the best state in the Conscious. What is the best state? That depends on what the client wants, therefore, to help the client find the best state the client needs to be asked.

For example, clients who want to enjoy intimacy with their partners, may want a part that can be relaxed in the moment, a part that can enjoy physical sensation, a part that might enjoy being playful.

You might wonder, why can't we just find the best part for a situation without resolving the Vaded State that has previously taken over the Conscious at the wrong time. A Vaded State is like a bear walking down the road. Other parts stay away when it is out. It will overpower other parts with its fear and take over the Conscious, until it is resolved. Choice follows resolution, and it cannot come before resolution. A person with a phobia of flying cannot just decide, "Here is how I want to feel," and make that the case. The unresolved Vaded State will drive the chosen state away. It is the bear coming down the road.

Instructions for "Find Resource"

To find the preferred Resource. the client's name is called, followed by the questions, "How would you like to handle this situation in the future? How would you like to act and how would you like to feel?"

After getting an answer to those two questions, the next question to ask is, "When in the past have you acted and felt like that?"

A time that state has been out needs to be vivified (using Vivify Specific). This brings the preferred state into the Conscious. It can then be asked, "What can I call you," and "Will you be willing to help in the future." Finding a state with the right skills ensures that it will want to help. States like to do what they are good at.

Examples

Examples of Find Resource may be found on the following pages, 188, 202 230, 251, 264, 282, 301, 319, 335, 352, and 360.

Step 6.1 Young state thanks the future acting state:

Purpose for saying, thank you.

Once you have found the best Resource State for the formerly problematic situation, you can get the resolved state (which is the state that had previously been Vaded with Fear) to say thank you to the new acting Resource. This confirms to it that it will no longer be responsible for adult situations, and it helps the volunteering Resource to feel appreciated and proud of what it is going to do.

Conceptual understanding

This step accomplishes two things.

- It provides a reassurance to the child state that a mature state is already lined up to handle the difficult situation in the future, so it helps relieve the child state of concern.

- It helps motivate the mature state to use its skills in the future to help. We all like to be appreciated and we like to help if we can. This step provides motivating appreciation to the mature state for helping in the future.

Instruction

After finding the best Resource to act in the difficult situation in the future (using the Find Resource Action), it is helpful to ask the young state if it would like to say, "Thank you," to the future acting Resource.

This is usually the final time the therapist will address the previously Vaded State. It has already been resolved, and it already has chosen a positive name for itself. The Find Resource Action has already located the preferred Resource State to handle the problematic situation in the future.

Immediately after speaking with the preferred, mature Resource State something like the following can be said.

"'PEACE', did you hear that? 'COMMUNICATE' has volunteered to talk to groups in the future, so you can stay there with 'HELPER'. 'PEACE', would you like to say thank you to 'COMMUNICATE' for doing this, so you won't have to worry about it?

(Following the thank you)

'COMMUNICATE', you are very popular now. 'PEACE' really appreciates that you will be helping in the future. Thank you for helping. You are a much better part to handle this situation.

Examples

Examples of young state saying thank you to future acting state may be found on the following pages, 189, 204, 232, 253, 267, 304, 319, 337, and 362.

Step 7) Ensuring the intervention was helpful

(The Imagery Check Action)

Purpose

The purpose of the Imagery Check action is twofold. It is to check and make sure that the needed work with the state has been completed, and it is to give the Find Resource State practice in applying its skills in the needed situation. This helps the client to gain confidence for the future.

Conceptual Understanding

Some therapies use a technique called future pacing to check that the client is ready for future situations. In future pacing, a new, imagined situation is presented for the imagery checking procedure.

The Resource Therapy Imagery Check action is different. Rather than use an imagined situation, Imagery Check uses the exact same situation that the client presented as problematic. An imagination is in the brain, created by an intellectual state. Reliving a real situation is a better test, and the situation presented in Vivify Specific is a real situation, not an imagined one.

The Vivify Specific action near the beginning of the session is used to help the client enter the Vaded State. The client is able to relive what was felt during the difficult situation. Since clients have already experienced the negative feelings about the difficult situation, they can notice the difference near the end of the session when they return to the same imagery.

If the client still feels the situation is difficult, then that is good information for the therapist that more work needs to be done. Possibly Bridging missed the ISE associated with the difficult situation, or possibly a second Vaded State is involved.

Occasionally, two Vaded States can be involved. Sometimes, when a client is asked during the Bridging step, "Where in the body is this emotion you are feeling right now?" (see page 83), the client will respond with two body locations. This is an indication that two separate Vaded States are involved.

After resolving the first one, Imagery Check can inform the therapist that negative emotions are still present, and ready for more work. This means starting again at step 3, Bridging to the ISE (see page 79) by using the negative feelings the client is reporting. Going through the steps a second time in the session is often very easy and quick.

During Imagery Check, if the client does feel empowered, then that is testimony to both the client and the therapist that a more appropriate state is able to help.

Instructions

The Imagery Check action is straightforward and easy. During the Vivify Specific action near the beginning of the session the therapist should take good notes, writing down things such as where the situation occurred, what was felt, who else may have been there, etc.

The Imagery Check action starts following the finding of the preferred state to handle the situation, and after it has been thanked by the previously Vaded State. The therapist says something like, "Okay, Sophie, let's go back to your office when your boss was criticizing you. Now you have STRONG there (the Find Resource State). STRONG, the boss is coming in with a disapproving look. STRONG, how do you want to handle this?"

The steps are to:

    a.   Call the client by name.

    b.   Return to the imagery of the difficult situation that was described in "Vivify Specific" at the beginning of the session.

    c.   Speak directly to the 'preferred state' from the Find Resource step and ask it how it would like to handle the situation.

Most usually the client will feel more confident and empowered. If there are still negative feelings present then the state that feels upset can be spoken with and worked with, usually very easily. For some reason, at this point, the session work can go very quickly.

If the new state is just a bit unsure you can say, "You are the very best part of Sophie to handle this, and you will be better at it the more you practice it. You are highly appreciated for helping."

Examples

Examples of Imagery Check may be found on the following pages, 190, 204, 234, 254, 284, 305, 338, and 363.

Step 8 Debrief with the client

Debriefing with the client allows any questions to be answered, and if the client needs further context, it can be given.

Immediately prior to ending the session, the client should be in a mature, positive state. Clients will move into a state that can answer the questions that are asked. Knowing that it is good to have a positive state in the Conscious, the therapist can, at the end of a session, ask questions of the client that will help a positive, mature state move to the Conscious. For example, a question like, "When have you felt the strongest, when communicating with your partner?" can help move the client into a strong state.

Likewise, observations about the client can move the client into the state that is the focus of the observation. The statement, "I have noticed you have the ability to see the best in people, even when they are struggling," can help move the client into the state that is mature and empathetic.

Helping a client be in a strong, positive state at the end of a session prepares the client to walk out and be ready to face the world. It does not solve the client's issues. Too often therapists think that moving a client to a more positive state is therapeutic. It is not. If a client has an Underlying State Vaded with Fear or Rejection it will still be there if a therapist merely helps them move to a more positive state. It will come out and feel overwhelmed in the future when it is triggered.

Finding the Vaded State and resolving it in the way discussed in this book (see Figure 16) leaves that state feeling positive rather than feeling overwhelmed. It will not come to the surface again with those overwhelming feelings, because it no longer has them.

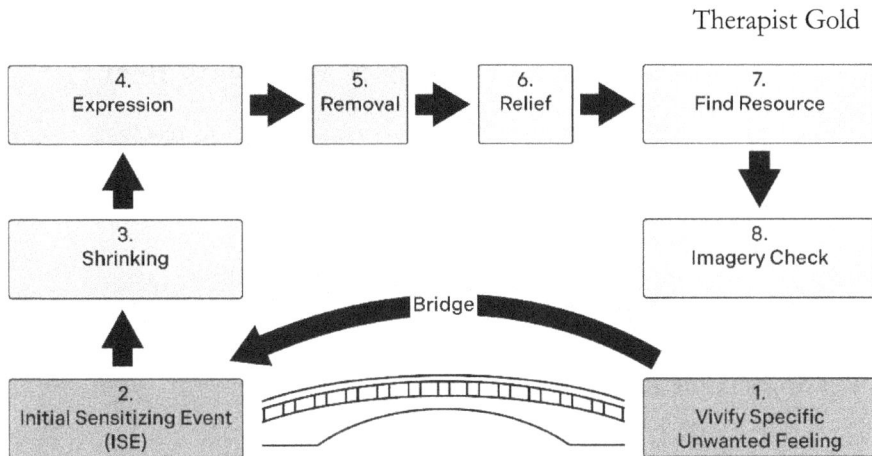

Figure 16: Treating a State Vaded with Fear

General Note: Each time we are asking the client something by calling the name of the client, we are asking the mosaic of states that **is** the client. When the client is addressed by name with a question the best state to answer that question most normally jumps into the conscious to respond. If you ask someone if he wants to play basketball, the state that likes playing basketball will most likely respond. Of course, if there is a disagreement among his states there may be a competition to respond. His basketball playing state may want to say, "Yes, let's play basketball," but he may have a work state or even a health state that says, "Not a good idea at this time." If the partner of that person asks him if he loves her, it is not his basketball state that will jump into the Conscious to respond. It is good that it works that way. Otherwise, life would be very confusing.

Takeaways from Chapter 3: Resolving Fear

This chapter outlines a structured, step-by-step approach to resolving trauma rooted in fear by working directly with the **Resource State** (referred to as the **Vaded State**) that holds the fear. The goal is to **move this state from a traumatized condition back to a functional one**.

Key Steps in the Resolution Process

1. **Diagnosis**
   Identify a Vaded State based on inappropriate fear responses in current situations.

2. **Vivify**   **Specific**
   Bring the fearful state into the Conscious so it can lead the therapist to the source of trauma.

3. **Bridging**
   Use the feelings of the Vaded State to access the Initial Sensitizing Event (ISE)—the original traumatic incident.

4. **Resolving the Trauma**

   o **Expression**: The Vaded State speaks to the **Introject** (internalized image of a person, animal, or event that caused the fear).

   o **Removal**: The state is empowered to remove the Introject, dismantling its lingering psychological power.

5. **Relief**
   Introduce a nurturing, supportive state. The formerly Vaded State acknowledges its strength and allows other states to assist in future.

6. **Find Resource**
   A more competent (usually adult) state is chosen to handle the current life situation, replacing the fearful child state.

7. **Imagery Check**
   The original fearful scenario is mentally revisited to ensure the new, stronger state can now handle it without distress.

8. **Client Debrief**

    The client reflects on the session and may ask questions, reinforcing integration and understanding.

Why Trauma Persists

- The Vaded State remains trapped in the belief that the original trauma is still happening.

- Without early intervention or support, this state can't distinguish past from present.

- The **ISE** holds the core feelings (fear, pain, helplessness) that continue to affect the person.

- **Symptoms** rooted in these unresolved states include: Phobias, Panic Attacks, PTSD, Nightmares, Anxiety Disorders, Self-Harm, Addictions, DID, Workaholism, and OCD.

Chapter 4: Resolving Attachment Trauma

Pathology: Vaded with Rejection

Vaded with Rejection is the most common diagnosis in our daily practice.

The steps for resolving a State Vaded with Rejection are similar to the steps for a State Vaded with Fear. We need Bridging for both, as the root of the symptoms is most normally unknown to the client. So, just as with States Vaded with Fear, we need to access the feeling memory (SEM) to find the cause and to be able to process it. We access this memory by bringing the Vaded State into the Conscious.

However, there is a big difference in what a State Vaded with Fear and a State Vaded with Rejection needs. A State Vaded with Fear is overwhelmed by fear. It needs to experience that the feared Introject no longer holds power over it, and it needs to feel that it is now safe.

A State Vaded with Rejection is left with an overwhelming experience of being rejected, not cared for, left alone, or somehow of not being good enough. These feelings are cemented in its psyche and have a great impact on the client's self-esteem, self-love and often also self-care. It can result in toxic stress, poor emotional regulation, poor working memory, poor immune system and an unhealthy sense of self, which can lead to other psychological issues.

In "Vaded with Rejection," the fear that is felt is a fear of "not being good enough," "not sufficing," "fear of making mistakes," "fear of being wrong," "having wrong feelings," "not being the best," "others being better/ prettier/ slimmer/ more intelligent." The State Vaded with Rejection can cause a deep belief of "having to be a certain way" in order to be loved and accepted. Sometimes a person may not know who they really are, as they are so busy trying to meet other people's expectations that they can't recognize themselves anymore.

This Vaded with Rejection state needs to experience that it, itself, is just fine the way it is, but that the person it was exposed to at the ISE was not the way they should have been. Whether that's a parent or a caregiver who (at the ISE within the interpretation of the Vaded State) wasn't able to love and accept the child unconditionally, whether that was a frustrated teacher who didn't treat children the way they should be treated, or a friend who didn't act like a friend should act.

The way this section is organized:

- First, the steps to move a State Vaded with Rejection back into a normal state will be listed, along with the page numbers where each is discussed.
- The techniques will be explained ("Instructions").
- Finally, several transcripts of clients are provided so you can see how the steps flow together, and so you can see how clients react to each step. There will be bracketed illustrative comments within these transcripts.

Steps to resolve Attachment Trauma:

1. Diagnosis: (page 116)

- The process begins by diagnosing a state as 'Vaded with Rejection', where the individual feels not good enough.

2. Getting the state feeling fear into the Conscious: (page 118)

- Once the therapist identifies the client has 'rejection-based trauma,' the next step is to bring the Vaded State into the Conscious. Only this vaded, traumatized state can lead the therapist to the trauma's cause.

3. Bridging to the Initial Sensitizing Event (ISE): (page 122)

- With the Vaded State in the Conscious, the therapist can bridge to the ISE using the feelings of the Vaded State.

4. Resolving the Trauma: (page 125)

- The Vaded State holds the false belief that the traumatic event is still occurring. By bringing the event's image into the Conscious, this illusion can be stopped.

4.1 Speaking to the rejecting person: (page 125) - Within the imagery of the ISE, it is crucial for the Vaded State to speak directly to the rejecting person. The Introject of the rejecting person causes the Vaded State to feel 'not good enough'. Speaking to the rejecting person helps the Vaded State gain a better focus on the ISE.

4.2 Client responds as the rejecting person: (page 129) - The client is asked to respond as the 'rejecting person'. This key step allows the Vaded State to learn that it was the other person who couldn't show unconditional love, not the Vaded State that was unlovable.

4.3 Removal of the provoking Introject: (page 133) - The client then has the power to decide that the provoking Introject is no longer needed in their inner space, known as 'removal'. At this point, the state is no longer vaded, but additional work can be done to help the state feel more positive.

5. Relief Phase: (page 137)

- A nurturing state of the client is brought to the previously Vaded State to provide support and connection. This step is crucial as it demonstrates the Vaded State is lovable, receiving unconditional love from a helping state.

6. Engaging a more mature state: (page 140)

- A more mature state is recruited to handle the current issue, as a child state, even if no longer vaded, may not be best suited for adult concerns.

6.1 Gratitude and Assurance: (page 141) - The previously Vaded State expresses gratitude to the adult helping state. This reassures the child state that it will no longer be responsible and motivates the adult state through appreciation.

7. Revisiting the original problem image: (page 143)

- The original image of the problem is reintroduced to demonstrate that the helper state can now manage the issue effectively, without trauma.

8. Client's questions: (page 146)

- Finally, the client is invited to ask any questions they may have.

Table 9 summarizes the Resource Therapy Actions to resolve a State Vaded with Rejection.

Table 9: Actions to resolve a State Vaded with Rejection

Steps to Resolve Attachment-Based Trauma:	RT-Action:
Find what the client is ready to change	Diagnosis
Get the pathological state into the Conscious	Vivify Specific
Get to the Initial Sensitizing Event (ISE) by bridging	Bridging
Express to the rejecting Introject	Expression
The state speaks as the rejecting Introject	Introject Speak
Removal of the rejecting Introject (or after Relief)	Removal
Find a nurturing state	Relief
Find a better state to face current problems	Find Resource
Check the efficacy of the therapeutic intervention	Imagery Check

Step 1) Diagnosis

If the client presents with self-worth-based problems or fears, Anorexia, Bulimia, or Over-Competitiveness, the diagnosis is "Vaded with Rejection".

Here are some statements that point to a State Vaded with Rejection:

- I'm afraid people will laugh at me.
- When my boss criticizes me, I feel like crawling into a hole.
- I feel terrible when I disappoint someone else.
- I only feel good about myself when I please others.
- I feel unlovable.

Purpose

Diagnosis leads us to the steps that will be needed to help the pathological state. If a state is diagnosed into the wrong diagnostic category, the wrong actions will be chosen and therefore the intervention may not have the desired effect.

Conceptual understanding

The client may present with a concern that is expressed as a fear, like for example, "I'm afraid to speak in front of a large group of people." When it is a fear of not being good enough or not doing well enough, the pathological state is Vaded with Rejection, not with Fear. A State Vaded with Fear feels physical fear, like for example, in panic attacks. It is afraid there is something that can hurt it or that may be life-threatening.

When it is not absolutely clear if we are working with a State Vaded with Rejection or a State Vaded with Fear, it will become clear at the ISE. There the state will either feel alone, not seen, not heard, not understood, not cared for (Vaded with Rejection), or it will be full of physical fear, feel in danger or threatened (Vaded with Fear). Since the course of actions up to the ISE is the same for both pathologies, it isn't problematic to make that distinction at the ISE. But, from this point on, it is important to know which pathological state we're dealing with, as a State Vaded with Rejection needs a different kind of support to heal than a State Vaded with Fear.

Step 2) Getting the state feeling rejected into the Conscious

(The Vivify Specific Action)

It is essential to bring the state that needs change into the Conscious With every RT-diagnosis. To access the state that is Vaded with Rejection, a situation must be re-vivified when the client felt the unwanted feeling. Again, it is important to make sure the client picks an isolated situation, a point in time, and no generalization.

Purpose

Like in Vaded with Fear, the State Vaded with Rejection must be in the Conscious to guide us to the ISE, so that it can be healed of its negative core-belief.

(The Vivify Specific Action)

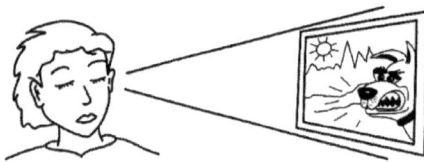

Figure 17: The Vivify Specific Action

Only the state that experienced the traumatizing event can lead us to the traumatizing event. The process of bringing the right state (the traumatized state) into the Conscious is called "Vivify Specific," because we need to re-vivify a recent specific event in which the client experienced the unwanted feeling of fear. It must be a specific event, as any generalizing is a mental process, and we need to bring the emotional state into the Conscious, not an intellectual state. When the client is re-experiencing these feelings of fear, it means that the Vaded State is holding the Conscious, and we can then work with it.

Conceptual Understanding

The Vaded State must be conscious to lead us to the event that vaded it. The Vaded State acts as our guide, someone who has been there before. However, it can't simply tell us what vaded it, but it can lead us there if we focus on the feelings.

When clients are asked why they are having an unwanted feeling, they often provide their best guess, which is frequently incorrect. For instance, a client who has experienced sexual abuse may attribute almost any negative feeling to that abuse. While sometimes true, often the negative emotion is connected to something else. Our goal is to identify and process what is necessary to help clients with their unwanted emotions.

To achieve this, we need to guide the client away from thoughts and intellectual attributions and instead focus on a specific recent situation where the unwanted feelings were experienced. By having the client re-experience this specific situation through imagery, the corresponding unwanted negative feelings are re-activated. The client can feel that fear now, allowing the Vaded State to move from a subconscious position into the Conscious, where it can be addressed immediately.

There is one exception to this process: When the client is already emotional and experiencing the fear. In this case, the Vaded State is already Conscious and can be worked with directly. Ensuring the Vaded State is conscious is the first step in reaching the Initial Sensitizing Event (ISE).

Often, clients will report the issue, but the Vaded State is not in the Conscious. One state will be discussing another state, often complaining about the Vaded State, saying things like, "I want this fear to go away!" Usually, an intellectual state is describing an emotional state.

When the vaded emotional state is not already in the Conscious, we need to use the Vivify Specific Action to bring the Vaded State into the Conscious so it can lead us to the root of the problem—the ISE.

Instructions for getting the right state into the Conscious (Vivify Specific)

a) Gain an understanding of which state is needed in the Conscious:

- To process fear-based trauma, we need the traumatized state in the Conscious, the state that is FEELING the fear.

b) Find one specific time this fear was experienced:

- Ask the client: "When was the last time you felt this way? I need to know one precise time you have felt that fear, one point in time."

c) Re-experience the situation in imagination:

- With the client's eyes closed, have them re-imagine the situation in their mind. Switch to present tense language and take verbatim notes:

    o "Now allow your eyes to close so you can really focus on this and describe the situation in the present tense, as if you were there now. What time of day is it? Is it light or dark? Are you standing or sitting? Who is there? What is the impression on this other person's face?"

d) Notice when the Vaded State is in the Conscious:

- Continue until you observe signs that the Vaded State is in the Conscious. These signs may include changes in voice, fear, tears, discomfort, changes in breathing, muscle tonus, etc. Another indication is when the client appears to be feeling the corresponding emotions, rather than just talking about an event.

Once the Vaded State is in the Conscious and displaying a level of the unwanted emotion, the next step can be taken: Finding the moment of the first traumatization. This process is known as "Bridging."

Important points in Vivify Specific Action

<u>Find a Specific Point in Time:</u>

- Ensure the client describes a specific point in time. If the client generalizes about an experience, it means an intellectual state is holding the Conscious, which is not what we want. For example, if the client says, "It happens when I am talking with someone who I feel is above me," they are generalizing. This indicates the client is speaking from a non-vaded, thinking state, about when the Vaded State is often out. We need to communicate directly with the Vaded State to find the root of the problem.

Wording:

- Never ask the client to 'think' during Vivify Specific, as an intellectual state will enter the Conscious to answer your question. Focus on feelings and experiences.

Use Present Tense Language:

- As soon as you locate 'one specific event', switch to and maintain present-tense language throughout the process. Instead of saying, "In this situation, who was there?", say, "You are in the living room now. Who is there? What is the expression on his face?" Insist that the client speaks in present-tense language.

Not too long and not too short:

- If you continue vivifying the situation after the Vaded State is already in the Conscious, there is a risk of losing the state. Conversely, if you move too quickly and the state is not yet in the Conscious, finding the first moment of traumatization will not be possible.

Core feelings:

- Watch for statements of core feelings. When the client expresses core feelings like, "I feel scared," "I'm horrified," or uses sentences that point to core feelings like, "I want to run," "My heart is racing," "I want to get out of here," it indicates the Vaded State is in the Conscious, and you can proceed to the next step. You should write these core feelings down so you can repeat them to keep the Vaded State in the conscious.

Examples

Examples of Getting the right state into the Conscious may be found on the following pages, 181, 193, 212, 238, 255, 269, 288, 307, 323, and 323.

Step 3) Getting to the Initial Sensitizing Event

(The Bridging Action)

Purpose

States Vaded with Rejection have had an overwhelming experience where they felt unworthy, incapable, or unlovable and, because they are frozen in this experience, they continue to hold these negative feelings. They also continue to hold an impression of the person rejecting them, the rejecting Introject. Every time this state comes to the Conscious it brings the unresolved feelings mentioned above with it. Bridging is necessary to locate the first situation when such an overwhelming amount of rejection has been experienced. The Vaded State is brought to the conscious using the Vivify Specific Action then, while conscious, Bridged back in time to the Initial Sensitizing Event, see Figure 18. There, at the ISE, the upset feelings and the resulting negative core beliefs can be resolved.

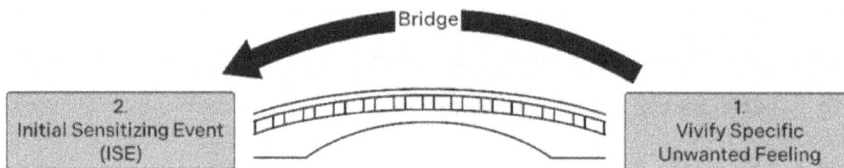

Figure 18: Bridging with Feelings of Rejection

Conceptual understanding

Some examples of parental rejection are indifference or neglect, belittling or shaming, making the child feel unloved, inadequate or unwanted, favoring one child over another, or a lack of warmth and caregiving. It is irrelevant if the rejection truly took place, or if it was just the perception of the child. Either way, feeling rejected is a painful experience and the state is left traumatized. Often moments of severe rejection take place at a very young age. Just imagine a baby or a small child left crying and upset with no one reacting to its physical or emotional needs. An experience like this can vade a Resource State. A parent with a new baby will not be able to pay as much attention to the older sibling. Then, when this older sibling acts out to get attention, the rebuke by the parent can vade the already emotionally fragile small child. Children with loving parents, doing their best, can still have States Vaded with Rejection. Childhood states can also be vaded in school settings, or in other places.

Just like in "Vaded with Fear," it is most likely that the traumatizing situation is not remembered intellectually. Bridging is necessary to find the ISE and to help the traumatized state. By using the feeling memory (SEM), it is possible to find the root of the problem: The therapist gold.

Instructions for Bridging

The instructions for Bridging with a State Vaded with Rejection are the same as Bridging with a State Vaded with Fear (see page 80).

What to expect at the ISE

Don't be surprised if, with this pathology, not much is happening at the ISE (unlike Vaded with Fear). While the State Vaded with Fear may describe a scene with other people, the State Vaded with Rejection is often simply <u>alone</u> somewhere. Alone in a forest, alone in its room, alone in the crib, alone in space, alone in a fog, or alone in the middle of a crowd. At other times a State Vaded with Rejection can be actively interacting with the rejecting person or persons.

Obviously, a problem can be that the child is feeling overwhelmingly alone, maybe also deserted, helpless, not understood, not important, not cared for, or whatever core feelings were expressed during Vivify Specific and Bridging. A question that needs to be asked is, "Being (for example) 5 years old, sitting in your room, feeling helpless, WHO SHOULD BE THERE?

You will read more about the importance of this question in the section "Expression."

Here are some examples, where the scene at the ISE is more concrete:

- Being in kindergarten, with the mother gone
- Being excluded from a group
- Being different and others don't like the child
- Having to perform well to feel loved and accepted by the parents

- Being scolded for making a mistake
- Having a baby sister or brother who takes a lot of the attention away
- Being responsible for a younger sibling at an early age
- Having very busy parents who never have time
- Being turned away by the father
- Feeling like a burden
- Being mocked or shamed, e.g. at home or in school
- Having to wear funny clothes or hairstyles, which makes it hard to connect with others

Examples

Examples of Bridging may be found on the following pages, 216, following pages, 182, 193, 216, 241, 256, 270, 291, 308, 325, 343, and 356.

Step 4) Resolving the Trauma

Now that the root of the problem is found, we can process the traumatic feelings of rejection the Vaded State is holding. To do so, a State Vaded with Rejection needs a different treatment than a State Vaded with Fear.

Let's look at the difference:

The de-traumatizing interventions for a State Vaded with Fear are to disempower the feared Introject and to empower the Vaded State by helping it realize that it can shrink the feared Introject, say anything it wants to it and send it out of its space. Then the state feels safe. To feel even better, it is provided with a nurturing, mature state that can always be there for it.

The de-traumatizing interventions for a State Vaded with Rejection are to also have the Vaded State express to the rejecting Introject, but then it needs to learn that it is the rejecting Introject that's failing, because it's not able to give the love and acceptance (or support, understanding, empathy, etc.) that every child should have. This is the important message that will resolve the feelings of 'not being good enough' and previous negative core beliefs. The nurturing, mature state, that helps in the relief step has an important function: It's not only there to make the Vaded State feel good, but it proves to the previously Vaded State that it is indeed lovable! It should be noted that the Introject that was rejecting at the ISE (mother, father, or other) was experienced by the Vaded State as being rejecting. That may or may not have been the case at the time. The important thing is that the experience of being rejected left the state feeling vaded, and the feeling of that state needs to change.

After Bridging, the next step is Expression.

Step 4.1) Expressing to the rejecting Introject

(The Expression Action)

Empowering the Vaded State Expression is the most important step to help the Vaded State realize that the past is not still happening. For States Vaded with Rejection, it is mandatory to express to the right Introject, which must be the rejecting Introject.

Conceptual understanding for Attachment Trauma

Like States Vaded with Fear, States Vaded with Rejection are stuck in their negative feelings and need to learn that the traumatizing event is a memory fragment from the past.

The difference here is that when working with a State Vaded with Fear, it is usually obvious who or what the feared Introject is. There is a bully at the ISE, an abusive parent, an accident, a flood or an enemy in a war scene, so we know exactly what needs to be worked with.

When we work with States Vaded with Rejection, they are often alone at the ISE. Then the crucial question is, who should the Vaded State express to? It's our challenge to make sure it's the rejecting Introject, <u>not</u> someone the state would like to have there. When the question "Who should be there?" is asked, the Vaded State sometimes chooses a person it has good feelings about, like for example, a loving grandmother. But the loving grandmother is not causing the problem. She's not the one who traumatized the state. We want the person there that is causing the problem by rejecting the child. Only by demasking the rejecting Introject as being not unconditionally loving and accepting can we enable the State Vaded with Rejection to understand that <u>it, the child,</u> was not the problem, but that it was the Introject who failed to give the child what every child deserves. So, when we talk to the rejecting Introject in the next step (Introject Speak), we need to talk to the mother who is not there for the child, or to the father who cares only about his work, to the parents that don't realize their child is struggling, to the teacher with the derogatory attitude, or to the friend who turned their back.

If the State Vaded with Rejection chooses a person it has <u>good</u> feelings about instead of the rejecting Introject, it is helpful to say "It's not about who you <u>would like</u> to be there! Please tell me who <u>should</u> be there with you, being 5 years old and feeling all alone and helpless? Your Mom or your Dad?"

When a child feels alone, not cared for, not heard, not seen, not important, it is obvious that the most important attachment figure should be there. These are usually the parents.

Note:

It is possible that the Vaded State needs to express to more than one rejecting Introject. When there are two people (like, for example, Mom and Dad), the Vaded State needs to express to both. "Who needs to hear how you feel first? Mom, or Dad?"

If the Vaded State feels rejected by a group, it can choose one person from the group who will be representing the whole group and express to this person.

Shrinking the Introject for a State Vaded with Rejection:

While this step is one of the most important steps for States Vaded with Fear, it is not always necessary when working with a State Vaded with Rejection.

A State Vaded with Fear is full of fear. By shrinking the feared Introject and being told to be careful not to step on it, this immediately resolves most of this fear.

A State Vaded with Rejection is longing for love and connection. It might want to have a parent to lean on and to find guidance. The rejecting Introject might be a good mother, who just happened not to be there when it was important for the child. In cases like these, it would be strange and even counter-productive to shrink the Introject.

If the State Vaded with Rejection shows any difficulties to express to the Introject it is then helpful to shrink it.

For example, "We know Mom is not really here, so let's just shrink her down to 1 cm tall and you can tell her exactly how you feel."

It is important that the Vaded State says something so it can gain an emotional understanding that the past is not still happening. It doesn't have to say much.

Be aware that when a state doesn't stop talking about all the things that went wrong throughout their childhood, this is a sign that we might have lost the Vaded State. Instead, a more mature state is speaking which is happy to be able to talk about all the bad things it remembers. When this happens, we need to return to the Vaded State so that it can benefit from the next steps. A Vaded State feels overwhelmed, and it will not be talkative.

Chapter 4: Resolving Attachment Trauma

Instructions for "Expression"

a) If it is not clear, find out who the rejecting Introject is
b) Empower the Vaded State and make it safe for it to express to the Introject by:
   - letting the Vaded State know that it's not happening right now
   - letting the Vaded State know that the Introject is not really here
   - only if necessary: shrinking the Introject and asking the Vaded State to be careful not to step on the Introject
c) Ensure the Vaded State expresses a few words to the Introject.

Important in this action:

The rejecting Introject

Make sure the Vaded State expresses to the rejecting Introject, the person who caused the problem.

It may occur that the Vaded State says, "No, I don't want to have Dad here." Sometimes states feel so rejected, they don't even want to talk to this person anymore. Then it's even more important to make sure this is the Introject the Vaded State will express to. You can say, "Well, we know he is not really here. That's a great opportunity to tell him how you feel."

You can shrink the Introject if the Vaded State shows a greater fear to speak.

Make sure that the Vaded States speaks directly to the Introject and encourage the state to do so in case it starts telling you about what it wants the Introject to know.

Take notes.

Examples:

Examples of Expression may be found on the following pages, 185, 198, 221, 247, 260, 275, 296, 313, 330, 346, and 358.

Step 4.2) Client responds as the rejecting person

(Introject Speak)

Purpose

The only reason we speak to the rejecting Introject is to reveal it was not able to demonstrate unconditional love. It is essential for the State Vaded with Rejection to understand, "It's not me who is unlovable, it's (e.g.) Mom who isn't able to be unconditionally loving!" This understanding creates a cathartic shift and helps the traumatized state to let go of the negative self-view and the resulting negative core beliefs.

Conceptual understanding

For States Vaded with Rejection this is an especially important step. When the client slips into the skin of the Introject and speaks as the Introject, it becomes clear that at that time unconditional love was not being offered. The therapist repeats to the rejecting Introject what the Vaded State said during "Expression" and asks the rejecting Introject how it feels about that. The rejecting Introject will often say something like, "I'm just too busy to give her what she wants. She is just too demanding. I have other kids, too," or "I should never have had a child. I did not want kids," or "I'm raising her the way I was raised. I don't know any other way to do it."

It does not matter what the Introject says. It will never be a demonstration of showing unconditional love. The Vaded State feels rejected by its Introject and was vaded by this Introject. Therefore, the reply of the Introject will always reveal that it rejected the state in one way or another.

We are not trying to villainize the provoking Introject. We want to hear an excuse for the rejecting behavior so when we return to the Vaded State we can show understanding. We want to be able to go back to the Vaded State and say something like, "'ALONE', I can really understand why you don't feel heard. Your Mom, at this time, is not able to give you the unconditional love and acceptance every child deserves. I would not feel heard, if it was me. No one would."

This moves the responsibility for the rejection from the child to the adult. The child had felt that something must be wrong with them, but after hearing and feeling how the adult is unable to give unconditional love, and after hearing the therapist confirm this, the state that was Vaded with Rejection moves toward normalcy (see 'Affirming the feelings of the state' below.).

Examples

Examples of Introject Speak may be found on the following pages, 199, 222, 247, 260, 276, 295, 314, 331, 347, and 358.

Affirming the feelings of the state

Purpose

Affirming the feelings of the Vaded State comes immediately after having spoken with the Introject. Introject Speak is done for the purpose of being able to affirm the feelings of the Vaded State.

This affirmation step is when the therapist makes a statement showing that feeling rejected is a normal reaction. It is normal to feel rejected after being rejected by the provoking Introject.

Conceptual understanding

A State Vaded with Rejection feels 'not good enough'. It feels like, "There is something wrong with me." It feels like 'it' is the problem. Something has happened where it feels rejected and it feels like it is its fault.

The Introject Speak step is when the client speaks as the rejecting person, being asked by the therapist to explain the rejection. Explanations range from being too busy to pay attention to the child, to statements like, "I never wanted to have a child." The Introject Speak step allows the client to feel the frustration of the provoking Introject in not being able to provide unconditional love. After the Introject Speak step, when the therapist calls the Vaded State back to the Conscious, it is still aware of those frustrated feelings of the Introject. At that point of awareness, the therapist expresses an ability to understand and affirm the rejected feelings of the Vaded State. The therapist normalizes those feelings, saying, "I would feel that same way if this happened to me."

It is important for the state that has 'felt not good enough' in the past to understand that the upset feelings it had were reasonable. It needs to understand that the problem was with the other person who was not at that time able to share unconditional love.

This process is instrumental in changing the feelings of the Vaded State from, 'there is something wrong with me,' to 'the other person was not able at that time to provide the love and support that every child should have.' It prepares the Vaded State to accept the love offered in the Relief action below, and by accepting this love there is further proof that, "I am lovable." There is a huge difference between, "there is something wrong with me" and "I am lovable." This is key to working with clients suffering from attachment disorder, and it is key to working with all States Vaded with Rejection.

Instructions for affirming the feelings of the state

After the client has spoken as the Introject, the therapist goes back to the Vaded State, calling it by name, and say something like, "Wow, I can understand why you feel upset. I would feel upset too. Anybody would. I'm sorry that other person was not able to give you the love that every child should have. I want to make sure you get it now."

Notice, I do not say, "I want to make sure you get the love **you** deserve." Clients will often rebel against the statement that they deserve love, but they do not rebel against the statement that, "Every child deserves love."

"Whether a child is good or whether a child makes a mistake, there should always be love. I want to make sure you get what every child should have."

This removes blame from the child part and gives permission for the state that was vaded to receive love. It places it within the group of all children, and all children should have love.

Examples

Examples of Affirming may be found on pages, 224, 249, 261, 296, 315, 332, and 348.

Overview of instructions for "Introject Speak"

a. Introduce the idea of speaking as the Introject.

b. Following the Expression Action, the therapist can say something like. "That was great. Now I want to hear from Dad. Just be a great actor and be Dad."

c. Thank the Introject for talking to you.

d. The therapist repeats to the Introject what the Vaded State said during "Expression".

"Dad, your son just said he can't please you. What is going on, Dad? Are you trying to teach him? Is that the way you were raised?"

e. Address the Resource State and affirm its feelings.

"Wow, I can understand why you feel upset. I would feel upset too. Anybody would. I'm sorry that other person was not able to give you the love that every child should have. I want to make sure you get it now."

Important to remember

Introject Speak is normally only used for States Vaded with Rejection. To be de-traumatized, they need to have the experience that they are lovable. States Vaded with Fear need to feel safe to be de-traumatized. This Introject Speak Action should not be used for the Vaded with Fear pathology. The only exception is, if the State Vaded with Fear demonstrates a need to understand, 'How can that person do that?" Otherwise, there is no benefit in giving the perpetrator a voice (Introject Speak, p. Step 4.2)

For example, if an unknown person is the provoking Introject that the State Vaded with Fear is afraid of, then the Vaded State will most usually have no need or desire to hear from that person. There is just a desire to feel safe and free of the person. But if a parent or schoolmate is the provoking Introject then the Vaded State may be curious why that person would want to hurt them.

Note:

Occasionally in Introject speak a younger client will speak in a way that shows an effort to make Dad look unreasonable. You will pick this up more from the tone than from what is said. If this happens you can say, "I want to hear directly from Dad. I want you to be Dad, like a great actor who forgets who they are, and really becomes the other person. Just be a great actor now." We all believe we can be a great actor, so it is a good way to motivate a client. You should listen to see if Dad's voice sounds like it is what Dad would say, not what the client wants you to hear. This is normally not an issue.

Step 4.3) Decision whether to move the rejecting Introject

Removal

The Removal Action results in more empowerment for the Vaded State by allowing it to decide who it wants in its space.

Purpose

The State Vaded with Rejection is asked if it wants the Introject to stay in its space or if it wants the Introject to leave. It is irrelevant how this question is answered. Being able to make this decision is another step in helping the Vaded State realize, "I have the power – this is **my** space!" and that's empowering.

While States Vaded with Fear usually want the Introject to be removed, States Vaded with Rejection may - or may not - want the Introject to be removed.

Conceptual understanding

While for States Vaded with Fear it is important to remove the feared Introject as soon as the State has expressed to it, a State Vaded with Rejection may prefer to not remove the parent who has been unable to share unconditional love. Here we have a choice to use this Removal Action either before or after the Relief Action, but Removal should not come before Expression. It is only after the empowering step of Expression that the Vaded State understands the past is not still happening. It is only after Expression that the Vaded State understands it has the power for Removal. Whether to use Removal before or after the Relief Action, depends on the feelings of the Vaded State. Let's look at two examples:

- Imagine a 5-year-old child at the ISE, feeling alone and not seen by Mom, longing for love and connection. When we ask the child at this point, "Do you want Mom to leave or do you want her to stay in your space?", the child may feel, "If I tell Mom to leave, I will be all alone again." If we ask this question after the next step ("Relief"), the child has a loving, nurturing State by its side and doesn't feel alone anymore. In this case the child-state might feel more comfortable making that decision because it already feels supported by the helper state we found in "Relief".

- Imagine a different State Vaded with Rejection at a different ISE, let's say 7 years old, in school, and the insensitive teacher is embarrassing the child in front of the class. In this scene the child state may feel happy to tell the teacher to leave its space immediately following Introject Speak.

Instructions for Removal (if done after Introject Speak)

"Now I want to get another part to come in and stay with you and make sure you feel loved and supported. In the meantime, do you want Dad in your space right now or not? It's totally up to you. It's your space and you can do what you want."

If the Vaded State says that he can stay, "Ok, that's nice of you, to let him stay."

If the Vaded State says that he can leave, "Ok, that's fine. Let's just clear the space, Swoosh, it's clear now,"

Instructions for Removal (if done after Relief)

"Now that you have HELPER with you, do you want Dad in your space, or not? It's totally up to you. It's your space and you can do what you want."

If the Vaded State says that he can stay, "Ok, that's nice of you, to let him stay."

If the Vaded State says that he can leave, "Ok, that's fine. Let's just clear the space, Swoosh, it's clear now."

Sometimes a client will say, "I want him to stay, but not when he is bad." Then you can say something like, "Is it okay to have a magic golden barrier where the good Dad can come through, but the bad Dad can't possibly enter?" The answer to this question is almost always, "Yes."

"Let's have an extremely powerful golden barrier. It's much more powerful than it needs to be. The good Dad can come through an spend time with you, but the bad Dad can't possibly come through. You can enjoy the good Dad."

Important in this Action

It is especially important to maintain the sequences of the steps during the resolution of a State Vaded with Rejection, with one exception. It is okay to interchange the order of the Removal and Relief steps, **Table 10**. The order of these two Actions therapeutically does not matter, but the flow of the session will dictate which one the therapist will want to start with.

Table 10: Interchanging Relief and Removal Steps

Steps for Vaded with Rejection – Default Path	Steps for Vaded with Rejection – Alternative Path
1. Vivify Specific	1. Vivify Specific
2. Bridging	2. Bridging
3. Expression	3. Expression
4. Introject Speak	4. Introject Speak
5. Removal	5. Relief
6. Relief	6. Removal
7. Find Resource	7. Find Resource
8. Imagery Check	8. Imagery Check

Examples:

Examples of Removal may be found on the following pages, 185, 224, 228, 249, 262, 279, 299, 315, 332, and 350.

Step 5) Creating a feeling of positivity for the state

(The Relief Action)

After the steps mentioned above, the formerly traumatized state is not vaded anymore. It has become empowered and has internalized the information that it had a right to feel the way it felt and that there's nothing wrong with it, because it was the Introject that was not unconditionally loving and accepting. The next steps are the same as in "Vaded with Fear," but the step "Relief" plays an especially important role for States Vaded with Rejection.

Relief: Helping the previously Vaded State to feel loved and lovable

Purpose of Relief

States Vaded with Rejection have felt rejected for a long time, often since early childhood. As a consequence, they have a low self-worth and a distorted self-view. After the resolution of the traumatic experience, these States Vaded with Rejection already feel better, but we can help them feel even better and increase their level of self-worth from the inside.

Conceptual understanding

In Relief, we find a state that will support the previously Vaded State by accepting it, appreciating it, loving it, or by just being there for it. The great advantage of this intervention is, that a nurturing state of a person can always be there. The nurturing state is part of the personality and can be there for the child state for as long as this person lives, constantly giving it the feeling of being lovable and loved. This makes the client more independent from external appreciation. Of course, appreciation feels good to everyone and is nice to get. But a State Vaded with Rejection has a hunger for it, which can cause people to do things they don't really want to do or can keep them from doing something because they fear to fail. The nurturing state we find in "Relief" proves to the previously Vaded State that, "Yes! I **am** lovable!" This may be a feeling it gets for the first time in its life.

Instructions for "Relief"

While this step has a different significance for States Vaded with Fear and States Vaded with Rejection, the course of action is the same. We need to:

a.	**Find a helping state.**
b.	**Get a name for the helping state.**
c.	**Instruct the helping state.**
d.	**Ask the previously Vaded State how it feels now with the helping state by its side.**
e.	**Rename the previously Vaded State if it has a negative name.**
f.	**Gain permission from the previously Vaded State for another state to act in the future.**

The steps are explained in "Relief" for States Vaded with Fear (see page 96), but it is a more important step in helping States Vaded with Rejection. It provides proof to the State Vaded with Rejection that it can be loved, because in this step it is loved.

Important in this action

Sometimes States Vaded with Rejection feel so deeply rejected that they cannot believe that the helping state will really be there for them. They might say something like, "What if 'HELPER' leaves me?" Then it's best to talk to 'HELPER' again and ask, "'HELPER', you said you were always going to be there for 'ALONE', is that right? Could you please tell 'ALONE' directly that you will do that?" After 'HELPER' has reassured the previously Vaded State, you can address the previously Vaded State again, and say, "'ALONE', you have heard what 'HELPER' said and felt how 'HELPER' feels. 'HELPER' will always be there with you!" The feeling memory (Sensory Experience Memory, SEM) created by this intervention will allow the previously Vaded State to experience the honesty and sincerity of the helping state and will take away the doubts.

Examples

Examples of Relief may be found on the following pages, 186, 200, 225, 245, 262, 279, 298, 316, 333, and 348.

Step 6) Finding a preferred State

(The Find Resource Action)

Purpose

At the beginning of the process, in "Vivify Specific", the client described a problematic situation from the present life, in which he experienced the unwanted feelings of the presenting concern. Now that the Vaded State is resolved and doesn't occupy the client's conscious with its negative feelings anymore, the client is free to have the mature state handle the situation that can handle it best.

Conceptual understanding

If a person previously felt extreme stress around public speaking, a childhood Vaded State was entering the Conscious with feelings of not being good enough or feelings of being judged. Although the previously Vaded State is now a healthy state, it's still a childhood state and certainly not the best state for public speaking. The client would want a mature state that is good at communicating, a state that can look at the faces of the audience to see their level of understanding. The client would want a state that enjoys sharing knowledge. Therefore, following the resolution of the Vaded State, the therapist can easily help the client find the best state for the client's needs, in this case, public speaking.

Instructions for "Find Resource"

The instructions for "Find Resource" are the same as for States Vaded with Fear. We need to locate the best Resource State the client has for this situation by asking, "How would you like to handle this situation in the future? How would you like to act and how would you like to feel?"

Obviously, the state that can answer this question is the best state to deal with the situation. It knows what it's talking about, which means it has a trained neurological pathway that has been active before. The client needs to describe a time this state has already been out before by answering the question, "When in the past have you acted and felt like that?" It's good to let the client know that this can be a very small situation, e.g., "When I'm playing with the grandchildren," or "When I read a book to my son," or "When I go for a walk with my dog."

This point in time needs to be vivified (using Vivify Specific) to make sure the preferred state is in the Conscious. When the preferred state is clearly in the Conscious, we can ask for its name and if it will be willing to help the client in the future. "NAME OF STATE, you have a real understanding of how to respond to a situation like this. Would you be willing to come out during these situations and help?" States love to help when they have the skills, and with this action we have found a state with the right skills.

Examples:

Examples of Find Resource may be found on the following pages, 188, 202 230, 251, 264, 282, 301, 319, 335, 352, and 360.

Step 6.1). Young state thanks future acting state

Purpose for saying, thank you.

Once you have found the best Resource State for the formerly problematic situation, you can get the resolved state (which is the state that had previously been Vaded with Fear) to say thank you to the new acting Resource. This confirms to it that it will no longer be responsible for adult situations, and it helps the volunteering Resource to feel appreciated and proud of what it is going to do.

Conceptual understanding

This step accomplishes two things.

- It provides a reassurance to the child state that a mature state is already lined up to handle the difficult situation in the future, so it helps relieve the child state of concern.

- It helps motivate the mature state to use its skills in the future to help. We all like to be appreciated and we like to help if we can. This step provides motivating appreciation to the mature state for helping in the future.

Instruction

After finding the best Resource to act in the difficult situation in the future (using the Find Resource Action), it is helpful to ask the young state if it would like to say, "Thank you," to the future acting Resource.

This is usually the final time the therapist will address the previously Vaded State. It has already been resolved, and it already has chosen a positive name for itself. The Find Resource Action has already located the preferred Resource State to handle the problematic situation in the future.

Immediately after speaking with the preferred, mature Resource State something like the following can be said.

"'PEACE', did you hear that? 'COMMUNICATE' has volunteered to talk to groups in the future, so you can stay there with 'HELPER'. 'PEACE', would you like to say thank you to 'COMMUNICATE' for doing this, so you won't have to worry about it?

(Following the thank you)

'COMMUNICATE', you are very popular now. 'PEACE' really appreciates that you will be helping in the future. Thank you for helping. You are a much better part to handle this situation.

Examples

Examples of young state saying thank you to future acting state may be found on the following pages, 189, 204, 232, 253, 267, 304, 319, 337, and 362.

Step 7) Ensuring the intervention was helpful

(The Imagery Check Action)

Purpose

The purpose of the Imagery Check action is twofold. It is to check and make sure that the needed work with the state has been completed, and it is to give the Find Resource State practice in applying its skills in the needed situation. This helps the client to gain confidence for the future.

Conceptual Understanding

Some therapies use a technique called future pacing to check that the client is ready for future situations. In future pacing, a new, imagined situation is presented for the imagery checking procedure.

The Resource Therapy Imagery Check action is different. Rather than use an imagined situation, Imagery Check uses the exact same situation that the client presented as problematic. An imagination is in the brain, created by an intellectual state. Reliving a real situation is a better test, and the situation presented in Vivify Specific is a real situation, not an imagined one.

The Vivify Specific action near the beginning of the session is used to help the client enter the Vaded State. The client is able to relive what was felt during the difficult situation. Since clients have already experienced the negative feelings about the difficult situation, they can notice the difference near the end of the session when they return to the same imagery.

If the client still feels the situation is difficult, then that is good information for the therapist that more work needs to be done. Possibly Bridging missed the ISE associated with the difficult situation, or possibly a second Vaded State is involved.

Occasionally, two Vaded States can be involved. Sometimes, when a client is asked during the Bridging step, "Where in the body is this emotion you are feeling right now?" (see Finding the body location of the core feeling, page 158). If the client responds with two body locations, this is an indication that two separate Vaded States are involved. After resolving the first one, Imagery Check can inform the therapist that negative emotions are still present, and ready for more work. This means starting again at step 3, Bridging to the ISE (page 79) by using the negative feelings the client is reporting. Going through the steps a second time in the session is often very easy and quick.

During Imagery Check, if the client does feel empowered, then that is testimony to both the client and the therapist that a more appropriate state is able to help.

Instructions

The Imagery Check action is straightforward and easy. During the Vivify Specific action near the beginning of the session the therapist should take good notes, writing down things such as where the situation occurred, what was felt, who else may have been there, etc.

The Imagery Check action starts following the finding of the preferred state to handle the situation, and after it has been thanked by the previously Vaded State. The therapist says something like, "Okay, Sophie, let's go back to your office when your boss was criticizing you. Now you have STRONG there (the Find Resource State). STRONG, the boss is coming in with a disapproving look. STRONG, how do you want to handle this?"

The steps are to:

    a. Call the client by name.

    b. Return to the imagery of the difficult situation that was described in "Vivify Specific" at the beginning of the session.

    c. Speak directly to the 'preferred state' from the Find Resource step and ask it how it would like to handle the situation.

Most usually the client will feel more confident and empowered. If there are still negative feelings present then the state that feels upset can be spoken with and worked with, usually very easily. For some reason, at this point, the session work can go very quickly.

If the new state is just a bit unsure you can say, "You are the very best part of Sophie to handle this, and you will be better at it the more you practice it. You are highly appreciated for helping."

Examples

Examples of Imagery Check may be found on the following pages, 190, 204, 234, 254, 284, 305, 338, and 363.

Step 8) Debrief with the client

Note:

If a provoking Introject from the past is currently problematic in the life of the client, the steps to process the Vaded State do not change, see Figure 19.

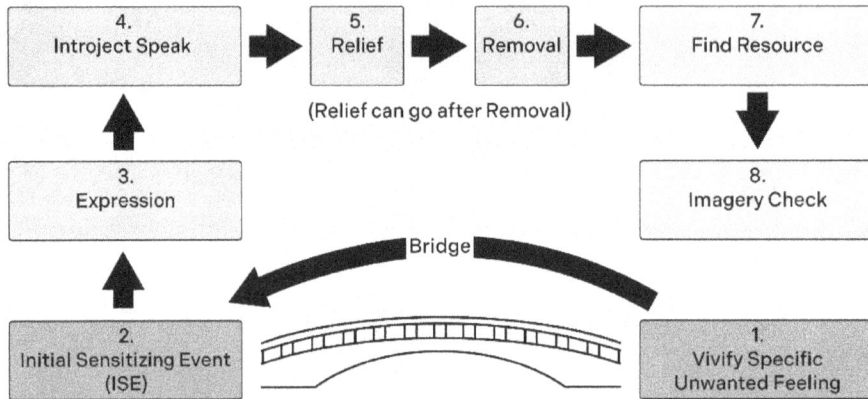

Figure 19: Treating a State Vaded with Rejection

Once the Vaded State is no longer vaded, no longer holding onto the illusion that the past is still happening, then the "Find Resource" action can be used to help clients decide how they want to deal with the provoking Introjects of today and then find their best Resource to do that.

Likewise, for States Vaded with Fear: If the provoking Introject is a spider from the past, once the childhood state is no longer holding onto the fear and that state feels safe and supported, then clients can define how they want to deal with a spider today, and we can use Find Resource to help them find their best state to do that.

Takeaways form Chapter 4: Resolving Attachment

Overview

This chapter focuses on how to resolve **Attachment Trauma**, specifically when a client has a **State Vaded with Rejection**—a deeply embedded part of the psyche shaped by early feelings of **not being loved, accepted, or valued**. It mirrors the structure used in fear-based trauma but with key emotional differences and therapeutic needs.

Key Differences from Fear-Based Trauma

- A **Vaded with Fear** state needs to feel *safe* and *powerful* over the fear-triggering Introject.

- A **Vaded with Rejection** state needs to feel *loved*, *worthy*, and *good enough*—as it often internalizes the belief that *it is inherently flawed or unlovable*.

This pathology affects:

- **Self-esteem**

- **Emotional regulation**

- **Physical health (via stress response)**

- **Identity and self-worth**

Steps to Resolve a State Vaded with Rejection

1. **Diagnosis**
   Identify the state as "Vaded with Rejection"—characterized by feelings of not being good enough or worthy.

2. **Vivify**   **Specific**
   Bring the Vaded State into Conscious awareness to begin healing work.

3. **Bridging**
   Use the emotions of the Vaded State to access the **Initial Sensitizing Event (ISE)**—the origin of the rejection wound.

4. **Expression Phase**

   o **Speak to the Rejecting Person (Introject)**: The Vaded State addresses the figure who caused the rejection.

   o **Client Speaks as the Rejecting Person**: The vaded state of the client responds in the role of the Introject, often revealing that the issue was with *them*, not the child.

   o **Removal**: The Vaded State removes the Introject, recognizing it no longer has a place in the client's inner world. (This step can follow the Relief Phase.)

5. **Relief Phase**
   A nurturing inner state offers unconditional love to the previously Vaded State, helping it feel accepted and lovable.

6. **Find Resource**
   A more capable adult state is brought in to manage the client's current situation.

   o **Gratitude and Assurance**: The healed state thanks the adult state, affirming the shift in responsibility and reinforcing the healing.

7. **Imagery Check**
   The client revisits the original rejection memory to confirm it no longer holds power.

8. **Client Debrief**
   The session ends with space for reflection, questions, and closure.

Core Insight

Healing rejection-based trauma means **helping the wounded state realize that it was not inherently flawed**, but that the *other person* failed to provide love and acceptance. This reframing, along with supportive inner states, restores emotional safety, self-worth, and internal harmony.

Chapter 5: Magic statements in therapy, and why

These are some statements and questions that can be very useful in therapy. These are statements that RT therapists use often and each is phrased to provide the most usefulness in the Resource Therapy process.

This chapter will provide:

- A short section introducing and highlighting the value of each statement

- A section that provides enough detail so you will be able to use these statements with clients if you choose

- Key takeaways to remember about the use of each statement.

The value of key statements

The Resource Therapy Magic Statements are designed to facilitate effective therapeutic interventions by focusing on client readiness, emotional processing, and empowerment. Here's a concise breakdown of their value:

1. **"What are you ready to change today?"**

   o **Value**: Defines the therapy focus, ensures precise diagnosis (e.g., unwanted feelings or behaviors), encourages client responsibility, aligns the session with the client's readiness, and confirms they are prepared to process issues. It sets a clear, client-driven direction for the session.

2. **"Tell me what I need to know."**

   o **Value**: Encourages client-driven information sharing, preventing the therapist from missing critical details. It avoids an interrogative tone, using active listening or reflective statements (e.g., "Your boss scares you?") to elicit deeper responses and build trust.

3. **"Where exactly in the body do you feel this?"**

   o **Value**: Used during Bridging to locate emotions in the body, keeping the client in a feeling state (not thinking) to trace the emotion to its root (Initial Sensitizing Event, ISE). It helps identify the age at the ISE by assessing the perceived size of the feet, securing the Vaded State in the Conscious for processing.

4. **"This is not happening right now."**

   o **Value**: Reassures the Vaded State during ISE imagery that the past event isn't current, reducing fear (e.g., shrinking the provoking figure to 1 inch). This empowers the client to safely express themselves, reinforcing that the past is an illusion while staying engaged in the therapeutic process.

5. **"I've got a secret for you."**

   o **Value**: Captures the attention of childhood states (often Vaded with Fear or Rejection), making them more receptive to key insights. It creates a safe space to reframe the situation (e.g., "He's not really here") or release emotional blame, using metaphors like "this space belongs to you" to shift focus to healing.

6. **"She is not here, so you can tell her exactly what you want."**

   o **Value**: Used in Expression Action, it paradoxically makes the provoking Introject feel present yet safe to confront by clarifying their absence. This reduces fear, enabling the client to speak freely, proving the past is no longer happening and fostering emotional release.

7. **"Let's just shrink him."**

   o **Value**: Empowers the Vaded State by reducing the perceived power of the provoking Introject (e.g., shrinking them to 1 inch). This gives the client (especially childhood states) a sense of control, enabling them to express suppressed feelings without fear.

8. **"Wow, I understand why you feel the way you do."**

    o **Value**: Validates the Vaded State's feelings after Introject Speak, especially for Rejection-vaded states. It shifts the belief from self-blame ("I'm flawed") to understanding external causes ("My parent couldn't give unconditional love"), paving the way for nurturing and healing.

9. **"Every child deserves unconditional love."**

    o **Value**: Reinforces the inherent worth of the client, countering feelings of rejection by highlighting that the lack of love stemmed from parental limitations, not the child's inadequacy. It promotes secure attachment and self-acceptance.

10. **"Swoosh"**

    o **Value**: A sound effect that dynamically signals a change (e.g., shrinking an Introject), making the shift more tangible and impactful during ISE imagery. It enhances the client's sense of transformation and control.

11. **"Client Name, how would you help a child like this?"**

    o **Value**: Engages a mature, nurturing state to support the previously Vaded State during Relief Action. It helps the client feel loved and safe, completing the catharsis from feeling unlovable to loved, and renames the state to reflect this shift (e.g., from "ALONE" to "LOVED").

12. **"You're not really feeling (OLD NAME) right now."**

    o **Value**: Facilitates the transition from negative to positive feelings by renaming the Vaded State (e.g., from "AFRAID" to "PEACE") after nurturing. This solidifies the emotional shift, making the change feel permanent and empowering the client with a new identity.

13. **"How would you like to feel and how would you like to act?"**

    o **Value**: Used in Find Resource Action, it identifies the client's desired emotional and behavioral response in triggering situations (e.g., feeling confident at work). It locates a resourceful state (e.g., "ASSERTIVE") to handle future challenges, ensuring the client responds maturely rather than from a Vaded childhood state.

14. **"Would you like to say thank you to the mature state?"**

    o **Value**: Encourages gratitude from the previously Vaded State (e.g., "PEACE") to the mature state (e.g., "ASSERTIVE"), fostering motivation and connection between states. It reinforces the mature state's role, ensuring the client feels supported and secure.

These statements collectively guide the client through identifying issues, processing emotions, confronting past traumas, and building resourceful states, ensuring a structured, client-centered therapeutic process that promotes healing and empowerment.

Magic Statements

What are you ready to change today?

(Used to define the focus for therapy)

Importance of the question: "What are you ready to change today?"

Asking the question, "What are you ready to change today?" at the beginning of a therapy session is crucial for several reasons:

Precise Diagnosis:

- The client's answer enables a precise diagnosis. By understanding their specific concern, we can categorize it into unwanted feelings, unwanted behavior, inner conflict, or the wrong state for the situation, and then apply the appropriate intervention.

Client responsibility:

- The response indicates the client's willingness to take responsibility for making a change. This verbal commitment makes the therapist's work easier, as the client has agreed to address the identified issue during therapy. The client will not be as willing to work on an issue that is not seen as important.

Avoiding misalignment:

- It prevents the therapist from working on an issue the client is not ready to address. This ensures that the therapy session is focused and effective.

Readiness for processing:

- Lastly, it ensures that the client is prepared to process the necessary issues on that particular day.

"Tell me what I need to know."

(used to hear information the client deems important)

When the client defines an issue, we often need contextual information about that issue. Therapists typically start asking a series of questions to gain this understanding. However, if we only ask questions, we might miss the precise information the client yearns to share.

Why It Matters:

- **Client-Driven Information:** By saying, "Tell me what I need to know," we encourage the client to share what they believe is necessary and appropriate. This helps us avoid missing key information.

- **Follow-Up Questions:** Once the client shares their perspective, we can ask further questions if needed.

Alternatives to questioning:

- **Active Listening:** Restating what the client has said in different words or making a simple statement of confusion often elicits deeper and more important information than questions do.

- **Avoiding interrogation:** Clients can feel interrogated with questions and may decline to answer in depth. However, they almost always want to help when we express confusion. For example: "I'm sorry, I'm just a little confused about... Can you help me understand?" This approach often yields a wealth of information.

- **Reflective statements:** Making a statement repeating what the client just said, as a question, also helps. For instance, "Your boss scares you?" This shows an initial level of understanding and introduces an element of confusion, prompting more detailed responses than, "Does your boss scare you?"

"Where exactly in the body do you feel this?"

(used during Bridging)

Bridging is a very important step in finding the root of the problem. Bridging follows the path from the state's sensory experience memory to where that feeling memory comes from. As soon as I see the State Vaded with Fear or rejection is in the Conscious holding the emotion, I like to ask, "Where exactly in the body do you feel *this*?" And rather than just say the word '*this*', I often say, 'this fear', 'this anxiety', or 'this feeling'.

It appears that feelings are located in some part of the body. My purpose is to keep the client from 'thinking', to keep the client feeling the emotion, and follow that emotion to the incident that caused it. By first locating where that emotion feels located in the body and then directing the focus to that location, I am holding the client in that feeling without asking the client to think about an answer. I am only wanting the client to talk about experiences and feelings. If the client goes into a 'thinking state' the process does not work. Finding the ISE requires the state that experienced that ISE to stay in the Conscious.

Upon finding a location in the body where the feeling is felt most, I next ask the client what it feels like in that location. This helps to better secure the Vaded State into the Conscious and it prepares for the next question about how big the feet are there in that space. As the Vaded State holds the Conscious it feels the age the client was at the ISE, therefore when the state holding the Conscious reports the size of its feet, that tells the therapist the age the client was at the ISE.

"This is not happening right now."

(used after Bridging)

A Vaded State feels the past is still happening. When it first arrives at the ISE the client may even hyperventilate if this state feels a lot of fear. If the client was afraid of dying at the ISE, that fear is still being held as if the past was still happening.

Because the Vaded State feels the past is still happening, I often say to the state, "This is not happening now. We are in a therapy room. This is just an illusion, so we can just shrink that other person down to two centimeters tall, just one inch. They are not really here, so let's make them one inch tall so you can tell them exactly what you want to say, Swoosh."

One might think that by saying, "This is not really happening now," the client would be jolted away from the ISE. But that does not happen. The client, with eyes closed, is securely visiting the ISE, and even though we can change the scene, change the size of the other person, or even of the client, the client is still at the ISE.

"I've got a secret for you."

(When I want a state to listen closely)

Let's face it. We all like secrets. We get privileged information. When I want a state to really listen to what I am going to say, I will say, "I've got a secret for you."

This is especially useful when talking with a childhood state. While working with States Vaded with Fear or States Vaded with Rejection at the ISE, we are almost always talking with childhood states. They really listen when I precede what I want them to hear with my declaration that it is a secret.

Examples include, "I have a secret for you. He is not really here. We are in a therapy room, so since he is not really here you can say anything you want to him. Tell him how you feel."

"I have a secret for you. I know it seems like you are in the ocean, but you really are not. You are in a safe place now and the ocean is really just pretend. Let's just make the water you are in knee deep since it is not real anyway. Now you can just stand up. Just go ahead and stand up now."

If the client's life is interrupted with blame for what someone has done in the past. "I have a secret for you. You don't have to give power to bad behavior by holding that emotional blame. The most powerful thing you can do is to decide to stop letting what he did emotionally impact you. You can intellectually remember it and know it was wrong, but let's not give him power in your life now. Are you ready to clear your emotional space of what he did? Are you ready to smell the flowers around you now?" (If yes.) "Let's just Swoosh that all away. You will have the intellectual memory and your life and happiness will be your own. Let's replace that emotional history and 'Swoosh', 'Swoosh', with a clean space now. You can replace it with light and flowers, if you like." This is using a metaphor to focus the intent of the client.

It is important to understand that "I've got a secret for you" needs to be said to the state that needs to change. It will not matter if you say it to a reporting state, or an intellectual state that is not the state that is holding onto negative emotions.

It is a powerful statement when made at a time an emotional state needs to really hear something.

"She is not here, so you can tell her exactly what you want."

(as used in the Expression Action)

It is an odd juxtaposition to say, "She is not really here, so you can tell her exactly what you want." The client hears 'she is not here', and that makes it safer to speak, but the client also hears, 'you can tell her exactly what you want', which places the other person in front of the client. (The client has her eyes closed at this time.)

I will say this when it is obvious that the client is afraid to speak. If the client has no fear of speaking to the provoking Introject, then this statement is not needed. The provoking Introject is the person that the client either feared, or the person that the client felt rejected by.

Actually, when you say to a client that a person is not here, that places the person here. If I say to you, "There is not a striped lizard on the floor in front of you," that places into your psyche the cognition of a striped lizard. It was not there before, but that statement places it there.

If I were to say to a Vaded State, "The bully is right in front of you. Tell him what you want to," the client might be too afraid of the bully to speak. But, by clarifying to the client that the bully is not here, the client is then better able to speak. When the client does speak that proves to the client that the past is not still happening because it is safe to speak now, so the past is past. It is safe now.

"Let's just shrink him."

(used in Expression)

This statement can be made when the Vaded State is experiencing the Initial Sensitizing Event imagery. It is made when the Vaded State shows some fear or inability to speak to the provoking Introject. It promotes a heightened sense of power that enables the state to express to the provoking Introject.

Let's just make him 2 cm, 1 inch tall, with a squeaky little voice, Swoosh. Be careful and don't step on him because I want you to be able to tell him what you want to.

This is immensely powerful. If I say to a Vaded State that feels 5 years old that it has more power than the bully, it will not believe me. It thinks, "Are you crazy. He is huge. He can have me for lunch."

But if we shrink the bully and then ask the 5-year-old state to, "Be careful not to step on him," then it understands that the bully has no power here. The bully has such little power that the child has to be careful not to step on him.

"Wow, I Understand Why You Feel the Way You Do."

(Used after Introject Speak)

This statement is crucial when addressing a State Vaded with Rejection. Such a state thinks it is flawed and that there is something inherently wrong with it. The individual feels rejected by another person and attributes this rejection to their own perceived shortcomings.

Process in Imagery of the ISE:

1. **Addressing the rejecting person:**

- After the Vaded State has spoken to the provoking Introject, sharply call out the name or title (e.g., Mom or Dad) of the rejecting person.
- Ask, "Why are you acting the way you are? Was this the way you were raised?" The answer doesn't matter, as the rejecting person (Introject) will always say something less than unconditionally loving. Example statements include:

    o "I don't have time to spend time with her. I have a new baby."

    o "I should never have had her. I'm not ready for kids."

    o "Her dad is too demanding. I can't go against him."

    o "I have to spend a lot of time at work. We have to eat."

2. **Accepting the rejecting Introject:**

- The client has internalized this Introject of the rejecting person. Attempting to change a rejecting person into a loving one would not feel realistic to the client.
- Respond to the rejecting Introject with, "Thank you for being honest. I hope your life improves in the future."

3. **Addressing the Vaded State:**

- Sharply call the name of the Vaded State and say, "Wow, I can understand why you feel the way you do. Every child should have parents who have time to spend with them, and who want to love them no matter what. I'm sorry your father has not been able to give you what every child should have. I want to make sure you get that now. I'm sorry it has taken so long."

- This statement shows the Vaded State that nothing is wrong with it and that anyone would have had those feelings.

Starting the Relief Action:

- A more nurturing part of the client is called upon to give love to the Vaded State.

- The name of the Vaded State is then changed to reflect its feeling of being loved.

Key points:

- The statement "Wow, I can understand…" cathartically transfers the belief from "There is something wrong with me," to "My parent was not able to give me the unconditional love that every child should have."

- There is no attempt to villainize the parent, but rather to convey that it is not the child's responsibility to be lovable; it is the parent's responsibility to show unconditional love.

"Every child deserves unconditional love."

(used after the Introject Speak Action)

Often parents are in a life situation in which they are unable to give their child what it needs. They can be too busy, overwhelmed, ill, or simply insensitive to the needs of the child. This often becomes clear at the ISE of States Vaded with Rejection. While it is obvious that every child deserves to be cared for and to feel safe, some nuances of "unconditional love" are not so obvious. Let's have a look at the deeper meaning of this sentence: Many children are raised in a parenting style that focuses on the behavior, and many of us were raised that way, too. When a child behaves well and does what the parents want it to do or has good grades, it receives praise and appreciation. Praise feels good. To gain more praise, it must please the parents more and excel, often at the expense of its own impulses and needs. When a child has a different opinion, acts out or when it makes a mistake, the parents make clear that this behavior is not appreciated. This can be by either scolding or criticising the child, by punishing it, or by withdrawal of love, the latter being a very effective but also very cruel form of controlling the child. Sadly, the focus often is on "how do I get my child to do what I say?" instead of "What does my child need?"

An unconditional loving parenting style means, that whether a child is good or whether a child makes a mistake, it always **feels** loved. Even though the great majority of parents surely love their children, they are often unable to transport this and to make their children feel loved in every situation.

Unconditional love means that there's someone who will offer the child guidance, orientation and support in a huge and sometimes confusing world. It means that how the child feels and what it's struggling with matters. It offers secure attachment, without the danger of love-withdrawal and makes the child feel seen and heard.

When we bridge with a State Vaded with Rejection, it often becomes evident that this is not what the child was offered, but it is what every child needs and deserves.

"Swoosh"

(used to indicate a change action)

Sound effects can be incredibly useful in therapy, especially during work within the image of the Initial Sensitizing Event (ISE) when the client has their eyes closed. Shrinking the image of the provoking Introject empowers the Vaded State to express itself and realize that the Introject is just a powerless image from the past.

While you could say, "Let's just shrink the bully to two centimeters tall. The bully is now two centimeters tall," this approach lacks the dynamic sense of change. By using the sound effect "Swoosh," it implies that something significant has occurred. Of course, if you prefer a different sound effect, it should work just as well.

"Client Name, how would you help a child like this?"

(used in Relief)

Part of the Relief Action is to find a mature state to come to the previously Vaded State to help it feel safe and loved. This is especially important for states that have been Vaded with Rejection, but it is also helpful for states that have been Vaded with Fear.

States that have been Vaded with Rejection have felt unlovable, or at least they have felt like they must work hard to get love. Following the Expression Action and the Introject Speak Action the state will understand that feeling unloved is not its fault. Still, it is important for it to feel loved to complete the catharsis from feeling 'unlovable' to feeling 'loved'.

To complete this step of helping the previously Vaded State feel loved, I clearly call the client by name (speaking to the mosaic of all states), and I ask the following question in relation to the location of the child state. "Kylie, if there was a little girl alone in her room who has just been through something, and, Kylie, if she was feeling a bit unsure of herself and just needing love what would you do to help her? If she is someone you know and love, like a daughter or a little sister, how would you help her?"

When I get the response to the 'how would you help' question I ask for a name for the helping state ("What can I call you, helping part?), then I instruct it to go to the child state ("*State name*, just go to 'ALONE' now, and give her a hug. The more things you do, the more powerful you become, and since you can do many things all at once you will always be able to be there with ALONE.")

Next, I ask the previously Vaded State how that feels, and if that state has a negative name, like ALONE, I ask it what it would like to be called now (see directly below).

"You're not really feeling (OLD NAME) right now."

(Used in Relief)

Immediate post-bridging question:

- After Bridging, ask the Vaded State, "What can I call you? What term fits you?"

- The Vaded State, feeling overwhelmed, will likely respond with a negative name such as 'AFRAID,' 'LOST,' 'ALONE,' or 'SCARED.'

- Using this negative name helps the state continue to hold the Conscious during the needed work.

Transition to positive feelings:

- As the state moves from negative feelings to feelings of being supported and loved, it is important to change the negative name it no longer identifies with.

Client feedback on name changes:

- Clients have reported that changing the name to reflect their peaceful feelings feels like an institutional, permanent change.

Nurturing phase:

- When the previously Vaded State is being nurtured by the helping state, ask, "Old name, how are you feeling now?"

- When the state reports feeling better, say, "You're not really feeling (OLD NAME) now. Now that you have 'HELPER' with you, what would you like to be called that better reflects your current feeling?"

New name selection:

- States often immediately provide a positive name such as 'FRIEND,' 'LOVED,' or 'PEACE.'

- If the state struggles to decide on a new name, ask what it enjoys doing when it feels good. For example, if it says 'dance,' ask, "Is it okay if I call you 'DANCER'?"

- Celebrate the new name: "That's a beautiful name. From now on I'll call you 'PLAY.'" You can add, "And PLAY, this is your space. You can have it any way you want. You can have lots of light if you want, or anything else."

Neutral names:

- Sometimes, the Vaded State might initially have a neutral name, such as 'FIVE' or 'BABY.'

- During the Relief action, ask if it wants a new name or if it would like to keep its current name.

- Respect the state's decision, "I'm happy to be called FIVE," and respond positively, "That's fantastic! That's a good name. I will continue to call you FIVE."

Showing enthusiasm:

- Show enthusiasm when working with childhood states. Positive confirmations like, "That's fantastic!" are often appreciated.

Chapter 5: Magic statements in therapy, and why

"How would you like to feel and how would you like to act?"

(used in Find Resource)

When the client came into therapy, during certain times an emotional Vaded State would enter the Conscious giving the client the unresolved feelings of that Vaded State. This state is almost always a child state, and it would not have come into the Conscious with upset feelings if it were not vaded.

For example, a childhood state that felt vaded by not being heard, came into the Conscious of an adult at work when she felt disrespected at work. The sense of feeling disrespected would cue the Vaded State and it would take over the Conscious, giving the adult the unresolved feelings of the Vaded State.

Resource therapy locates the event that vaded the state in childhood and processes it so that state no longer feels overwhelmed with feelings of not being respected. It will therefore no longer jump into the Conscious when someone is rude to the adult.

Now, when someone is rude to the adult a childhood state would not be the best state to respond, even if that state was not vaded. The adult would want to respond with a skillful, confident, assertive adult part of the personality.

Because of this, an important step in helping the client is to find their best and most preferred Resource to handle the situation at hand. The Find Resource Action quickly and easily accomplishes this.

Following the Relief Action, where the previously Vaded State learns to feel loved and supported, I will move the imagery back to the initial situation, "Okay, now, let's go back to your office! Your boss has just come in and he is not happy." Then I ask, "How would you like to feel and how would you like to act?"

I make sure I get a good understanding of exactly how the client wants to feel and act in the situation, then I ask, (using the information from the client's response, i.e., confident and assertive) "When in the past have you been confident and assertive? It can be any time, at work, with a friend, with a child, anytime. When has someone questioned you about anything and you felt confident and assertive?"

Upon getting a time, I will vivify that time with them in that imagery until I see that the wanted state is speaking, then I ask, "What can I call you, this confident, assertive part that I am speaking with?"

After I get a name for that Resource State, I merely say something like, "ASSERTIVE, you are a great part. You have been helpful in the past and you can be even more helpful in the future. When *client's name* needs you at work, will you use your skills and respond to her boss with your confidence and assertiveness? Because the state has been chosen specifically because it has the right abilities, it will say yes. Then later, during the Imagery Check Action I call that state by name and ask it how it would like to respond.

The example above is just for a situation where a client felt overwhelmed at work. A different client who had not been able to feel relaxed and present during intimacy may answer the "How would you like to feel and how would you like to act" question with, "I would like to feel present, to feel physical, and to feel positive." A client of mine responded in this way and when I asked her when she had felt present, physical and positive in her past, said "At yoga."

So, I vivified her at her yoga class and when I asked the state that had entered the Conscious for a name, she said, "YOGA". I ask YOGA if she would be present with her skills during times of intimacy. Then YOGA was the Resource that allowed her to enjoy intimacy with her partner.

It is important to note that Find Resource could be used without first resolving the Vaded State, but it would not be able to help when it is needed. The overwhelmed Vaded State will take over the Conscious as long as it is vaded. So first, resolve the Vaded State, then use Find Resource.

If you consider someone with a phobia this becomes clear. If someone has a phobia of spiders and goes into a feeling of panic when a spider is seen, you cannot just ask them "How would you like to feel and act?" As long as that state is vaded it will take over the Conscious. After it is resolved then the client will be able to use a preferred Resource, and the Find Resource Action helps the client to find their best Resource for the situation.

"Would you like to say thank you to the mature state?"

(used in Find Resource)

After all of the following:

> - The Vaded State was brought into the Conscious,
> - it was bridged to the ISE,
> - the Vaded State was resolved,
> - a helping state helped it feel connected and positive,
> - and the Find Resource Action was used to find the best mature state to handle the problematic issue when it arises.

It is time to go back and call the positive name of the previously Vaded State and ask that state to say thank you to the 'best Resource State to handle the issue.'

For example, if the Vaded State was at first named 'FRIGHTENED', then during the relief action took the new name, 'PEACE', as soon as I lined up an appropriate mature state to handle the situation and got a name for that state, e.g., 'ASSERTIVE', I would be ready to ask this question. 'PEACE', ASSERTIVE is going to take care of that adult stuff on the outside so you can stay with 'CARE'. Would you like to say thank you to 'ASSERTIVE'?

Our parts are us, and we feel motivated and positive when we are appreciated and when we understand we are doing important work. So, encouraging the 'thank you' at once places the previously Vaded State at ease and motivates the mature state.

You can see several transcript examples of the previously Vaded State saying thank you below under the headings, "Young state thanks future acting state."

Takeaways from Chapter 5: Magic Statements

Chapter 5 outlines key statements and questions used in Resource Therapy (RT) to enhance therapeutic effectiveness, particularly when addressing states vaded with fear or rejection. Each statement serves a specific purpose to guide the client through diagnosis, emotional processing, and resolution of pathological states.

1. **"What are you ready to change today?"**

   o **Purpose**: Defines the session's focus.

   o **Why it matters**:

      ▪ Enables precise diagnosis by identifying the client's concern (unwanted feelings, behavior, conflict, or wrong state).

      ▪ Encourages client responsibility and commitment to change.

      ▪ Aligns therapy with the client's readiness, avoiding ineffective focus.

      ▪ Confirms the client is prepared to process issues.

2. **"Tell me what I need to know."**

   o **Purpose**: Gathers contextual information the client deems important.

   o **Why it matters**:

      ▪ Allows client-driven sharing, reducing the risk of missing key details.

      ▪ Avoids interrogation-like questioning; reflective statements (e.g., "Your boss scares you?") or expressed confusion elicit deeper responses.

      ▪ Supports active listening to uncover critical information.

3. **"Where exactly in the body do you feel this?"**

   o **Purpose**: Used during Bridging to locate emotions and maintain the Vaded State in consciousness.

Chapter 5: Magic statements in therapy, and why

- o **Why it matters**:
    - Keeps the client focused on feelings, not thoughts, to trace the emotion to the Initial Sensitizing Event (ISE).
    - Identifying the feeling's bodily location and characteristics (e.g., size of feet) reveals the client's age at the ISE, securing the Vaded State for processing.

4. **"This is not happening right now."**
   - o **Purpose**: Used post-Bridging to reassure the Vaded State that the past event (ISE) is not current.
   - o **Why it matters**:
       - Reduces fear or panic by grounding the client in the therapy room (and allows shrinking the provoking Introject to 1 inch tall).
       - Maintains the client's connection to the ISE imagery without disruption, enabling safe expression.

5. **"I've got a secret for you."**
   - o **Purpose**: Captures the attention of a childhood Vaded State to deliver key insights.
   - o **Why it matters**:
       - Engages the state (especially child states) by framing information as privileged, encouraging openness.
       - Used to reassure the state of safety or empower expression (e.g., "He's not really here, so you can say anything").
       - Must target the Vaded State, not a reporting or intellectual state, for impact.

6. **"She is not here, so you can tell her exactly what you want."**
   - o **Purpose**: Used in the Expression Action to empower the Vaded State to confront the provoking Introject.
   - o **Why it matters**:
       - Reduces fear by clarifying the Introject's absence, making it safer to speak.

- Paradoxically places the Introject in imagery, enabling expression while proving the past is not current.

7. **"Let's just shrink him."**

   o **Purpose**: Empowers the Vaded State during Expression by reducing the Introject's perceived power.

   o **Why it matters**:

      - Shrinking the Introject (e.g., to 1 inch tall) gives the state (often child-like) a sense of control, enabling fearless expression.

      - Shifts power dynamics without denying the ISE's reality, fostering confidence.

8. **"Wow, I understand why you feel the way you do."**

   o **Purpose**: Used after Introject Speak to validate the Vaded State's feelings (especially rejection-based).

   o **Why it matters**:

      - Shifts the belief from "I'm flawed" to "My parent couldn't provide unconditional love," relieving self-blame.

      - Validates the state's experience without villainizing the Introject, preparing for nurturing in the Relief Action.

      - Introduces the concept that every child deserves love, initiating catharsis.

9. **"Every child deserves unconditional love."**

   o **Purpose**: Reinforces the Vaded State's worth after Introject Speak.

   o **Why it matters**:

      - Highlights that the lack of love was due to parental limitations, not the child's unworthiness.

      - Clarifies unconditional love as a need for guidance and acceptance, not behavior-based praise, addressing rejection-based trauma.

10. **"Swoosh"**

   o **Purpose**: Signals a dynamic change during ISE imagery (e.g., shrinking the Introject or moving the Introject away).

   o **Why it matters**:

   - Adds a vivid, sensory cue to empower the Vaded State and mark transformation.

   - Enhances the sense of action compared to verbal descriptions alone.

11. **"Client Name, how would you help a child like this?"**

   o **Purpose**: Used in Relief to engage a mature state to nurture the previously Vaded State.

   o **Why it matters**:

   - Calls on the client's compassionate states to provide love and safety, completing the shift from unlovable to loved.

   - Strengthens the Vaded State's sense of connection by involving a named helping state (e.g., giving a hug).

12. **"You're not really feeling (OLD NAME) right now."**

   o **Purpose**: Facilitates renaming the Vaded State during Relief to reflect positive feelings.

   o **Why it matters**:

   - Transitions the state from negative (e.g., "ALONE") to positive names (e.g., "LOVED"), marking permanent change.

   - Respects the state's choice (even neutral names like "FIVE") and celebrates with enthusiasm to reinforce positivity.

13. **"How would you like to feel and how would you like to act?"**

   o **Purpose**: Used in Find Resource to identify the preferred state for handling triggering situations post-resolution.

   o **Why it matters**:

   - Locates a mature, skilful state (e.g., "ASSERTIVE" for work conflicts) to replace the Vaded Child State.

- Ensures the client responds effectively in future scenarios, but only after resolving the Vaded State to prevent its interference.

14. **"Would you like to say thank you to the mature state?"**

o **Purpose**: Encourages gratitude from the previously Vaded State to the mature state in Find Resource.

o **Why it matters**:

- Reinforces collaboration among states, easing the previously Vaded State and motivating the mature state.

- Enhances the client's sense of internal harmony and appreciation for their parts.

These "magic statements" streamline RT by targeting specific states, fostering emotional safety, and guiding clients toward resolution and empowerment with precision and empathy.

Chapter 6: Generic walkthrough of steps

for Vaded with Fear and Vaded with Rejection.

These first two examples are created, not from actual therapy sessions, but they may be useful to gain a better understanding of the Resource Therapy process.

Vaded with Fear

This case example will follow the list of steps. At any time, you can review more information about the step by referring to the page in brackets for an explanation for that step.

Steps to resolve Fear Based Trauma:

1. Initial Diagnosis: (page 73)

2. Getting the state feeling fear into the Conscious: (page 75)

3. Bridging to the Initial Sensitizing Event (ISE): (page 80)

4. Resolving the trauma: (page 88)

    4.1 Addressing the provoking Introject: (page 88)

    4.2 Removal of the provoking Introject: (page 93)

5. Relief Phase: (page 96)

6. Engaging a more mature State: (page 102)

    6.1 Gratitude and assurance: (page 103)

7. Revisiting the original problem image: (page 105)

8. Client's questions: (page 108)

Diagnosis (page 73)

Therapist:

What are you ready to change today?

Tony:

It sounds crazy, but I am afraid to walk in the forest.

Therapist:

Tell me more about it.

Tony:

I don't have a problem walking in the city, or walking in a building, but I get terribly frightened about walking in the forest.

Therapist:

How long has this been a problem for you?

Tony:

As long as I can remember.

Therapist:

Tell me what I need to know.

Tony:

Well, when a friend asked me about going for a walk in the forest, I always have to make an excuse. I know if I go, I won't be able to take it. It is very embarrassing for me.

Therapist:

Exactly what happens when you attempt to walk in the forest?

Tony:

I get terribly frightened, like I'm going to die. It's like I can't breathe and everything goes fuzzy.

Getting the state feeling fear into the Conscious (page 75)

Therapist:

Tell me about one specific, single time, you had these feelings.

Tony:

Well, the reason I came here is because my friends are going for a walk in the forest. They asked me if I would like to come. I would love to be part of the group, but I cannot go into the forest.

Therapist:

Did you feel these frightening feelings when you thought about accepting?

Tony:

Boy, did I? My heart started racing and I could barely talk on the phone.

Therapist:

Just allow your eyes to close so you can really focus on this. What room are you in while you're talking with your friend on the phone?

Tony:

I'm in the living room.

Therapist:

Are you standing, or sitting?

Chapter 6: Generic walkthrough of steps

Tony:

I'm standing next to the couch.

Therapist:

Who are you talking with on the phone?

Tony:

My friend, John.

Therapist:

You are talking to John on the phone, and how are you feeling?

Tony:

I'm feeling OK until he asked me to go on the walk.

Therapist:

You are in the living room, standing, talking to John on the phone, feeling OK, and now he asked you about going on a walk. Tell me what's happening.

Tony:

As soon as he asks a walk on the weekend, I start feeling really strange.

Bridging (page 80)

Therapist:

He has just asked you about walking in the forest. Tell me about this feeling you are having as he is asking you about going on a walk in the forest.

Tony:

It's hard to breathe, and I know there's no way I'm going on that trip.

Therapist:

It's hard to breathe, and what are you feeling emotionally?

Tony:

It's like, danger, danger. I feel like if I go, I will die.

Therapist:

Are you feeling some of this danger/danger now?

Tony:

Yes, I am.

Therapist:

Where in the body is this danger/danger feeling right now?

Tony:

It's in my chest.

Therapist:

In your chest right now, this danger/danger, I might die feeling, how big an area in the chest is this, the size of a golf ball, a tennis ball, or football?

Tony:

It's big. It's the size of a football, even bigger.

Therapist:

Inside that big danger area, is it dark or light?

Tony:

It's dark grey.

Therapist:

I know it is not comfortable, but if you're standing in that dark grey danger area is it easy to move or hard to move?

Chapter 6: Generic walkthrough of steps

Tony:

It's hard to move.

Therapist:

You are a child sitting just above it, letting your feet dangle in that dark grey hard to move area. Your child's feet are pushing back and forth in that dark grey danger area. How big are those feet? How old are they?

Tony:

They are about five or six years old.

Therapist:

Being five or six years old, right now with those same feet, feeling danger/danger I could die, are you inside a building or outside in the open air?

Tony:

I'm outside.

Therapist:

Are you alone or is there someone else there?

Tony:

I'm alone.

Therapist:

Tell me what's happening?

Tony:

I'm up a tree and I can't get down. It was not that hard to climb up, but I can't get down. I'm afraid I'm going to die here.

Therapist:

What can I call you here, FRIGHTENED, SCARED, PANIC?

Tony:

PANIC.

Expression (page 88)

Therapist:

PANIC, thank you for talking with me. I know it seems really scary where you are right now, but I have a secret for you. This is not really happening now. I know it seems like you're up a tree and it is dangerous but you're actually sitting in a therapy room. This tree is not real, PANIC.

So, PANIC, we can do whatever we want to with this tree. Let's just shrink it down to the same height you are. Swoosh, it's small now. You can set your foot on the ground and step away from it. Go ahead and do that now. What do you want to say to that small little tree? Do you want to say, stupid tree you should not have scared me, you are just a little thing now? Go ahead and tell us what you want to say.

PANIC:

I don't like you, tree. Stay away from me.

Therapist:

That's very good. It better stay away from you, or you could make toothpicks out of it. PANIC, you have done really well, and I want to make sure you feel even better.

Removal (page 93)

Therapist:

Panic, since this is not happening now you don't even have to have that tree in your space. Do you want it here, or do you want it gone?

Chapter 6: Generic walkthrough of steps

PANIC:

I don't want it here at all.

Therapist:

Good. Let's just Swoosh it away. Swoosh! It's gone. Very good.

Relief (page 96)

Therapist:

Tony, if there was a 5- or 6-year-old boy who had had a frightening experience and this boy is someone you know and love, like a son or a little brother, what would you do to help him?

Tony:

I would put my arm around him and let him know everything is safe now.

Therapist:

That's great, and would you give him a hug?

Tony:

Yes, I would give him a hug too.

Therapist:

What can I call you, part?

Tony:

BIG BROTHER.

Therapist:

BIG BROTHER, right now I want you to go to PANIC right there, put your arm around him, give him a hug, and let him know you will always be there for him. BIG BROTHER, the more you do the more powerful you become, and because you can do many things all at once you will always be able to be there for PANIC. Go to him now and give him a hug.

Therapist:

PANIC, how does it feel having BIG BROTHER with you now?

PANIC:

It feels really good.

Therapist:

That's great. Can you give BIG BROTHER a hug also? That will make both of you feel good.

PANIC:

Yes.

Therapist:

That's great. I can see you feel a lot better. Since you're not feeling panic anymore what would be a good thing for me to call you? What new name would you like?

PANIC:

SAFE.

Therapist:

That's a wonderful name. From now on I'll call you SAFE. SAFE, is it OK with you if you stay here with BIG BROTHER and a more mature adult part takes care of some of the things on the outside?

SAFE:

Yes, that's alright.

Therapist:

That's great, thank you.

Find Resource (page 102)

Therapist:

Tony, when your friends ask you about going to the forest, how would you like to feel and how would you like to respond?

Tony:

I would like to feel thankful that they are asking me, and I would like to be able to say yes, I'll go and I'm looking forward to it.

Therapist:

So, you would like to be thankful, it sounds like calm, and you would like to look forward to going on the trip with your friends.

Tony:

That's right.

Therapist:

Tony, when in the past, at any time, have you felt thankful to be included, and confident and calm?

Tony:

Lots of times. When my friends asked me out for a drink, I feel confident and calm and thankful to be included.

Bringing the future acting state to the Conscious:

Therapist:

OK, you are being asked now by one of your friends to go out for a drink. Where are you as you are being asked?

Tony:

I'm at work. It's the end of the day. And I'm looking forward to the drink.

Therapist:

That's great. What can I call this confident part of you that's looking forward to going out? What can I call you, part?

Tony:

You can call me CONFIDENT.

Therapist:

CONFIDENT, you are a great part of Tony. You are grateful and like socialising and you like to go out and have an experience. You are a mature part of Tony. CONFIDENT, now that the part that used to feel panic is feeling safe, would you be willing to be the part of Tony that goes out with friends for a walk in the Bush? You are a much better part to do that than a child part.

CONFIDENT:

Yes, I could do that.

Young state thanks future acting state (page 103)

Therapist:

Fantastic! SAFE, did you hear that? CONFIDENT is going to go to the forest with his friends, and you can stay with BIG BROTHER. Is that OK with you, SAFE?

SAFE:

Yes, that's OK.

Therapist:

SAFE, would you like to say thank you to CONFIDENT for going to the forest, so you don't have to worry about it? You can tell him thank you right now if you want to. Go ahead and tell him.

Chapter 6: Generic walkthrough of steps

SAFE:

Thank you CONFIDENT for going to the forest for me.

Therapist:

Did you hear that, CONFIDENT? SAFE really appreciates you. You are much appreciated for doing something that you have the ability to do. Thank you for helping.

CONFIDENT:

That's OK.

Imagery Check (page 105)

Therapist:

Now, CONFIDENT, your friend John has just called, and you are on the phone with him. CONFIDENT, you have strength, and you like new experiences, and John is asking about you coming on a walk to the forest with your friends. CONFIDENT, what do you want to say?

CONFIDENT:

I'm a little bit nervous, but I do want to go, and I think it will be OK.

Therapist:

CONFIDENT, it makes sense that you are a little nervous because you have not done this before, but the more you practise the better you will get at it, and you are the very best part to practise doing this.

CONFIDENT:

Yes, I want to do it.

Debrief with the client (page 108)

Therapist:

Tony, how does that feel? Can you feel the difference?

Tony:

Yes, there's a big difference. Before, I would not have been able to even consider going on the walk. Now it seems like something I can do.

Therapist:

That's great, and the more you practise the better you will get at it. Do you have any questions?

Tony:

No, not right now. I'm looking forward to seeing how this works.

Chapter 6: Generic walkthrough of steps

Vaded with Rejection

This case example will follow the list of steps below. At any time, you can review more information about the step by referring back to the listed page for an explanation for that step.

Steps to resolve Attachment Trauma:

1. Diagnosis: (page 116)

2. Getting the state feeling rejected into the Conscious: (page 118)

3. Bridging to the Initial Sensitizing Event (ISE): (page 122)

4. Resolving the trauma: (page 124)

> 4.1 **Speaking to the rejecting person:** (page 125)
>
> 4.2 **Client responds as the rejecting person:** (page 129)
>
> 4.3 **Removal of the provoking Introject:** (page 133)

5. Relief phase: (page 137)

6. Engaging a more mature State: (page 140)

> 6.1 **Gratitude and assurance:** (page 141)

7. Revisiting the original problem Image: (page 143)

8. Client's questions: (page 143146)

1) Diagnosis (page 117)

Therapist:

What are you ready to change today?

Ava:

I've been feeling really bad about myself.

Therapist:

Tell me what I need to know.

Ava:

I was in a relationship for over a year, and I knew it wasn't the right relationship for me. I broke it off with him, but ever since then I feel like I'm a failure. I get excited about seeing another person but when he is not right for me, I feel horrible about myself. I don't think I feel good enough for anyone.

Therapist:

It sounds like you've been having a hard time. Tell me more about the exact feeling you've been having. What does it feel like, and what are your thoughts when you have the feeling.

Ava:

I get really upset and I cry a lot. Sometimes I can hardly catch my breath. I recently saw a man a couple of times and it was clear we were not a match, but I still felt a big sense of rejection when I told him I didn't want to see him again. I questioned whether I did the right thing.

It is clear that Ava has a State Vaded with Rejection. She feels like she is not good enough. Therefore, it will be important to Bridge to the ISE, and the first step is to make sure that the Vaded State is in the Conscious so it can guide us to the ISE.

2) Getting the right state into the Conscious (page 118)

Vivify Specific

Therapist:

Thank you. That helps me understand more. Tell me one specific time you were having these feelings of not being good enough. Exactly where were you?

Chapter 6: Generic walkthrough of steps

Ava:

I've been having them a lot lately.

Therapist:

I understand that, but what I need is one time that you felt that. Where were you?

Ava:

Well, just last night I was crying, feeling like I'm never going to find a partner.

Therapist:

Where were you when you were crying?

Ava:

I was at home.

Therapist:

What room were you in, and about what time was it?

Ava:

I was in my dining room having just sat down to eat and I was thinking I'm always going to be eating alone.

Therapist:

Just allow your eyes to close now so you can really focus in on it. You are in your dining room ready to eat, and you are feeling alone. About what time is it?

Ava:

It's about 6:30 PM.

Therapist:

Is it quiet or are you hearing noises?

Ava:

It's pretty quiet, although sometimes there's a car.

Therapist:

Are you alone in the house?

Ava:

Yes, very.

Ava starts to cry. This is an indication that the State Vaded with Rejection has taken the Conscious. This means that Bridging may begin.

3) Getting to the ISE by Bridging (page 122)

Therapist:

I can see you're feeling alone. Where in the body is this feeling right now?

Ava:

It's in my chest.

Therapist:

You are feeling alone. What other feelings are you having?

Ava:

Nobody is ever going to love me.

Therapist:

How big is this area in the chest where you are feeling alone, where you are feeling nobody is going to love me? Is it the size of a golf ball, a tennis ball, a football?

Chapter 6: Generic walkthrough of steps

Ava:

Its big. It covers my whole chest.

Therapist:

It must not feel good in there. If you are inside that area in your chest where you were feeling alone, where you are feeling nobody is going to love me, is it dark or light?

Ava:

It's a dark grey.

Therapist:

Is that the same dark grey all the way across the area, or is it darker in the middle?

Ava:

It's darker in the middle.

Therapist:

Right now, if you are sitting in the middle letting your feet dangle, they are child's feet, how big are those child's feet, dangling in that dark grey nobody's going to love me area?

Ava:

I don't know, maybe 5.

Therapist:

Being 5 right now, with those feet, feeling alone, feeling nobody is going to love me, are you inside a building, or outside in the open air?

Ava:

I'm inside.

Therapist:

Are you alone or is there someone else there?

Ava:

I'm alone.

Therapist:

What room are you in?

Ava:

I'm in my bedroom. I'm sitting on my bed.

Therapist:

What is happening?

Ava:

I'm crying.

Therapist:

What can I call you, here sitting on your bed, crying, ALONE, LOST, HURT, or something else?

Ava:

ALONE.

4) Resolving the trauma (page 125)

4.1) Expressing to the rejecting Introject (page 125)

Expression

Therapist:

ALONE, thank you for talking with me. ALONE, who is not loving you. Who would you really like to love you right now?

> *(Here, we want the rejecting Introject, as it is the one that is internally causing the bad feelings for the Vaded State.)*

ALONE:

My Dad.

Therapist:

ALONE, this is not really happening right now, so we can do anything we want. Let's have your Dad standing right in front of you, right now. Tell him how you feel. You can say anything to him now because he is not really here. Go ahead and tell him.

> *(Telling ALONE that Dad is not here now makes it easier for her to speak and telling her to speak to him places him in front of her.)*

ALONE:

Why don't you love me? You are always angry with me. I try really hard and I'm never good enough for you.

4.2) Hearing from the rejecting Introject (page 129)

Introject speak

Therapist:

That was really good, ALONE. Now, ALONE, I want you to be a great actor. Forget about who you are and be your Dad. I want to talk directly with Dad right now.

Dad, your little girl feels like you don't care about her. What is going on with you dad? Are you busy or do you care?

Dad:

I've got a lot going on. Her mother and I aren't getting along and I'm very busy.

Therapist:

Dad, it sounds like you're grumpy with the world. Thank you for talking with me, Dad, and I hope your life improves in the future. Thank you for being honest with me.

> *(Here, all that is needed is an indication that Dad is not able to be unconditionally loving at this time. The conversation with the rejecting Introject does not need to be long.)*

ALONE, I can see why you feel upset. I would feel upset too. Anyone would. Your Dad isn't handling things very well right now. Every child should have parents who love them, who adore them, and who always let them know they are loved. I'm sorry you're not getting that right now from your Dad. I want to make sure you finally get what every child should have.

4.3) Decision to remove the rejecting Introject (page 133)
Removal

Therapist:

But first, do you want your Dad in this space. This is your space, and we brought him in. Do you want him to be in this space, or do you want him somewhere else?

ALONE:

He can be somewhere else.

Therapist:

That's fine. Let's just clear the space. Swoosh, he is gone. You have a nice clear space, and you can have lots of light if you want it.

5) Creating a feeling of positivity for the state (page 137)

Relief

Ava, if there was a 5-year-old child who you know and love, like a daughter or a little sister, and if she was alone in her room feeling upset and unloved, how would you help her? What would you do?

Ava:

I would go and put my arm around her and tell her that she is loved. I would hold her and let her know I will listen to her.

Therapist:

That's fantastic. What can I call you, part, who will put your arm around her and let her know she is loved? What can I call you?

Ava:

You can call me CARE.

Therapist:

CARE, you are a great and loving part of Ava. You have helped her in the past and you can help her more in the future. The more you do the more powerful you become, and you can do many things all at once, so you can always be there with ALONE. CARE, go to ALONE right now and put your arms around her. Send your wonderful love to her so she can feel it all through her body. This will feel good to you too, CARE.

(Pause)

Therapist:

ALONE, what does that feel like having CARE with you?

ALONE:

It feels good.

Therapist:

ALONE, can you give CARE a hug too. That will make both of you feel better.

ALONE:

Yes.

Therapist:

How are you feeling now?

ALONE:

Much better

Therapist:

That's fantastic! It sounds like you are not feeling alone anymore, now that you have CARE with you. What would be a better name for you now. What name would you like, now that you are getting all this love from CARE?

ALONE:

You can call me PEACE.

Therapist:

That's a wonderful name. From now on I will call you PEACE. I really like that name.

6) Finding a better state to face current problems (page 140)

Find Resource

Therapist:

Ava, let's go back to your dining room. When you are in your dining room on your own, eating, how do want to feel and how do you want to act? What would you like?

Ava:

I would like to just enjoy my space and the food I have fixed. I would like to be able to reflect on my day.

Therapist:

And when in the past have you been present, enjoying what you are doing, and being able to reflect. It could be anywhere or anytime. When have you been calm, present and reflective.

Ava:

I guess when I am at work in my office, I feel like that. I can be present and reflect on my work and what I need to do.

Therapist:

That's great. I want you to be at work right now (Ava's eyes are still closed). Describe what you see and how you feel.

Ava:

I see my desk, and things I need to do. I feel good. I like tasks.

Therapist:

What can I call you, part, the part that is calm and is in the present?

Ava:

FOCUS, I guess.

Therapist:

FOCUS, you are a great part of Ava. You have helped her in the past and you can help her even more in the future. FOCUS, Ava needs your skills to be in the present, to be calm, and to be reflective at other times, like when she is having a meal at home. Would you be willing to use your great skills to help her feel calm and focused at home?

FOCUS:

Sure.

Therapist:

That's great, FOCUS. FOCUS, I want you with your ability to focus, to sit at the table with food. You can focus on the food, the day, anything you want in your calm way. How does that feel?

FOCUS:

Good. I like being here. I like focusing on the food. It's good.

Therapist:

That's great, FOCUS. Thank you for using your skills to help Ava more.

(Resource States love to help when they can. It makes them feel useful.)

6.1) Young state thanks future acting state (page 141)

Therapist:

PEACE, (pause) PEACE, FOCUS is a mature state who is going to feel strong during quiet times. Would you like to say thank you to FOCUS. You can stay there with CARE, and FOCUS can take care of the adult stuff. Would you like to say thank you to FOCUS?

PEACE:

Yes, thank you, FOCUS.

Therapist:

Thank you, PEACE.

7) Imagery Check (page 143)

Therapist:

Ava, let's check this once more, now that you have a strong, mature part with permission to help. You have just finished cooking, and you're sitting down at your table to have a meal. FOCUS is calm and knows how to focus on what is in the immediate surroundings. FOCUS, how does that feel, focusing on the food and on the day, and tomorrow.

FOCUS:

It feels good. I like doing this.

Therapist:

That's great. And you are helping. Ava, anytime you want to, you can remember FOCUS and bring those resource skills so you can use them.

I want to say thank you to all the parts, FOCUS, PEACE (the part that used to be ALONE), and CARE. You are all good parts. Ava, you can allow your eyes to open so we can talk about the session.

8) Debrief with the client (page 146)

Therapist:

Ava, how are you feeling?

Ava:

Really good.

Therapist:

How does that area in your chest feel?

Ava:

It feels good too. That bad feeling is gone.

Therapist:

That's great. Do you have any questions?

Ava:

What is going to happen next time? What do I need to do to keep this feeling from coming back?

Therapist:

We can never be sure, but that bad feeling you had belonged to the part that is now called PEACE. PEACE used to feel alone and the upset emotions of that feeling kept you from being able to respond as an adult. Now, PEACE is feeling loved and secure, so that gives room for FOCUS, a mature part, to respond in the way you would like. PEACE will always feel loved from now on. It is possible that you have other parts that still hold negative feelings, so our work may not be done, but we have made a good start.

Ava:

I do feel much better.

Takeaways from Chapter 6: Generic Walkthrough

Chapter 6 provides a step-by-step guide for resolving trauma in Resource Therapy (RT) for states Vaded with Fear and Rejection, illustrated through two fictional case examples: Tony (fear-based trauma) and Ava (rejection-based trauma). Each case follows a structured process to diagnose, process, and resolve the trauma, ensuring the client can respond to triggers with a mature, resourceful state.

Vaded with Fear: Tony's Case (Fear of Walking in the Forest)

Steps to Resolve Fear-Based Trauma:

1. **Initial Diagnosis** (p. 61):

    o   Therapist asks, "What are you ready to change today?" Tony reveals his fear of walking in forests, feeling panic and inability to breathe, present since childhood.

    o   Identified as a State Vaded with Fear, requiring Bridging to the Initial Sensitizing Event (ISE).

2. **Getting the State Feeling Fear into the Conscious** (p. 62):

    o   Therapist vivifies a specific moment (e.g., Tony on the phone with friend John, feeling panic when invited for a forest walk) to bring the Vaded State forward.

3. **Bridging to the ISE** (p. 66):

    o   Therapist asks where Tony feels the fear (chest, size of a football, dark grey, hard to move) and determines the age (5-6 years old) by visualizing child's feet.

    o   Tony recalls being stuck in a tree, alone, fearing death, naming the state "PANIC."

4. **Resolving the Trauma** (p. 74):

    o   **Addressing the Provoking Introject** (p. 74): Therapist reassures PANIC the tree isn't real, shrinking it to a small size ("Swoosh") to empower expression. PANIC tells the tree, "I don't like you, stay away."

- o **Removal of the Introject** (p. 78): PANIC chooses to remove the tree entirely ("Swoosh, it's gone").

5. **Relief Phase** (p. 80):

- o Therapist asks Tony how he'd help a scared child, identifying a nurturing state, "BIG BROTHER," who hugs PANIC.

- o PANIC feels better, renames itself "SAFE," and agrees to stay with BIG BROTHER.

6. **Engaging a more mature State** (p. 86):

- o **Find Resource**: Therapist asks how Tony wants to feel about forest walks (thankful, calm). Identifies "CONFIDENT," a state from past social outings, to handle future walks.

- o **Gratitude and Assurance** (p. 87): SAFE thanks CONFIDENT for taking over forest walks, reinforcing internal cooperation.

7. **Revisiting the Original Problem Image** (p. 89):

- o In imagery, CONFIDENT responds to John's invitation, feeling slightly nervous but willing to go, with encouragement to practice.

8. **Client's Questions/Debrief** (p. 92):

- o Tony feels a significant difference, now able to consider the walk. Therapist explains practicing will strengthen CONFIDENT's role and addresses any questions.

Vaded with Rejection: Ava's Case (Feeling Unlovable)

Steps to Resolve Attachment Trauma:

1. **Diagnosis (p. 97):**

- o Ava shares feeling like a failure and unlovable after ending relationships, triggered recently while dining alone.

- o Identified as a State Vaded with Rejection, needing to locate the ISE.

2. Awareness and Conscious Recognition (p. 62):

- o Therapist vivifies a specific moment (Ava crying at the dining table, feeling "nobody will love me") to bring the Vaded State into consciousness.

3. Bridging to the ISE (p. 99):

- o Therapist locates the feeling in Ava's chest (dark grey, darker in the middle) and determines the age (5 years old).

- o Ava recalls crying alone in her bedroom, naming the state "ALONE."

4. Resolving the Trauma (p. 106):

- o **Speaking to the Rejecting Introject** (p. 106): ALONE expresses to her father, "Why don't you love me? I'm never good enough," after being reassured he's not really present.

- o **Client Responds as the Introject** (p. 110): Ava role-plays Dad, admitting he's busy and struggling, revealing his inability to love unconditionally.

- o **Removal of the Introject** (p. 114): Therapist validates ALONE's feelings, noting Dad's limitations, and ALONE chooses to remove him ("Swoosh, he's gone").

5. Relief Phase (p. 80):

- o Therapist asks Ava how she'd help a lonely child, identifying "CARE," who comforts ALONE with love and hugs.

- o ALONE feels better, renames itself "PEACE," reflecting its new state of feeling loved.

6. Engaging a More Mature State (p. 120):

- o **Find Resource**: Ava wants to enjoy meals calmly and reflectively. Identifies "FOCUS," a state from work, to handle dining alone.

- o **Gratitude and Assurance** (p. 87): PEACE thanks FOCUS for taking on adult responsibilities, fostering internal harmony.

7. **Revisiting the Original Problem Image (p. 89):**

   - o In imagery, FOCUS enjoys focusing on the meal and day, feeling calm and present, confirming its suitability.

8. **Client's Questions/Debrief (p. 123):**

   - o Ava feels good, with the chest discomfort gone. Therapist explains PEACE now feels loved, enabling FOCUS to respond maturely, and notes further work may address other Vaded States if needed.

Key Points

- Both processes use structured RT steps: diagnose, vivify the Vaded State, bridge to the ISE, resolve trauma through Expression and Removal, provide Relief with a nurturing state, engage a mature state for future scenarios, and debrief.

- **Fear-Based**: Focuses on reducing physical fear by proving the threat (e.g., tree) is not real, empowering the state to feel safe.

- **Rejection-Based**: Addresses feelings of unworthiness by validating the state's experience and providing unconditional love, shifting blame from self to parental limitations.

- The therapist uses "magic statements" (e.g., "This is not happening now," "Swoosh," "Every child deserves unconditional love") to facilitate emotional shifts and empowerment.

- Outcomes ensure the Vaded State is resolved, renamed positively (SAFE, PEACE), and supported by mature states (CONFIDENT, FOCUS) for adaptive responses to triggers.

Appendix 1: Therapy Transcripts

Several steps and suggestions relating to Therapist Gold have been provided in this book. A theoretical understanding of personality and familiarity with the intervention steps are both essential. However, it is equally important for the reader to see these steps applied within a practical context to fully comprehend their implementation and impact. The way each step is used will vary depending on the client, and the conversation.

Below are several transcriptions from video recordings. They are presented to assist the reader in understanding real world applications. They are accurate and unchanged other than the names and some awkward phrasing has been made more clear. The pictures are not pictures of the actual clients.

Ellie: Afraid of violent thoughts

Presenting Concern:

Ellie presented with a concern about having thoughts of acting out in a violent manner. She had never given into these thoughts, but they were troubling to her.

Diagnosis:

(Having violent thoughts or actions is the reaction of a Retro Avoiding part that is trying to protect a Vaded State. Therefore, understanding that Ellie is having unwanted violent thoughts tells us that a State Vaded with Fear or Rejection is in need of resolution. That means we will need to bridge to the ISE to help this state, and we may not know if it is Vaded with Fear or Vaded with Rejection until we reach the ISE. We do know what we need to, how to proceed. We need to get the related Vaded State into the Conscious so we can bridge and resolve it's upset feelings.)

Getting the right state into the Conscious

Emmerson:

When recently, did you feel some of this anxiety? You know, since you've been on medication, when recently have you been able to feel some of this?

(Ellie has already told me she feels anxiety about having thoughts of becoming violent. She has also told me that she is on medication. When a client is taking anti-depressants, states can be blocked, so we can only work with the states that can be accessed. Ellie has told me that she was still having violent thoughts even on the medication. It is important for me to find a time she has experienced these thoughts after going on the medication, as that is an indication that that state is not being blocked by the medication. When a client tells about a feeling that was experienced prior to starting a medication it is possible that the state that

experienced that feeling will not be able to come to the Conscious for therapeutic work, because it may be being blocked from the Conscious.)

Ellie:

Yeah, well, recently I was doing a hypnotherapy course, and I was in a hypnotherapy session. I was scared in that session that I'm going to have the thought because then I'm scared that I'm going to get stuck on my own with the thought and not be able to come out of a hypnotherapy session. So that was a recent thing that made me go, oh God, here's the anxiety. And here are the thoughts that go along with it.

Emmerson:

So that was the anxiety that you were feeling or fear of the anxiety?

Ellie:

Probably fear of the fear of anxiety.

Emmerson:

Okay, is it that the anxiety is going to come, then the anxiety comes?

Ellie:

And I've had this in so many different ways in my life, I used to have insomnia, and then I would have fear of having insomnia, so then I would have insomnia.

Emmerson:

Okay, so just allow your eyes to close so you can focus on this. You're in the hypnotherapy session and lead me through what's happening.

> *(As soon as one specific time is found, ask the client to allow the eyes to close, then begin using present tense language to help bring the Vaded State into the conscious.)*

Ellie:

Okay.

Emmerson:

You're in a therapy room? Where are you?

Ellie:

I'm in my home, and I'm doing training. And I'm with another student. And we're practicing and (pause)

Emmerson:

You're sitting down?

Ellie:

Yeah.

Emmerson:

Is the other student sitting down?

Ellie:

Yeah.

Emmerson:

And tell me more. What's happening?

Ellie:

So, then I had the thought of, 'Oh, my God, what if I have the thought?' That gives me anxiety during this process.

Emmerson:

What time of day is this now?

Ellie:

Probably about three o'clock in the afternoon.

Emmerson:

It's in the afternoon, and the other student is there, and what exactly are you doing with the other student?

Ellie:

So, we're practicing as a hypnotherapist.

Emmerson:

Are you the hypnotherapist, or is the other student?

Ellie:

They're a student and I'm a student.

Emmerson:

But who, you're practicing? Who's practicing as a hypnotherapist?

Ellie:

The other student.

Emmerson:

The other student. And are your eyes closed or open?

Ellie:

Closed.

Appendix 1: Therapy Transcripts

Emmerson:

And, and you're sitting here, around 3:30, with your eyes closed and the other student is going to practice, and this feeling comes up for you. Describe this for me. You can hear the other student's voice. What are you feeling?

Ellie:

I'm feeling really scared that I'm on my own with my eyes closed.

Emmerson:

Yeah. And you're on your own with your eyes closed and sort of defenseless.

Bridging

Ellie:

Yeah.

> *(Here, I can hear in the voice of the client the anxiety of the Vaded State. Now that the right state is holding the Conscious, Bridging can begin. The right state must be holding the Conscious otherwise Bridging will not work.)*

Holding the state in the Conscious

> *(The Vaded State can be held in the Conscious by continuing to repeat the core feelings of the Vaded State, represented in all the shaded comments.)*

Emmerson:

And where, where are you feeling this defenseless scared feeling?

Ellie:

In my chest.

Emmerson:

Chest. Yeah. And are you feeling some of that defenseless scared feeling right now, in the chest?

Ellie:

Yeah.

Emmerson:

And this defenseless, scared feeling in the chest. Something could happen here. I might not be able to stop it. In the chest. What is that? Golf ball size? Tennis ball size football size? How big is that?

Ellie:

Probably like soccer ball size.

Emmerson:

Soccer ball size. And it's a big area in the chest. If you were to go inside that area, that defensive scared area if you were to go inside that would it be dark in there? Is it dark in there? Is it white? What's it like in there?

Ellie:

Yes. Probably black?

Emmerson:

It doesn't feel very good in that defensive scared area, does it? Like out of control?

Ellie:

Yeah.

Appendix 1: Therapy Transcripts

Emmerson:

And is it darker in the middle or is it dark all the way across in that soccer ball sized area? Defensive scared area.

Ellie:

Yeah. Just all, all black.

Emmerson:

All Black? And that doesn't feel good. Being in that all black. Is it thick stuff or thin stuff?

Ellie:

Thick.

Getting the age

Emmerson:

If you're just sitting on the edge of that thick stuff, letting your feet dangle. They're little kid's feet pushing back and forth in that big dark, defenseless scared area stuff. It's not very easy. What does it feel like trying to push your feet back and forth in that defensive scared area?

Ellie:

It kinda feels sticky.

Emmerson:

Sticky, and it's also child's feet. Look at those feet? How big are they? How old are they?

Ellie:

Maybe about 3.

Emmerson:

And being about 3 right now. Feeling defenseless and scared and not really knowing what's going on. And not really very safe being about three, does it feel like you're inside a building or outside in the open air?

Ellie:

Inside.

Emmerson:

And being defenseless and scared inside, are you alone or is somebody else there?

Ellie:

My parents.

Emmerson:

What room are you in?

Ellie:

Like, our loungeroom.

Emmerson:

What's happening?

Ellie:

Like we made this shed in the bush, and we didn't have a lot. And my Mom so we're all just, Yeah, in the shed.

Appendix 1: Therapy Transcripts

Emmerson:

It's scary here, isn't it?

Ellie:

Yeah.

Emmerson:

Well, can I call you scared? What can I call you?

Ellie:

 Yeah, it's like scared or alone.

Emmerson:

I'll call you ALONE.

> *(Because the client introduced the name, ALONE, I decided to use that name.)*

Ellie:

(nods)

Emmerson:

ALONE, thank you for talking with me. ALONE, the other people don't understand you. Do they?

ALONE:

No.

Emmerson:

ALONE. What's your Mum and Dad doing? Are they arguing, or what's happening?

ALONE:

Yeah, they're always arguing.

Emmerson:

Is that scaring you?

ALONE:

Yep.

Emmerson:

ALONE, thank you for talking with me, ALONE. I've got a secret for you, ALONE. This isn't really happening now so we can do anything we want. And let's just take both of your parents and shrink them down Swoosh to two little people two centimeters tall, one-inch tall, tiny little parents with squeaky little voices. They still get the same expression on their faces. ALONE, please don't step on them because I want you to be able to tell them how you feel. But you're a lot bigger than they are. What do you want to say to them?

> *(The parents were shrunk here because they were loud and arguing. I wanted the Vaded State to have the courage to speak.)*

Expression

Emmerson:

What are they making you feel like, ALONE?

ALONE:

They're making me feel really scared.

Emmerson:

Tell them that. Tell them.

Appendix 1: Therapy Transcripts

ALONE:

All right, guys. You make me feel really scared.

Emmerson:

Yeah, it's not nice, is it? Which ones making you feel the most scared, Mom or Dad?

ALONE:

My Dad.

Emmerson:

Tell your dad. Say Dad, you're making me feel scared.

ALONE:

Dad, you're making me really scared.

Emmerson:

That's not right for you to do that...

ALONE:

No, that's not right.

Emmerson:

Thank you, ALONE. That's really, really good. You're doing a great job, ALONE.

Introject Speak

Emmerson:

Dad. I want to talk directly with Dad. Dad. Your little girl. She's only little, Dad. You're scaring her, Dad. What's it make you feel like?

Dad:

Bad.

Emmerson:

Yeah, did you know you were scaring her dad?

Dad:

Yeah, but I'm angry.

Emmerson:

Life's not that easy for you right now. Is it Dad?

Dad:

No.

Emmerson:

You're not coping very well, are you?

Dad:

No.

Emmerson:

You get angry and you say things, don't you, Dad?

Dad:

Yeah.

Emmerson:

Dad, thank you for being honest with me. I hope your life improves in the future. But thank you for being honest with me.

Affirming the feelings of the state

Emmerson:

ALONE, I can understand why you feel scared and alone. Your Dad isn't coping. This is too much for him. I know he's an adult and he's a big guy. But he's not coping very well. I've got a secret, ALONE. Every child deserves to feel safe and loved. Every single child deserves to feel safe and loved and taken care of. And they especially deserve to feel safe and loved with their parents.

Removal

Emmerson:

I want to make sure you get what every child deserves, and I know that it's been a long time, and I'm sorry it's taken so long. ALONE, right now, do you want your dad in this space? This is your space you can have it any way you want. Do you want your Dad in this space right now? Or do you want it clear of him? Other parts can have him, this is up to you, ALONE. You can make up your mind later if you want to.

ALONE:

No, I think he can go.

Emmerson:

Okay, let's just have a nice clear space of him, Swoosh.

Relief

> *(Next, I will call the client by her name and ask the mosaic of parts that is the client, how she would help a 3-year-old girl. The part that wants to help will answer.)*

Emmerson:

Ellie, if there's a little girl around three years old, who really feels isolated and alone and scared and not attended to and not loved all the time. It is somebody you know, and love, Ellie, what would you do? How would you help her, Ellie?

Ellie:

I would take her away from that.

Emmerson:

Would you give her a hug?

Ellie:

Yeah, yeah.

Emmerson:

You would send her some love. Fantastic. What can I call you part, that is talking with me?

CARER:

CARER.

Emmerson:

CARER, thank you for talking with me, CARER. You're a wonderful part of Ellie, and I'm sure you care for other people too. But you can do many things at once CARER, and the more you do, the more powerful you become. So, you can always be there for ALONE, so CARER, just go to ALONE right now, this will feel good to you, too, to put your arms around ALONE. And let her know you can take her away, you can help her in a nice safe place. Maybe don't take her away quite yet because she may want to say something to her mother. But let her know that she's safe with you. And send her love into every cell and fiber. Let her feel your love, CARER. And that's going to feel really good to her, and to you too.

Emmerson:

ALONE. How does that feel having CARER there?

ALONE:

It's Good.

Emmerson:

It's nice, isn't it, ALONE? Is it okay with you to give care a bit of a hug also?

ALONE:

Yep.

Emmerson:

That's nice. That's really nice. I can see you're a really nice little girl. That's fantastic. And I'm sorry it's taken so long to get all this love that CARERs got to offer. ALONE, do you want to say something to your Mum?

ALONE:

I think you should leave him. (laughs)

Emmerson:

Okay, that's fantastic. And do you want to hear what your mom's got to say, or not?

ALONE:

Sure.

Introject Speak

Emmerson:

Mum, your little girl has been afraid of her father. And she's felt alone and not really cared about that much. Mum, what does that make you feel like?

Mum:

Sad.

Emmerson:

What do you want to say to ALONE, Mum?

Mum:

I'm sorry.

Emmerson:

You've not been paying much attention to her, as your life has been so full and busy. You've not been able to pay attention to her the way she really deserves, have you Mum?

Mum:

No.

Emmerson:

Thank you for being honest, Mum. And I hope your life improves.

Affirming the feelings of the state

Emmerson:

ALONE. I'm sorry again, your Mom wasn't able to step above this and give you the love that every child deserves.

Removal

Emmerson:

Do you want your Mom in this space, or not? This is up to you. You can let her stay or can let her leave. You have CARER there, so what do you want?

ALONE:

(garbled)

Emmerson:

Pardon me?

ALONE:

She can stay.

Emmerson:

She can stay. That's very nice. I can see you're a really nice little girl. And Mom can stay there, and you've always got CARER. And you can feel those hugs from CARER, and you can give hugs to CARER. That feels good, doesn't it?

ALONE:

Yeah.

New name for the resolved state

Emmerson:

And this is your space so you can have lots of light in it if you like. You can have a nice bright space. You can have anything you want in your space because this belongs to you and to CARER. And you're not alone anymore. You've got CARER there.

Emmerson:

What would you like to be called now? What do you like? What do you like to do? Or what would you like to be called?

Ellie:

What would ALONE like to be called?

Emmerson:

Yeah. ALONE, what would you like to be called?

ALONE:

Neckted

Emmerson:

Say it again.

ALONE:

CONNECTED. Connect. Like Connect.

Emmerson:

Connect. Sorry. I couldn't hear that. Connect. Thank you. That's a beautiful name, Connect. Connect or CONNECTED?

CONNECTED:

CONNECTED.

Emmerson:

Fantastic CONNECTED. From now on I'll call you CONNECTED, and you've always got CARER there and that's great having such a beautiful name like that. And I'm going to want to talk to you again in a minute, CONNECTED. But you just enjoy your space right now and think about how much light you want in it. Think about anything else you might want in your space because this is yours. And you can give CARER hugs and receive hugs from her.

Find Resource

Emmerson:

And, Ellie, when you're in this place like the hypnotherapy session, and you're going to be hypnotized, how do you want to feel? And how do you want to act in spaces like this?

Ellie:

I want to feel calm and safe.

Emmerson:

Fantastic, calm and safe, and you want to act that way too, don't you? Calm and safe?

Ellie:

Yeah.

Emmerson:

Fantastic. And, Ellie, when are you in a space where you feel calm and safe? When have you been someplace where you felt calm and safe?

Ellie:

When I'm at home.

Emmerson:

When you're at home. Okay, and where are you at home feeling calm and safe?

Ellie:

In my kitchen.

Emmerson:

And what are you doing in the kitchen?

(It is important to vivify enough to make sure that the state with the needed skills is holding the Conscious, so it will be able to directly respond to the call for help. It is always important to vivify and speak directly with the correct state for these processes to work.)

Ellie:

I'm cooking and I'm listening to music.

Emmerson:

You're cooking. Okay, you're in the kitchen right now. Cooking, feeling calm and safe. What time of day is it?

Ellie:

Like, lunchtime.

Emmerson:

And it feels good, being calm and safe while you're cooking here in the kitchen, doesn't it?

Ellie:

Yeah.

Emmerson:

What can I call you, part?

Emmerson:

What name or term fits you?

Ellie:

Like, Peaceful? Peace. Yeah, like a peaceful spirit.

Appendix 1: Therapy Transcripts

Emmerson:

Okay, Peace or Peaceful? What would you like?

PEACE:

PEACE.

Emmerson:

Fantastic, PEACE. You're a wonderful part of Ellie, and you help her a lot. You help her while she's cooking. And she needs your skills even more. And now that CONNECTED is feeling connected. There's more opportunity for you to help. Would you be willing, like if Ellie is getting hypnotized or in places like that? Would you be willing to come in? And do what you do best to feel calm and safe so she can enjoy that experience and enjoy life more? Would you be willing to help, PEACE?

PEACE:

Yeah.

Emmerson:

Fantastic. Thank you, PEACE.

Young state thanks future acting state

Emmerson:

CONNECTED, I know you're there with CARER. I don't know if you are listening, CONNECTED. But there's an adult part, PEACE, that's going to take care of those big adult things on the outside and feel calm and safe. At times like when Ellie's getting hypnotized. Is that okay with you, CONNECTED, that PEACE does this and you can stay down there with CARER.

CONNECTED:

Yeah.

Emmerson:

CONNECTED, would you like to say thank you to PEACE for helping you?

CONNECTED:

Thank you, PEACE, for helping.

Emmerson:

That's fantastic. And I want to say, CONNECTED, you're a sensitive part. And that's fantastic. Sensitive parts can really enjoy things like, like a nice taste, or a beautiful night sky. And you might be able to help this person enjoy those things. But if there's any kind of trauma or danger or something like that, it's nice to let the adult parts take care of that because that's not what you specialize in. So, thank you, CONNECTED. And thank you for being thankful to PEACE. You can settle in there CONNECTED with CARER. And enjoy those hugs.

Emmerson:

PEACE, did you hear what CONNECTED said? She really appreciates what you're doing.

PEACE:

Yeah.

Emmerson:

And you're going to be helpful and you're a great member of this team, PEACE. And so, thank you, PEACE, for being there and for offering your services. And I think you will enjoy it because you know how to be calm and safe. And this will help Ellie enjoy life more, so thank you, PEACE. Is there any other part that has anything they would like to say?

Long pause

Appendix 1: Therapy Transcripts

Ellie:

Just a grateful part, to say thank you.

Imagery Check

Emmerson:

Oh, that's fantastic. Let's do one more thing. Let's go back to the room. You're closing your eyes and you're going to practice hypnotherapy. And there's a part there that's called PEACE, and it's coming out now. It is feeling very calm and safe. And it's going to help you practice this and enjoy it. How does that feel?

PEACE:

It feels good.

Emmerson:

Thank you, Ellie.

Ellie:

Thank you, Gordon.

Debrief with the client

Emmerson:

How was that for you?

Ellie:

Yeah, that was pretty... That was a journey. It's a lot. It's a lot.

Ellie:

Yeah, it's great.

Emmerson:

How does it feel in your body?

Ellie:

It feels really good. Right? And it feels really hopeful.

Emmerson:

We want peace within.

Ellie:

Yeah. And I'm thinking a lot of people have things in their childhood.

Audrey (1st Bridge): Feeling Panic about leaving the womb

Presenting Concern: Audrey wanted to feel more confident, and she said she often did not feel good enough.

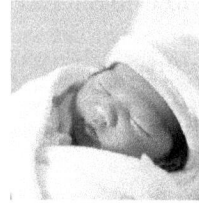

Diagnosis:

Emmerson:

Okay, Audrey, what are you ready to change today?

Audrey:

I would like to feel confident.

Emmerson:

Okay, in which circumstances?

Audrey:

I would like to feel good enough, really.

Emmerson:

And tell me what I need to know.

Audrey:

Ah, it's been around forever, this feeling of not being good enough. I think it comes from feeling like I didn't really belong in my family, and where I grew up, and that I didn't have a very good upbringing. And so, I sometimes feel like I don't really (it's mainly in family situations) I don't feel good enough.

Emmerson:

Can you give me an example?

Audrey:

It's hard because I'm actually feeling a bit of fear now. I feel really exposed. So that's really present. So, I'm having trouble moving past that.

Emmerson:

This fear that you're feeling right now, is that the same feeling you're talking about when you say in family situations? Is this that, I don't feel good enough feeling, or is this different?

Audrey:

This is a different one, I think. Yeah. This is that feeling that I'm being watched, and people will judge me.

Emmerson:

So, it's, it's Vaded with Rejection also, but it's a different state.

(Note: This client already knows RT terms, such as Vaded with Rejection.)

Audrey:

Yeah, I think so. Yeah.

(Here I needed to decide whether to go back to the presenting issue, or to see if Audrey might want to work with the state that is conscious now. I decided to go back to the presenting issue and vivify to bring the state that feels uncomfortable in family situations to the Conscious so we could work with it. Had the state currently conscious been more highly emotional I would have gone ahead and bridged to see where that emotion was coming from.)

Emmerson:

Okay.

Appendix 1: Therapy Transcripts

Audrey:

Blocking access from the other one.

Emmerson:

So, the other one, you said it happens in family situations? Is that like, in your parental family or marital family? Or?

Audrey:

Um, probably? All of the above? It's more in my family of creation, I think. So, it's more with my stepchildren and my husband's family. So, his sister and his brother think that I'm not good enough.

Emmerson:

And is that while you're all getting together, or when you're thinking about getting together, or *(Interrupted)*

Audrey:

I used to be quite crippled by when we had to get together with them. I would feel just really sick, and nervous and like, I was going like, you're asking me to go into a lion's den.

Emmerson:

Okay.

Audrey:

Or a nest of vipers would probably be more accurate.

Getting the state feeling fear into the Conscious

Emmerson:

When does this feeling hit you? Before you got together or during?

Audrey:

I think it's been around for a long time. But I think my husband, marrying my husband, he, like they are very middle class. I, I come from working class stock. And yeah, they all went to private schools. I went to a public school.

Emmerson:

This nest of Viper's feeling. Is that like when you're preparing, or on the way over, or is that when you're actually there with them?

> *(In order to vivify and bring the Vaded State into the Conscious I need to get one specific time it was out, so I can re-create that seen. I cannot do it when Audrey is generalizing, as an intellectual part generalizes. An emotional part experiences. I need to re-create the experience.)*

Audrey:

Both. Yeah, so it would be, but it starts before I even see them. So, it starts as soon as my husband says, we've been invited to a family get together.

Emmerson:

Okay. So what room are you in?

Audrey:

I'm in the kitchen.

Emmerson:

You're in the kitchen. Just allow your eyes to close so you can really focus. Where's your husband?

(After finding one specific time that state was out, it is important to use present tense language to give the state the feeling that it is happening now.)

Audrey:

He's at the bench.

Emmerson:

Are you standing or sitting?

Audrey:

I'm standing.

Emmerson:

You're standing, and he's at the bench.

Audrey:

Yeah.

Emmerson:

And, he's saying something to you.

Audrey:

Yeah.

Emmerson:

What's he saying?

Audrey:

We've been invited to Beck's for Christmas.

Emmerson:

And you hear that? And that gives you …

Audrey:

My heart is like, really racing. I feel really hot, like my hands are sweaty.

Emmerson:

Are you feeling some of that right now?

Audrey:

Yeah.

(Because the client is feeling the vaded feeling, Bridging may begin.)

Bridging

Emmerson:

Where in your body is this emotion right now?

(Emotions feel like they are located in a specific part of the body. It helps the client get into the feeling when they are encouraged to focus on that particular part of the body. It helps bring the Vaded State more fully into the Conscious.)

Audrey:

It's in my chest and my shoulders. I feel like, like I've got hackles on my back. Like, like a cat with its hackles up.

Emmerson:

Yeah. You've gotta defend yourself.

Audrey:

Yeah, absolutely.

Appendix 1: Therapy Transcripts

Emmerson:

And in that chest area. Is that like a big area in your chest?

Audrey:

It's my whole chest.

Emmerson:

In the whole chest and on the inside of the hackled chest, where you have to defend, is it dark in there or light or what's it like inside there right now?

(Holding the state in the Conscious: It is very important to continue to repeat the feelings of the state to keep the Vaded State in the Conscious (in these transcripts, the feelings of the Vaded State, when repeated, are shaded. If you don't keep repeating its feelings, another state may come into the Conscious then Bridging will not work. You can only bridge by holding the state in the Conscious so it can locate the time it was vaded.)

Audrey:

Yeah, it's like red, like, pulsating kind of red. Reddish black.

Emmerson:

And, in that pulsating red and black, that's not an easy place to be, is it?

Audrey:

I don't like it at all.

Emmerson:

Really quite uncomfortable.

Audrey:

Yeah.

Emmerson:

If your feet are in that, your feet are dangling down in that pulsating red and black. What do they feel like?

Holding the state in the Conscious

(The shaded statements repeat emotive statements that define the feelings of the state, so it continues to stay in the Conscious and respond.)

Audrey:

I can't move.

Emmerson:

You can't move. And what feeling are you having?

Audrey:

Pa..Pa..Pa..Panic! (hyperventilating)

Getting the age

Emmerson:

Can I ask you, you can't move. It's pulsating red and black, does it feel like you're in the womb?

(I have found when a client describes their location as red and black, and they are stuck and can't move they often later say they are in the womb. Therefore, when I get that description, I just ask.)

Audrey:

(Shakes her head, yes.)

Appendix 1: Therapy Transcripts

Emmerson:

Okay, Can I call you STUCK, HOT, PANIC? What can I call you?

Audrey:

PANIC.

Emmerson:

PANIC, thank you for talking with me. I really appreciate you talking with me, PANIC. I've got a secret for you, PANIC, that you are going to be born and it's going to be okay. But I want somebody else to tell you that PANIC.

Emmerson:

Right now, I want you Audrey to imagine being a baby held in really loving arms. A mother that loves this baby so much this baby can do nothing wrong. Just be a baby held in these amazing loving arms where it's just totally unconditional. It's just extraordinary. Total unconditional love. Can I call you BABY?

Audrey:

Yes.

Emmerson:

BABY, that feels good, all that love, doesn't it? And there is lots of air around you. And light, and that love is just amazing. I've got one thing I want you to do for me BABY. I want you to let PANIC know that there's love out here. There's air and there's love out here. And so, let's go to PANIC. And just let PANIC know that and then you can leave if you want to BABY you can go back to those arms. But just let PANIC know. There's love and there's air out there. Plenty of air.

Emmerson:

PANIC, I know that you feel panic and you're not sure about things. PANIC, what are you feeling? Is it? Are you feeling like I can't get out of here or it's scary out there? What are you feeling, PANIC?

PANIC:

I'm just trapped. I can't get out.

Emmerson:

Well, I've got a secret for you. You do get out, PANIC. The person that I'm talking with now is the adult that you grew into. So, you do get out, but I want to make sure you feel good now.

Relief

(It is unusual to bring in the helping state so early, but with a state feeling stuck in the womb, it is helpful for it to gain some relief early. This step usually comes after Expression and Removal.)

Emmerson:

Audrey, if there's a tiny little baby who really is afraid and needs love and security and safety, what would you do to help that baby, Audrey?

Audrey:

I'd just hold it and rock it, and sing to it.

Emmerson:

And what can I call you part?

NURTURE:

NURTURE.

Emmerson:

NURTURE, thank you for being here. NURTURE, right now, just go to PANIC and hold her and rock her and sing to her and let her feel love from you going into every cell and fibre, let her feel how safe you are. Let her know that you can always be there with her, NURTURE, because the more you do, the more powerful you become. And you can do many things all at once, and this will feel good to you too, NURTURE

Emmerson:

PANIC, how does that feel having NURTURE hold you?

PANIC:

Better.

Emmerson:

And PANIC, this is an illusion right now. So, you don't even have to move. Let's just have lots of light around you. You're out now. You're in the air you can breathe. You're in a sea of air. You can bring that air in, and NURTURE is holding you and loving you.

PANIC:

I don't want to be out.

Emmerson:

You don't want to be out?

PANIC:

(Shakes her head, no)

Emmerson:

Tell me about that, PANIC.

PANIC:

They don't want me.

Emmerson:

PANIC, you're thinking your parents don't want you, is that right?

PANIC:

(Nods in agreement.)

Expression

Emmerson:

That may be true. I don't know. We can do anything we want now PANIC, because this isn't a real situation. This is a figment of our imagination. So PANIC, let's have your mother, your real mother in front of you. And tell her I'm afraid you don't want me.

(Here, this is a good example of not trying to change Introjects from the past. Introjects are real impressions held by Resource States, and Resource States see them in a certain way. If we say they are different from that, the Resource State will not accept that. It is better to empower the Resource State within the reality it holds.)

PANIC:

I'm afraid that you don't want me.

Introject Speak

Emmerson:

Real Mum, you heard your little girl say she's afraid you don't want her. Real Mum, is that true, or not true? How does that make you feel?

Real Mum:

I want her, it's just her Dad.

Appendix 1: Therapy Transcripts

Emmerson:

You want her? So, tell me about that. You said I want her. I didn't feel a lot there.

Real Mum:

Well, she's kind of problematic, because her Dad, her Dad's changed. Her Dad doesn't really want her. So that's going cause problems for me. (Spoken in a matter-of-fact way.)

Emmerson:

You want her? But, but she's a problem?

Real Mum:

Yeah

Emmerson:

I understand, Real Mum. Thank you for being honest with me.

Emmerson:

Dad. Dad, thank you for talking with me. Dad, PANIC's mother said you don't want her. Is that true?

Dad:

No, not really. I just don't know what to do with her. (Spoken in a confused voice.)

Emmerson:

You don't? You're lost, aren't you Dad?

Dad:

I've got no; I've never even held a baby. I don't know what on earth I'm supposed to do.

Emmerson:

You're, you're not very educated on this, are you. Dad?

Dad:

No.

Emmerson:

So, it's not that you don't want her, you just don't know what to do. Is that what I'm hearing?

Dad:

Yeah. And I'm making jokes to cover my own. Because I feel uncomfortable. So, I say that I don't want her. I didn't even know that, I just fell over. That I didn't mean to have her.

Emmerson:

Yeah, that's sort of sad but hopefully you get over that. But thank you for being honest with me, Dad, I really appreciate that. Thank you.

Affirming the feelings of the state

Emmerson:

PANIC. PANIC, I can see why you would feel that way. Your Mom thinks your Dad doesn't want you. And he, he really sort of does want you, he just he's just confused and makes stupid jokes. But PANIC, the real truth is this person you are is an adult now.

Removal

Emmerson:

And you can have your situation now any way you want. And you can have NURTURE there with you. And you can let your parents be there with you, too. But that's up to you. They don't have to be there at all. This is your space, now PANIC. This is the space that that you want it to be. How do you want it? Do you want your parents there or do you just want NURTURE there?

PANIC:

I don't want them there, just NURTURE.

Emmerson:

NURTURE. Fantastic. Let's just clear the space of parents, Swoosh, and parents are gone, and NURTURE's there, and you've got lots of air, and you can remember how that baby felt. And there's love in this world. And this adult knows that, and NURTURE knows that, and NURTURE can give that to you right now. NURTURE wants you. You are wanted, and you are free. And you can feel air and there's a lot of amazing, beautiful things. How are you feeling now, PANIC.

PANIC:

Good.

New name for the resolved state

Emmerson:

That's nice, isn't it? And I'm glad that you're feeling better and that you're being loved. And, you know, there's love and you're really going to have an amazing time. Different parts of this person's going to have an amazing time. And what would you like to be called now, hugged, or free or …

PANIC:

MIGHTY. (She interrupts with the name.)

Emmerson:

Pardon?

MIGHTY:

MIGHTY? (spoken loudly with a smile)

Permission for another state to act in the future

Emmerson:

MIGHTY, that's a fantastic name. MIGHTY. I like that, so from now on, I'm going to call you MIGHTY and MIGHTY, you've got NURTURE there. And MIGHTY, is it okay with you, if you stay there with NURTURE and let Audrey's more mature parts handle the silly things on the outside that the adult needs to handle.

MIGHTY:

Uh-huh (shakes head yes)

Find Resource

Emmerson:

You're not the best part for that. You're the best part for getting those hugs and being MIGHTY. Fantastic. Thank you, MIGHTY, it is really good to meet you.

Emmerson:

And Audrey, how would you like to respond when your husband says we're going to be with the family? How would you like to act and how would you like to feel?

> *(This is the Find Resource Action, to locate and prepare Audrey's best Resource for dealing with the family.)*

Audrey:

I would like to take a deep breath. And I would like to feel calm. And I would like to say family's important. So, let's go.

Emmerson:

So, you'd like to feel calm, and nothing says you have to feel like `this is going to be a wonderful thing', that you will be calm, and you want to feel like you want to say family is important.

Audrey:

Yeah. Something like that.

Emmerson:

And when have you had that kind of feeling in life, feeling calm, and you know, it's important, and feeling mature.

Audrey:

Okay, today.

Emmerson:

Today?

Audrey:

Yeah.

Emmerson:

When?

Audrey:

I went and saw my stepson and his partner and their three children.

Emmerson:

And how are you feeling? Right there seeing them?

Audrey:

Great.

Emmerson:

What should I call you part?

Audrey:

LOVE.

Emmerson:

LOVE, you're a wonderful part of Audrey. LOVE, would you be willing to be helpful to Audrey, other times also, like when her husband says we're going to get together with the family? Would you like to step in and handle it in a mature adult way that this person can appreciate?

LOVE:

Sure.

Emmerson:

Your fantastic, thank you, LOVE.

Young state thanks future acting state

Emmerson:

MIGHTY? Is that okay with you? If LOVE does that?

MIGHTY:

Yeah.

Appendix 1: Therapy Transcripts

Emmerson:

That's fantastic, isn't it? Do you want to say thank you to LOVE?

MIGHTY:

Thank you.

Emmerson:

Fantastic! LOVE, did you hear that?

LOVE:

Uh-huh.

Emmerson:

You're really going to be appreciated for doing this.

Imagery Check

Emmerson:

So, let's go back and you're in the kitchen. And your husband has just said we're going to get together with the family. LOVE, you are there. LOVE, how do you want to handle this?

LOVE:

Okay, well, family's important. So, let's work out how we can do that.

Emmerson:

Fantastic. Thank you LOVE. That's really good. Audrey, how did that feel to you?

Audrey:

Um. Much better.

(The following is Bridging to a second state in the same session.)

254

Audrey (2ⁿᵈ Bridge): A bully who wanted to cut her down

Presenting Concern: Audrey originally presented with wanting to feel more confident. There was a second state that was related to her concern. This presentation is how we dealt with the second state.

Diagnosis:

Emmerson:

Yeah. Fantastic. And, Audrey, while your eyes are closed, there was a moment there when after you decided to volunteer there was some fear, because you're going to be watched. But that was another part of you. And tell me about that part.

Audrey:

It's just that I, I, feel like people will think badly of me.

(It is already clear that there is a State Vaded with Rejection. Audrey is afraid of not being liked, and she feels she is not liked.)

Getting the right state into the Conscious

Emmerson:

You're feeling a little bit of that right now, aren't you?

(Audrey is showing emotions that indicate the Vaded State is already holding the Conscious. When it is evident that the emotional state that

> *needs work is already in the Conscious there is no need to use the Vivify Specific Action to find a time when it was conscious in order to bring it into the Conscious.)*

Audrey:

Yeah.

> *(The second Bridging in a session normally goes quickly and easily.)*

Bridging

Emmerson:

And where in the body are you feeling that?

Audrey:

That's kind of in around my midriff.

Emmerson:

And tell me the emotion that goes along with that fear.

Audrey:

Fear.

Emmerson:

It's fear of them thinking badly of you.

Audrey:

That I'm too much.

Emmerson:

And, what's the fear?

Audrey:

That they'll talk about me behind my back.

Emmerson:

That they won't accept you?

Audrey:

Yeah.

Emmerson:

And that's not an easy feeling, is it?

Audrey:

No.

Emmerson:

In that area in the midriff, is it dark in there? Is it light? Is it red? Is it white?

Audrey:

Some. It's kind of, yeah, it's darker. It's got red in it, but it's got black as well.

Emmerson:

And how big an area is it?

Audrey:

About bigger than maybe two footballs.

Emmerson:

That is big, isn't it? And is that blacker in the middle, or does that black go all the way across?

Audrey:

It's blacker in the middle.

Holding the state in the Conscious

> *(There are not as many shaded areas here, showing a repeating of the core feelings, as this is the second Bridging, but repeating the feelings is still important to hold the state in the Conscious.)*

Getting the age

Emmerson:

In the middle. It's not easy being in the middle, is it? They might not accept you the way you are. And if you're sitting on the edge of that, and you're a little girl dangling your feet into that blackness, into that black stuff, feeling not accepted, what do those feet look like? How big are they?

Audrey:

Six.

Funneling into the ISE

Emmerson:

And being six right now, feeling like I may not be accepted, they may talk about me, does it feel like you're inside a building or outside in the open air?

Audrey:

I'm outside.

Emmerson:

Alone, or are there other people there?

Audrey:

There's other people.

Emmerson:

What's happening?

Audrey:

I'm walking into the school grounds.

Emmerson:

And, what's happening? Are you seeing other students?

Audrey:

Yeah, I know that they'll, they'll look at me and then they'll whisper something.

(When Bridging goes to the right place the client will have the same emotion at the ISE as the client felt before Bridging. This is a way you can understand that you have bridged with the right state.)

Emmerson:

Look at the one that you're worried the most about. Is that a male or female?

(When there is a group at the ISE, there is usually one person who has the most focus of the Vaded State.)

Audrey:

It's a female.

Emmerson:

Let's have her right in front of you. We know she's not really here.

Emmerson:

What can I call you? Can I call you AFRAID, or what can I call you?

Audrey:

Yeah, AFRAID.

Expression

Emmerson:

AFRAID, thank you for talking with me. AFRAID, you can say anything you want to that girl, Because she's not really here. Just tell her how you really feel.

AFRAID:

It's not nice to leave people out. You should be nice.

Emmerson:

Yeah!

AFRAID:

I haven't done anything wrong.

Emmerson:

I'm just doing the best I can, and I just want to be accepted.

AFRAID:

I'm just doing the best I can, and I can't help it. If I use big words. It's just the way that I am.

Introject Speak

Emmerson:

Girl, AFRAID just said she is really upset. She doesn't feel accepted, Girl. How does that make you feel when you hear her say that, Girl?

Girl:

Oh, I don't care. She thinks she's better than us. (Spoken loudly, like a bully.)

Emmerson:

That bothers you, doesn't it, Girl?

Girl:

Yeah.

Emmerson:

You don't mind cutting her down, if you can, do you?

Girl:

Yeah. I can turn everyone against her.

Emmerson:

Oh, I can hear, Girl, that you're not real comfortable with yourself. Because, if you were comfortable with yourself, you'd be happy for everybody to be happy. And I hope, Girl, in the future you become more comfortable with yourself. But I want to thank you for being honest with me. Thank you for being open and honest with me, and letting me know what's happening with you now.

Affirming the feelings of the state

Emmerson:

AFRAID. AFRAID, I've got to tell you. If I'm your age, and that girl's around me, I'm going to feel afraid too. She is a wrecking ball.

(This confirms that the feeling that the state has had is normal and that there is nothing wrong with the state.)

AFRAID:

Yeah, she's not very nice.

Emmerson:

Yes. That's not very nice, and that's not going to feel very good to anybody. It wouldn't feel good to me. It wouldn't feel good to anybody.

Appendix 1: Therapy Transcripts

AFRAID:

I don't think I'm better. I just want friends.

Removal

Emmerson:

I know. You just want friends. And do you want that wrecking ball in this space or not?

AFRAID:

No.

Emmerson:

Let's just shrink her to tiny and then, Swoosh, she's out of this space. She's totally out of this space, because this isn't happening now, anyway. This is just a memory fragment.

Relief

Emmerson:

And Audrey, if there's a little girl around six years old, who just feels like she just wants to be friends, and other kids have been mean to her. How would you help her, Audrey?

Audrey:

I just would take her hand, and I'd play with her.

Emmerson:

And what can I call you, part?

Audrey:

FRIEND.

Emmerson:

FRIEND, thank you for being here. I can tell you are a really nice part. FRIEND, go to AFRAID and take her hand and let her know how silly that girl is. And, that girl is not here anymore, so now you can be friends with AFRAID, and you can take her hand, and you can play with her. You can send her love, and you can get love from her. And she's never ever going to be alone. She's never ever going to be without a friend. And FRIEND, the more things you do, the more powerful you become, so you can do many things all at once. You can always be there with AFRAID. You can tell her secrets, and she can tell you secrets.

Emmerson:

AFRAID, how does that feel?

AFRAID:

That's good.

Emmerson:

That's good, isn't it? That silly girl. I'm glad she's not around here. And FRIEND is really nice, and every child deserves a friend like this. Every child deserves to have somebody they can confide in and talk with and play with. That's fantastic. And I'm sorry it's taken a while for you, but you've got it now and you always will have it.

Name for the resolved state

Emmerson:

What do you want to be called now?

AFRAID:

I don't know.

Appendix 1: Therapy Transcripts

Emmerson:

FRIENDLY, MATE, HAPPY, PLAYFUL?

AFRAID:

HAPPY.

Emmerson:

HAPPY, fantastic. That's a great name, HAPPY. HAPPY, you can be just as happy as you want to be with FRIEND, and you can be in any place you want to be. You don't have to be right there where you are. You can be in a beautiful place with lots of green or whatever you want. You have got friend there and enjoy that, and you can even have fun in dreams having happy dreams with friends if you want to.

Permission for another state to act in the future

Emmerson:

And so, is it okay with you HAPPY, if Audrey's more mature parts handle the sticky situations on the outside, and you can have a good time there with FRIEND.

HAPPY:

Nods yes.

Find Resource

Emmerson:

Fantastic! Audrey, if you're in a group and you're going to say something, how would you like to act and how would you like to feel?

Audrey:

I just like to feel calm and interested and engaged.

Emmerson:

You just want to be happy to be there, don't you?

Audrey:

Yeah. Just relaxed to be contributing, or to not have to.

Emmerson:

You want to just be relaxed toward others and feel positive feelings from others.

Audrey:

Yeah.

Emmerson:

When have you felt this, relaxed and engaged in positivity going both ways?

Audrey:

When I used to teach.

Emmerson:

You are teaching now and there are people here. How are you feeling?

Audrey:

I know that they're thinking good things because that's what we've been trained to do.

Emmerson:

What can I call you?

Audrey:

TEACHER.

Appendix 1: Therapy Transcripts

Emmerson:

TEACHER, thank you for talking with me, TEACHER. That's a great name. TEACHER, would you be happy, you're a wonderful part of Audrey, and would you be happy to help Audrey out now that you've got such skills.

Audrey:

Okay, of course.

Emmerson:

Fantastic, TEACHER. So, TEACHER, let's just imagine Audrey has got something to say in the group and you're there, TEACHER, and you've got all these TEACHER feelings, these happy feelings with the other people, and feeling positivity from you to them, and from them to you. Everything is okay. And, if somebody else is having a bad day, or they're having a hard time feeling positive, we can feel a bit sorry for them, TEACHER, but you're happy and you're understanding and everything is okay.

TEACHER:

(Shakes head yes.)

Emmerson:

All right TEACHER, fantastic. So, TEACHER, you can hang around and does any other part want to say anything?

Audrey:

No.

Emmerson:

Fantastic. And TEACHER, you can be here while we debrief. It would be a good time for you to be here, TEACHER.

Young state thanks future acting state

Emmerson:

HAPPY, is that okay with you? If TEACHER does that?

HAPPY:

Nods yes.

Emmerson:

Fantastic. 'HAPPY', would you like to say thank you to 'TEACHER'.

HAPPY:

Thanks TEACHER.

Emmerson:

Fantastic. TEACHER, you're really appreciated.

> *(When a previously Vaded Part says thank you to the more mature part that further allows the child part to understand the mature part is going to handle things now, and it helps motivate the mature part to help.)*

Emmerson:

Okay. All that settles in. As it settles in you can just allow your eyes to open.

Audrey:

Oh, my goodness. Oh, wow! Oh, thanks, Gordon. Wow. What a trip?

Emmerson:

Yeah, it's interesting, isn't it?

Appendix 1: Therapy Transcripts

Audrey:

Oh, yeah. My goodness. Ah, I didn't expect that. …

Audrey:

Yeah, who would have thought that that's where it started. Logically, I would have thought, all sorts of other things, but I didn't think that, so, it's amazing.

Emmerson:

Yeah, it's really interesting.

Audrey:

Thank you.

Emmerson:

Thank you.

Sharon had a spider phobia

Presenting Concern: Sharon presented with a phobia of spiders. She was afraid to even look at a picture of a spider. She was a workshop attendee who volunteered for a demonstration.

Vaded with Fear

Diagnosis:

Emmerson:

Sharon, what are you ready to change?

Sharon:

I'm afraid of Spiders (laughs).

Emmerson:

(laughs) Alright, my example.

Sharon:

(laughs) Yeah.

(In a workshop I had given an example of a phobia as having a fear of spiders that did not match any real danger. Sharon, a workshop participant, is indicating that she has this phobia.)

Getting the right state into the Conscious

Emmerson:

Tell me what happens.

Sharon:

Ah... My heart is beating right now if I think of spiders. I don't like them moving and ... scrambling around. It makes me nervous.

> *(It is evident that the State Vaded with Fear is already holding the conscious, therefore there is no need to vivify to another time to get this state in the Conscious. Work can immediately start to bridge to the ISE.)*

Bridging

Emmerson:

Mm. Okay. And ... Just allow your eyes to close. And where in the body are you feeling this right now?

Sharon:

The fear?

Emmerson:

Yes.

Sharon:

My heart is beating.

Emmerson:

And how big an area is that heart beating area?

Sharon:

Uh ... (makes a big circle with her hands in front of her chest)

Emmerson:

Big ... huge ... alright. And ... Put more adjectives to your fear. It's like ... terrified or ... they could hurt me or ... I've got to run away...

Sharon:

Uh, I want to run away. It makes me nervous and- and- and- shaking and …

Emmerson:

Panic?

Sharon:

Uh, almost.

Emmerson:

Yeah. Okay, and that big area in your chest, is it light or dark in there?

Sharon:

(sighs)

Emmerson:

That spider area.

Sharon:

Right now, it's … it's … bright … bright grey.

Emmerson:

Are you feeling the fear now?

Sharon:

I'm feeling my heart beating. (chuckles nervously)

Emmerson:

And it's bright in there?

Appendix 1: Therapy Transcripts

Sharon:

Mmm

Emmerson:

And ... and ... is it bright in the whole area or is that brightness different across the area?

Sharon:

It's very bright in the middle and ... getting darker to the outside.

Emmerson:

Which feels more dangerous, the middle or the outside?

Sharon:

The middle. I feel- it´s like fire that ... uhm, like burning.

Emmerson:

And ... and ... if you're in that middle its really uncomfortable, isn't it? In that burning hot fire?

Sharon:

Yeah

Emmerson:

And if you're just sitting on the edge of that burning, just letting your feet dangle back and forth in that burning... They don't feel good either, do they? Inside that really bright area, like fire burning...

Sharon:

(Sighs uncomfortably, moves around on the chair.)

Emmerson:

What's it like letting your feet dangle in there?

Sharon:

I'm afraid to burn my feet (chuckles nervously).

Emmerson:

What do they look like? If you're a child, what size of feet are they? You don't want to burn them…

Sharon:

Small, yeah, small…

Emmerson:

Yeah, what size … how big are they … how old is the person with those feet?

Sharon:

Little. Very little. Mmmmh…

Emmerson:

About what?

Sharon:

Maybe two … two years.

Emmerson:

Yeah. And being maybe two years old right now, having this fear, like this bright white fire … Bright. Being two. Does it feel like you are inside a building or outside in the open air?

Sharon:

Outside.

Appendix 1: Therapy Transcripts

Emmerson:

Are you alone or is somebody else there?

Sharon:

I'm alone.

Emmerson:

And where are you? What's around you? Is it daylight or dark?

Sharon:

It's daylight. In maybe a garden or something.

Emmerson:

What's happening?

Sharon:

... I'm seeing something ... scrambling around and I ... I was afraid and nobody was there to save me.

Emmerson:

What can I call you, AFRAID?

Sharon:

Yeah, AFRAID.

Emmerson:

AFRAID, thank you for talking to me, I really appreciate you talking to me, AFRAID. AFRAID, I've got a secret for you: this isn't really happening now, so we can do anything we want to with this. So, AFRAID, I want you to get far enough away from that stuff that is scrambling around, where you can look at it, and we're going to change that into something else. What would you like to change it into? Play-dough? Or something else, AFRAID?

AFRAID:

Change what?

Emmerson:

The stuff that's scrambling around. It's not really here, it's not in the room. It's not where we are, AFRAID. It's an illusion, what would you like it to be?

AFRAID:

Lay down. And...

Emmerson:

Lay down?

AFRAID:

And be calm.

Emmerson:

Calm? So, you would like the things that are scrambling to be ... to be calm right?

AFRAID:

Yeah.

Expression

Emmerson:

Okay. Let's just ... tell them to be calm.

AFRAID:

Calm down. Do nothing to me.

Appendix 1: Therapy Transcripts

Emmerson:

And ... and ... I want you to be one of those scrambling things and ...

AFRAID:

I think they are ants! They aren't ... they are not spiders.

Introject Speak

(Most often with Vaded with Fear the Introject Speak Action is not used, but in this instance, I decided to use it to show the fear the ANT had of the much bigger human.)

Emmerson:

Okay, they're ants, that's fine. I want you to be an ant. Just ... in your imagination, imagination's fun, and look back up at AFRAID. Look at that huuuge person up there. ANT. ANT, look at that huge person, have you noticed her before, ant? She's a lot bigger than you, isn't she, ant?

ANT:

It's afraid ... it wants to run away ...

Emmerson:

It's wanting to run away from you, isn't it?

ANT:

Yeah.

Emmerson:

And it doesn't know who you are, does it? It doesn't know you don't want to hurt it. Or maybe you do, I don't know,

ANT:

I don't know! (laughs) Maybe it steps on me!

Emmerson:

And ant, would you like to go away from that person?

ANT:

Yeah, I want to run away.

Removal

Emmerson:

Okay, thank you, ANT, AFRAID, is it okay if ANT runs away from you?

AFRAID:

Yeah, go away.

Emmerson:

Tell it to go away. Let's have a nice, clear space.

AFRAID:

Go away.

Emmerson:

Fantastic. That's very good! And … and now let's have a nice, clear space, do you want the grass to be there? Do you want it to be wood? Or pavement?

AFRAID:

Pavement.

Appendix 1: Therapy Transcripts

Emmerson:

Let's have nice pavement in front of you. This is your space, AFRAID, so you can have it any way you want. Let's have a nice, clear pavement. That's really good, AFRAID. You've talked to the ANT, and you've heard the ANT and now you know, there's an ANT. Ah, and AFRAID, you're feeling a bit more calm now, aren't you?

AFRAID:

Ah, not safe at the moment.

Emmerson:

Are you still afraid of the ants?

AFRAID:

Yeah.

Emmerson:

Uh huh … and … would you like to step on the ants? What would you like … well, you've sent the ants away, what would you like to do with the ants? Would you like to change the ants into a friend?

AFRAID:

No.

Emmerson:

No? Okay, what would you like, AFRAID? This is your space; you can have anything you want.

AFRAID:

I want them to go away. And … leave me alone. Don't bite me. Calm down.

Emmerson:

Okay.

AFRAID:

Don't come over the edge of the pavement.

Emmerson:

Alright, would you like a magic shield around where the ants can't get through?

AFRAID:

Yeah! (smiles)

Emmerson:

Okay. Let's have this magic shield, it's like this amazingly powerful shield. And you're safe in it, you can have everything you want in it, but the ants can't come through. They cannot come through the shield. That feels better, doesn't it?

AFRAID:

Yeah.

Relief

Emmerson:

That beautiful, strong magic shield. And I'm going to get something else for you too AFRAID, I'm going to get you somebody there who can care for you and help you feel safe. Uh, I'll be right back.

Sharon, if there was a little child who … had been afraid and is feeling much better now. But she's been really afraid, and she could benefit from support and love. How would you help her, Sharon?

Sharon:

I would take her up so she's away from the ants.

Appendix 1: Therapy Transcripts

Emmerson:

And you would give her love and support?

Sharon:

Yeah, carry her, calm her down, give her a hug.

Emmerson:

And what can I call you, part?

Sharon:

It's kind of … It's kind of MOTHER…

Emmerson:

Can I call you INNER MOTHER? So, we know it's the mother in you?

INNER MOTHER:

Yeah

Emmerson:

INNER MOTHER, thank you for talking to me. INNER MOTHER, go to AFRAID right where she is, pick her up and let her know she's safe with you. And you like looking after her. And INNER MOTHER, the more you do, the more powerful you become. And you can do many things all at once so you can always be there with AFRAID. And this will feel good to you too, INNER MOTHER. And you can hold AFRAID and you can feel her energy. And you can give her love and calmness. And let her know that she's safe in your arms. AFRAID, how does that feel?

AFRAID:

I'm safe now.

Emmerson:

That's nice, isn't it?

AFRAID:

Yeah

Emmerson:

And AFRAID, is it okay with you, if you stay there with INNER MOTHER and let Sharon's more mature parts handle things on the outside? And you can just be safe inside that magic shield and with INNER MOTHER.

AFRAID:

Yeah, that feels good.

Emmerson:

And can you give INNER MOTHER a bit of a hug, too?

AFRAID:

Yeah.

Name for the resolved state

Emmerson:

That's nice, isn't it? And uh, you're not feeling afraid and so what would you like to be called now?

AFRAID:

STRONG.

Emmerson:

STRONG. That's fantastic. STRONG. From now on, I'll call you STRONG and you are with INNER MOTHER and you're safe and you can look around and appreciate things around you. And appreciate the hugs you're getting from INNER MOTHER. So, thank you, STRONG, it's been really nice to meet you.

And you can stay there with INNER MOTHER and let the mature adult parts handle things on the outside.

Find Resource

Emmerson:

Sharon. It may take you a little while because you've got the habit of ... of ideas about spiders, but when you get to where you want to be with spiders, how would you like to react when you see a spider? How would you like to feel and how would you like to act?

Sharon:

I want to be more calm and have the feeling, the spider also is afraid.

Emmerson:

Yeah.

Sharon:

So maybe I could take it out where it's safe and I'm safe.

Emmerson:

And ... So, you would like to be more calm and remove it from your space.

Sharon:

Yeah.

Emmerson:

And when have you been calm and able to manipulate things in the past? With a pet or ... kitten or something like that? When have you been calm and able to ... to gently help an animal? With care and respect. Or a person.

Sharon:

What time, or ...?

Emmerson:

Yeah, like, a time … a specific time when you were helping a cat or a pet or a dog or a person and you're calm and you're helping them a bit. Helping them, maybe to be safe…

Sharon:

Yeah … Yeah, I got one!

Emmerson:

What is it?

Sharon:

Uhm … A swallow was getting into our sleeping room, and it hung up on the curtains and didn't find the way out.

Emmerson:

And what are you doing?

Sharon:

I took a towel and put it around, my boyfriend opened the window, and I let it out.

Emmerson:

What can I call you, part?

Sharon:

SAVIOUR.

Appendix 1: Therapy Transcripts

Emmerson:

SAVIOUR, fantastic. SAVIOUR. SAVIOUR, you had to be careful with that swallow, didn't you? You had to plan, do it right, but you helped save the swallow didn't you?

SAVIOUR:

Yeah.

Emmerson:

Fantastic, SAVIOUR. SAVIOUR, would you be willing to be helpful to Sharon again if she chooses to help get a spider out like in a glass or something, it's a tiny little thing that is afraid, like the swallow was, SAVIOUR. And if you don't want to do this, it's fine but would you be willing to be helpful to Sharon if she needs help from you SAVIOUR?

SAVIOUR:

I could try. (chuckles)

Emmerson:

And you would be thinking "This little animal is afraid" and you'd be careful. And help it escape. And SAVIOUR, Sharon has a history of being concerned about spiders, so you can anticipate being a bit nervous, okay SAVIOUR?

SAVIOUR:

(nods)

Imagery Check

Emmerson:

Okay, so let's allow a little spider to be, let's say, on the table. SAVIOUR, you helped the swallow in the past. You got the swallow in a cloth; you helped it out. And this little spider is afraid. And SAVIOUR, what do you want to do with it?

SAVIOUR:

I need a glass.

Emmerson:

Yeah. A nice big glass.

SAVIOUR:

Yeah.

Emmerson:

Yeah. Let's have a big glass. And you put it over the spider, is that what you do? And you're going to slide something under the glass...

SAVIOUR:

Yes, and ... that's a magic shield.

Emmerson:

That's fantastic. And you are going to take it out and put it into the garden?

SAVIOUR:

Yeah.

Emmerson:

Okay, go ahead and do that and tell me how you feel.

SAVIOUR:

I can let her out.

Appendix 1: Therapy Transcripts

Emmerson:

That's fantastic. And you're the SAVIOUR. How does that feel?

SAVIOUR:

Good!

Emmerson:

Fantastic. And that's something, SAVIOUR, you can get better and better at. And at first you may be a little bit reluctant, but you are the SAVIOUR. And you're a wonderful part of Sharon and the other parts can pat you on the back. I would like to ask STRONG … STRONG, would you say "thank you" to SAVIOUR?

STRONG:

Yeah, thank you.

Emmerson:

Yeah. And you can pat her on the back a little bit. And you don't have to worry about it at all. You can stay there with INNER MOTHER, and you don't even have to be aware of it. So, SAVIOUR, did you hear, STRONG really appreciates you.

SAVIOUR:

Yeah. It was a pleasure.

Emmerson:

I would like to say thank you to all the parts, thank you SAVIOUR and STRONG and INNER MOTHER and all the other parts, and they can go and settle in where they belong and when that happens you can just … is any other part there that needs to say anything?

Sharon:

(Shakes head, no.)

Emmerson:

Fantastic. Thank you and you can allow your eyes to open.

Sharon:

(sighs deeply, opens her eyes) That was a challenge.

Emmerson:

Yeah? Well, it would be, I mean … Phobias are … are pretty big.

Sharon:

And … that was interesting, because … what I don't like about spiders is when they're scrabbling around. And I remember, in the … imaginary? Uhm, that as a child I was standing in a hill of ants, and nobody was there to take me out!

Emmerson:

Yeah, and you were almost trapped at that time.

Sharon:

Yeah.

Emmerson:

And then that state became vaded and … I call it a Sensory Experienced Memory that … the Sensory Experienced Memory is an emotional memory that can get separated from the intellectual memory. And then the emotional memory comes up and we feel whatever we feel. And Bridging reconnects the Sensory Experienced Memory with the intellectual memory, so you know exactly where it's coming from, and you can resolve the state with the … with the steps that we do.

Teara: Distancing after feeling rejected by friends

Presenting Concern: Teara presented with the issue that she would pull away from friendships when small events would cause her to feel rejection. She would hold onto these feelings of rejection, and those vaded feelings are even evident during the initial stages of this intervention.

Diagnosis:

Emmerson:

Teara, what is it that you're ready to change?

Teara:

Okay, so I believe that I have a part that's fed up with rejection. I, I get upset with people. So, I feel that I don't always stay in touch with people. Because people, you know, upset me in the past may have upset me. You know, they say that they're going to do stuff and then they don't. And then I feel rejected. So, for an example, in my mother's group, they were planning on going to the beach, and they asked me if I wanted to go to the beach, but then it came to that time when they went to the beach together, and the time had been gone, and they hadn't asked me. So, then I kind of start to distance myself from them, and I feel hurt and then I can't be bothered with them so much anymore. And I'd really like to change that.

(It is clear from this presentation that Teara has a part Vaded with Rejection.)

Getting the right state into the Conscious

Emmerson:

Okay, so would that be a good example to take how you felt after the mother's group?

Teara:

Yeah. Let's do that.

Emmerson:

Tell me about finding out that they had been to the beach, and you had not been invited?

Teara:

Well, it really hurt.

Emmerson:

Where were you when you found out?

Teara:

I was at home. Yeah, phone call. And when I say they had gone to the beach. It was a holiday. It was a trip away, you know, for a couple of nights. So, it wasn't just a, you know, a little drive. It was like, go away for a couple of days.

Emmerson:

So, you're at home? And who tells you?

Teara:

My friend, Amy.

Emmerson:

Where are you when you get the telephone call?

Teara:

I was at home.

Appendix 1: Therapy Transcripts

Emmerson:

What room?

Teara:

I can see the kitchen.

Emmerson:

Just allow your eyes to stay closed so you can really zero in on it. You're in the kitchen and the phone rings and you got a phone call from Amy. And as you're answering the phone, you're probably fine. Is that right?

Teara:

Uh-huh.

Emmerson:

And then Amy is talking. Tell me what is happening.

Teara:

Well, she ended up telling me that she, and one of the other mothers from mother's group, had gone to the beach. I was hurt because she had said that she would invite me.

Emmerson:

So, she's telling you now that they've already gone.

Teara:

Yes.

Emmerson:

And this is hitting you on the inside.

Teara:

Uh-huh.

Emmerson:

What's that feel like right now, as you're hearing Amy tell you that she's gone to the beach with these other people?

Teara:

It feels heavy in my heart.

Bridging

Emmerson:

It's sort of like being hit by something?

Teara:

No, just heavy.

Emmerson:

Heavy.

Teara:

Just heavy and like a dark circle.

Emmerson:

Where in the body, you said the heart, is that where it is that you're feeling it right now.

Teara:

So yeah, I can feel it like all now.

Holding the state in the Conscious

(By continuing to repeat all the shaded comments)

Appendix 1: Therapy Transcripts

Emmerson:

Right there in the heart. That heavy dark circle, how big is that?

Teara:

Yeah. I'd say like a football.

Emmerson:

It's pretty big. And in that football area, if you were to go inside that heavy, dark area, is it really dark inside?

Teara:

Yeah, when you said go inside, I just felt like the pictures were gone, and everything just went black.

Emmerson:

So, it's really dark, and it's not a good feeling in there, is it?

Teara:

No.

Emmerson:

Is that darker in the middle or is that the same darkness all around?

Teara:

It's just dark all around.

Emmerson:

Yeah, left out and heavy and is there any color in there or just dark in that left out heavy area?

Teara:

It's just dark.

Getting the age

Emmerson:

It's just really dark, and if you're just sitting on the edge of that really dark, just letting your feet dangle into the darkness, little feet dangling into the darkness, you're a child, what do those feet look like, dangling into that left out darkness, that area? What do the feet look like as they dangle back and forth in that darkness?

Teara:

They are young.

Emmerson:

What do they feel like? How old do they feel, dangling there?

Teara:

I'm not sure. They look young, and I can see my legs.

Emmerson:

About how old are those legs?

Teara:

Maybe five or six, I think.

Funneling into the ISE

Emmerson:

Around five or six, feeling this heaviness, this, I've been left out, somebody may not like me feeling, are you inside or are you outside in the open air?

Teara:

I'm outside.

Appendix 1: Therapy Transcripts

Emmerson:

And being outside, is it dark or daylight?

Teara:

It must be daylight because I feel like I can see the grass.

Emmerson:

Are you alone or is somebody else there? Is there another person, or people, around you?

Teara:

 I feel like I can see my grandmother, and my grandfather.

Emmerson:

What's happening?

Teara:

I have come over to show them my shoes, my new shoes, and they're not happy because they're planting zucchini. And they told me to go away because I'd get my new shoes dirty.

Emmerson:

What can I call you there? What, what term or name fits you right here where you are with your new shoes. SAD or REJECTED or what can I call you?

HURT:

I think, HURT.

Expression

Emmerson:

HURT, thank you for talking with me. I really appreciate you talking to me, HURT, and I know you really wanted one of them to be excited about your new shoes. HURT, let's just allow Grandma and Grandpa to be right there in front of you. We can do anything we want, HURT, because this isn't really happening now. This is a past thing so now we can do anything we want. HURT, what would you really like to say to Grandma and Grandpa?

HURT:

You've really hurt my feelings.

Emmerson:

Tell them directly, "You hurt my feelings." Who are you talking to the most, Grandma or Grandpa?

HURT:

Um, Grandma. You've really hurt my feelings. I just wanted to come and show you my new shoes, and to feel included, and be here and help you.

Introject Speak

Emmerson:

Thank you HURT. That was really good. Grandma, I want to talk to Grandma directly. Grandma, thank you for being here, Grandma. You know your little granddaughter, HURT, has just told you you've hurt her feelings. How does that make you feel?

Grandma:

She was silly. She came. She was being silly because she's just got these new shoes, and she was going to get them dirty.

Emmerson:

You're very practical, aren't you Grandma?

Appendix 1: Therapy Transcripts

Grandma:

Yes.

Emmerson:

You think about the shoes more than you think about her feelings right now, don't you Grandma?

Grandma:

Yes, well, it's silly.

Emmerson:

Thank you for talking with me, Grandma. I really appreciate your honesty, and I hope that in the future you can learn to understand the value of sharing excitement but thank you right now for being honest.

Affirming the feelings of the state

Emmerson:

HURT, I can see why you feel hurt. Your Grandma's not noticing you. She's just thinking about shoes and getting them dirty you're not. HURT, I can really understand why you're upset. I would be upset too.

Expression

Emmerson:

What do you want to say to Grandpa, HURT?

HURT:

To Grandpa, he just never seemed bothered by anything. So, Grandpa, you never notice anything, you're not bothered by anything.

Emmerson:

I'd like you to pay some attention to me, Grandpa.

HURT:

Yeah, I'd like you to pay some attention to me Grandpa.

Emmerson:

Make me feel important.

HURT:

Yeah, I'd like you to make me feel important. I'd like Grandma to make me feel important, too.

Introject Speak

Emmerson:

Grandpa, did you hear what your granddaughter said? She would like to feel important, and she doesn't feel like you pay attention to her, Grandpa. Tell me what's happening, Grandpa.

Grandpa:

She's just young. She's a kid.

Emmerson:

You have other things to do, don't you Grandpa?

Grandpa:

Yeah.

Emmerson:

You don't really pay that much attention to her, do you?

Grandpa:

No. No.

Emmerson:

Thank you for being honest with me. I really appreciate that. And I hope you learn to value people more in the future. I don't know if you will, but I hope so. But thank you for being honest with me.

Affirming the feelings of the state

Emmerson:

HURT, HURT. My goodness. I can see why you feel hurt. Every child, HURT, every single child should feel very important and special and loved, and they should have adults that show them that and get excited. And I'm sure your grandma and Grandpa are fine people but they're just not connecting, as a Grandma and Grandpa can. They're not showing you all that love. And every child deserves and needs and should have a lot of attention and love and I want to make sure, HURT, that you get what every child deserves.

Relief

Emmerson:

Teara, if there was a little girl like HURT that was like your daughter or a little sister, Teara, who really just wanted to be noticed and get some love and attention. Teara, how would you help that child? What would you do to help, Teara?

Teara:

I'd probably go to her and put my hands on her shoulders and just give her a big hug.

Emmerson:

Fantastic. What can I call you, Part?

COMFORT:

COMFORT.

Emmerson:

COMFORT, that's fantastic. That's a great name, COMFORT. I would like you to go to HURT right where she is there in the garden. COMFORT, you can do this and everything else you do. The more you do the more powerful you become, and you can do many things at once, so you can always be there with HURT. Go to HURT and put your arms around her and let her know how special she is. Look at her shoes and let her know how special you think those shoes are. But especially her, and how special it is that she's excited about those shoes. Give her love, a hug, and love, and let that love flow to every cell and fiber of HURT's being. Let her fill up with your love.

HURT, how does that feel?

HURT:

It's nice. It's really good.

Emmerson:

Is it okay with you, HURT, to give COMFORT a little bit of a hug? That will make both of you feel good.

HURT:

Yeah.

Removal

Emmerson:

Fantastic. And feel that love coming in from COMFORT. It's always going to be there. Do you want your Grandma and Grandpa in the scene, or not? It doesn't matter. It's up to you. This is your scene you can have it any way you want. Do you want them here, or not?

HURT:

No, they can leave.

Appendix 1: Therapy Transcripts

Emmerson:

They can leave, Swoosh. They're not in the scene and it's you and COMFORT. And you can have lots of light. You can have whatever you want. You can have your shoes, and they can even be a little bit shinier if you want them to be. This is your scene, and you've always got COMFORT there, and you can feel that, and you can survey your body and any part of your body that can use more love, it can just go into that part and fill up.

Name for the resolved state

Emmerson:

Fantastic, you're feeling a bit better now, aren't you?

HURT:

Yeah.

Emmerson:

What do you like to do when you're having fun?

HURT:

Laugh.

Emmerson:

You like to laugh? What would you like me to call you now? Since you're not feeling hurt anymore? What name would you like?

HAPPY:

HAPPY.

Emmerson:

HAPPY, fantastic. From now on I'm going to call you HAPPY. And HAPPY, you are always going to have COMFORT there. And HAPPY, I am going to come back to you in a minute. But you just stay there with COMFORT, and HAPPY I've got a secret for you.

Permission for another state to act in the future

Emmerson:

Young sensitive parts like you are wonderful. Because you can experience things with a lot of feeling and awe and surprise and you could look at the night sky and see beauty, so this adult could really use you HAPPY. But if there's ever a time when something bad's happening on the outside, you can just stay there with COMFORT and let the more mature parts handle that. Would that be okay with you, HAPPY?

HAPPY:

Yeah.

Find Resource

Emmerson:

Fantastic. Teara, when Amy is telling you about going away or when there's something that's happened like that where maybe somebody did something wrong, how would you like to feel, and how would you like to act? How would you like to respond?

Teara:

Like, I actually don't care.

Emmerson:

You'd like not to really care.

Teara:

Yeah.

Emmerson:

Just let it be. And, so you'd like to feel strong?

Appendix 1: Therapy Transcripts

Teara:

Yes, Strong. Yes! That's exactly how I'd like to be. I'd like to be happy for them.

Emmerson:

Fantastic. When are you able to do that, like if a child is telling you something they've done, or friends telling you something they've done, when you're able to be happy for somebody else, and let it be their moment?

Teara:

When somebody else has achieved something.

Emmerson:

Tell me sometime when somebody did and you were happy for them, a friend or relative, an adult or a child.

Teara:

My daughter recently got into university, so I was really happy about that.

Emmerson:

You felt happy for her, didn't you?

Teara:

Uh-huh.

Emmerson:

Where are you with her, feeling happy for her? Where are you?

Teara:

In my body, or where am I feeling happy?

Emmerson:

Are you at home or in the car or where are you when you are feeling this happy feeling?

Teara:

Oh, when I'm having this happy feeling? Okay, so I was on the phone.

Emmerson:

Um, so you're on the phone and your daughter just now telling you she got into university.

Teara:

Yes.

Emmerson:

Fantastic, and you're feeling proud for her, aren't you, and happy and you sort of want to help her enjoy it?

Teara:

Uh-huh.

Emmerson:

What can I call you, part?

PROUD:

I don't know if this is the right name, but PROUD.

Emmerson:

PROUD. That's a fine name. PROUD, you can be proud at different times in different ways. PROUD, you are a very useful and strong part of Teara. PROUD, Teara needs a part to respond in situations, like to Amy. Would you be pleased, PROUD, to help Teara and be there for her at times when someone like Amy is telling her something, and you can share that understanding and happy achievement with the other person. Would you be happy to help Teara, PROUD?

PROUD:

Yes.

Emmerson:

Fantastic. Thank you for your wonderful help. I want to talk to that little part again, HAPPY, down there with COMFORT. HAPPY, you're such a wonderful sensitive part.

Young state thanks future acting state

Emmerson:

HAPPY, I just talked to PROUD, and she is now willing to take over times when in the past you felt hurt. PROUD is going to take those times now. Is that okay with you, HAPPY, and you can stay there with COMFORT and enjoy that place?

HAPPY:

Yeah.

Emmerson:

Would you like to say thank you to PROUD?

HAPPY:

Yes, thank you PROUD.

Emmerson:

Fantastic. Thank you HAPPY. You enjoy your time there with COMFORT.

Emmerson:

PROUD, did you hear that? You are really popular. What you're doing for Teara, the other parts are going to really appreciate it, and Teara's going to have a better life. She's going to have a more comfortable life. So, this is fantastic. Thank you, PROUD.

Imagery Check

Emmerson:

PROUD, right now, let's go back to that telephone call. And you can take that telephone call, PROUD. You can help enjoy. Help Amy enjoy her experience. So, Amy is telling you PROUD, she's saying that we went to the beach. PROUD, how do you want to respond?

PROUD:

That's great. I hope you had a good time.

Emmerson:

And DO hope she had a good time, PROUD.

PROUD:

Yeah. Yeah.

Emmerson:

Fantastic. And PROUD, thank you very much for being here. Thank you for always being here for Teara. And is there any other part that has something that it needs to say, or would like to say?

Teara:

No, I think I'm good.

Appendix 1: Therapy Transcripts

Emmerson:

Fantastic. Thank you PROUD. Thank you HAPPY. Thank you, COMFORT. What's the team color of your parts? Like if you're a football team, what color is your jersey?

Teara:

For some silly reason I can say like a blue and green. Those colors do not go together.

Emmerson:

Maybe a turquoise, or is it blue and green, blue or green or let's just have the color that feels like it fits. And all the team can have that color, working together. And knowing that I don't have to do anything that I don't want to do. Because there's another part that's good at it. PROUD is probably not the best part to have a little bite of ice cream, but HAPPY might be. HAPPY might really enjoy it. So, let's be thankful for all the parts with their blue and or green. And they can, they can have peace within. And as that settles in, you can just allow your eyes to open.

Emmerson:

What was that like for you?

Teara:

That was great! So, when you were talking to PROUD, I felt it across my chest. So, I felt it. It's strength. And yeah, it changed in my chest. HAPPY, you know, couldn't get the smile off my face, which was a change. So, in COMFORT I felt filled with warmth and with comfort.

Emmerson:

That sounds great. A Vaded State is a state that has something unresolved. And it will come back out when it's reminded of that, and once that gets resolved, then it doesn't have to come back out with bad feelings. It doesn't have bad feelings. It's now feeling quite good.

Sophia: Bridged to the first day of school

Presenting concern: Sophia presented with a physical pain which she felt might have to do with her past. This part of the session is following work on pain, with the client sitting with her eyes still closed.

Emmerson:

And is there any other part that would like to say anything?

Sophia:

There is a little bit of fear.

> *(When a part says it is afraid during a session that is an indication of a State Vaded with Fear or Rejection. It may be physically afraid, or it may be afraid of not being good enough. There is nothing to fear during a therapy session, so when a part is feeling fear other than telling about a fearful time, that is an indication that the fear is coming from an unresolved Resource State. This means a Resource State is holding onto a fear from the past.)*

Getting the right state into the Conscious

Emmerson:

Tell me about that. Fear of?

Sophia:

Fear of the future.

Emmerson:

Where in the body are you experiencing that right now?

Appendix 1: Therapy Transcripts

Sophia:

In my leg.

Emmerson:

And the emotion of fear. The actual emotion of fear of the future, where in the body is that?

Bridging

(While Bridging it is highly important to continue to repeat the emotion in order to keep the Vaded State in the Conscious. All statements and questions need to be about feelings and experiences, never anything about thinking. Never ask why, while Bridging.)

Sophia:

It's in my knee.

(It is unusual for a client to say the feeling is anywhere other than the chest or the stomach, but it does happen.)

Emmerson:

In your knee. And how big an area is that in your knee? Is that like a golf ball, a tennis ball, a football?

Sophia:

Bigger than a tennis ball, smaller than a football.

Holding the state in the Conscious

(By continuing to repeat all the shaded comments.)

Emmerson:

It's a lot of fear. If you go inside that knee, inside that big ball of fear, what color is it in there?

(I keep repeating the emotion to hold the state in the Conscious.)

Sophia:

Grey.

Emmerson:

Grey. So, is that a dark grey or light grey?

Sophia:

Light to mid grey.

Emmerson:

And is it the same greyness all the way across that area? Or is it darker in the middle?

Sophia:

It's a little bit lighter in the middle. No, it's pretty much consistent.

Emmerson:

And that fear in there, that fear of the future, what other adjective can you give me for that feeling?

Sophia:

Uh, Trepidation.

Emmerson:

Okay, am I going to be good enough? Can I do it?

(This indicates the state is Vaded with Rejection, because the fear was about being good enough, not about physical fear. This means it will be important to have the rejecting Introject to speak, so the Vaded State can

> *better understand that it was not that it was not good enough, it was because the other person was not able to be unconditionally loving.)*

Sophia:

Yeah, is it all going to turn to shit?

Emmerson:

It's all going to be bad?

Sophia:

Well, what's going to happen next will blow it out of the water.

Emmerson:

In that grey area, that trepidation, that it is all going to be bad area, being inside that, is it thin in there, or is a thick? Is it easy to move around in that or is it hard?

Sophia:

It's kind of misty. It's ethereal, I suppose.

Getting the age

Emmerson:

Misty. And if you're sitting in that mist, sitting up above in that mist, letting your feet dangle back in that misty ethereal area. That is all going to be bad? You know. It is going to be awful. I don't know if I can take awful stuff. I don't know if I can take it. Letting your little girl feet dangle back and forth. It's all going to be bad? How old do you feel? How old are those feet?

Sophia:

Um, five.

Emmerson:

And being five right now. Fearing, it is all going to be bad? It is going to be horrible? Are you inside a building or outside a building?

Sophia:

I'm, I'm outside. I'm, I'm going to school.

Emmerson:

Are other people around you?

Sophia:

Yeah.

Emmerson:

Tell me what's happening.

Sophia:

I'm, I'm just afraid of going to school.

Emmerson:

Can I call you, AFRAID? What can I call you?

Sophia:

Yeah.

Appendix 1: Therapy Transcripts

Emmerson:

AFRAID, thank you for talking with me. I really appreciate you talking with me, AFRAID. I understand this can be scary. Is this your first day or is this later on?

AFRAID:

Uh, no it's my first day.

> *(I am amazed about how many Vaded States became vaded on the first day of school.)*

Emmerson:

I can understand that. AFRAID, look around you. What is it that you're afraid of?

AFRAID:

So many children, and they all know where they are going, and I don't?

Emmerson:

Is there any one child that you see that causes you to have more fear than the others or just all of them?

AFRAID:

All of them. Some of them are big.

Emmerson:

And they make you a little bit more afraid, the big ones?

AFRAID:

Yeah.

Emmerson:

Let's take a big child there. Is that big child a male or female?

AFRAID:

Uh, it's a girl.

Expression

Emmerson:

Let's take that big girl. And we know this isn't really happening, AFRAID, so now we can say anything we want to that big girl. What do you want to tell her about how you feel? We know she's not really here, so you can say anything you want. What do you want to say to the big girl?

AFRAID:

It's all quite overwhelming. Really.

Emmerson:

Yeah.

AFRAID:

And, and everyone seems to know their place and I don't know mine.

Emmerson:

You want to tell her that she scares you some?

AFRAID:

Yeah, she does.

Emmerson:

Tell her that.

AFRAID:

You scare me.

Introject Speak

Emmerson:

That's really good, AFRAID. You've done a great job. Big girl, that little girl there, AFRAID, said you scare her, and everything is overwhelming. What does that make you feel like, Big Girl?

Big Girl:

I'm just having fun.

> *(It seems to help a small part to realise that a bigger child does not have anything against them. It seems to help the small child just to know that the bigger child is going about their own business.)*

Emmerson:

You're not really thinking of her, are you, Big Girl?

Big Girl:

No. She is just a little girl.

Emmerson:

You didn't really think about trying to help her either, did you, Big Girl?

Big Girl:

No.

Emmerson:

You're just having fun. I understand, Big Girl. Thank you for talking with me, Big Girl.

Affirming the feelings of the state

Emmerson:

AFRAID, I think those kids are just in their own world. And nobody's coming up to help you. That's sad.

Removal

Emmerson:

AFRAID, this is an imaginary space.

Do you want those kids here, or do you want it clear right now?

AFRAID:

No, I want them there. But I just want them to slow down.

(This is the Removal Action. Here the state learns it has the power to either remove the provoking Introjects from the scene or allow them to stay. It does not matter what the decision is. Having the choice helps the state feel more secure. Had she said, "I don't want them here," I would have said, "That's fine, we can just swoosh them away. Swoosh, they are gone now, because this is your space."

The Vaded State has carried the illusion that the past is still happening, that there is something to fear now. The Removal Action is further proof to the state that, "This scene from the past is not happening now.")

Emmerson:

Is there a nice girl there?

AFRAID:

Yeah.

Appendix 1: Therapy Transcripts

Emmerson:

Well, what do you want to say to her?

AFRAID:

Hi.

Emmerson:

Okay, Nice Girl. She just said hi to you. How does that make you feel, Nice Girl?

Nice Girl:

Um, I need a friend.

Emmerson:

That's nice. Maybe the two of you can be friends. That would be really good.

Relief

Emmerson:

Sophia, if there is a five-year-old, experiencing her first day of school, and she's really afraid. And it's a new setting for her. How would you help her? How would you make her feel loved and appreciated, and okay?

Sophia:

I'd be there with her and tell her that it's okay. And that she'll make friends easily, and that she will know her place. It's all good.

Emmerson:

Fantastic, and would you give her a bit of a hug?

(Vaded parts need to feel loved. It is important they receive a hug to feel loved.)

Sophia:

Yeah.

Emmerson:

What can I call you, Part?

Sophia:

Mother

Emmerson:

Can I call you INNER MOTHER?

> (*When a part gives a name like Mother that could be confused with the client's mother, I always ask if I can call it INNER MOTHER so there is no confusion later if I ask to speak with that part.*)

INNER MOTHER:

Yeah, INNER MOTHER.

Emmerson:

INNER MOTHER, just go to AFRAID right there. You sound really relaxed and calm. Just give her a bit of a hug. Let her know that you're there for her, that you can be visible or invisible, but she knows you're there. And she can play with her new friend, but you can give her a hug and let her know that she's never ever going to be alone. And that everything is going to be okay. And you're going to give her love. AFRAID, how does that feel, with INNER MOTHER there?

AFRAID:

It feels good.

Appendix 1: Therapy Transcripts

Emmerson:

Can you give INNER MOTHER a bit of a hug also, AFRAID, to make her feel good?

> *(I often ask the child part to give the helper part a hug. This helps the child part feel good and connected and rewards the helper part for helping.)*

Emmerson:

That's fantastic. And then you've got this other girl who wants to be your friend. And I've got a secret for you, AFRAID, none of this is happening now so we can have it any way we want. So, INNER MOTHER can always be there, and this girl can be a wonderful friend. And that big girl can go off and do her thing because she's just oblivious. She's neither here nor there. So, you can have plenty of sun. You can have it any way you like. And this can be fun.

New name for the resolved state

Emmerson:

How are you feeling now, AFRAID?

AFRAID:

Good, excited.

Emmerson:

Can I call you EXCITED? Or what can I call you?

AFRAID:

Yeah, you can call me EXCITED.

Emmerson:

That's fantastic. That's a great name.

(I like to give positive feedback for the name that was chosen.)

Permission for another state to act in the future

Emmerson:

So, I'll call you EXCITED, and you can have fun there with INNER MOTHER, and with your new friend. And, EXCITED, is it okay with you if Sophia's more mature parts handle the outside and live in a balanced way and deal with adult things the way adults do. Is that okay with you?

Find Resource

(Because this Bridging occurred in the later part of a longer session, I had already found a relaxed part earlier in the session. Therefore, I did not have to look for a helpful part with the skills Sophia needed. This relaxed part had already volunteered to help, and the Vaded Part was discovered during the Imagery Check at the end of the session. Now, after the Vaded Part was resolved, it can just say thank you to the helpful state, RELAXED.)

EXCITED:

Okay. Yeah.

Young state thanks future acting state

Emmerson:

Fantastic. Thank you. And would you like to say thank you to RELAXED, EXCITED, because RELAXED is going to help a lot on the outside? As are some other parts.

319

EXCITED:

Thank you RELAXED.

Emmerson:

Did you hear that, RELAXED? And would you like to say thank you to STRONG, EXCITED, because STRONG is going to help too.

EXCITED:

Thank you STRONG.

Emmerson:

STRONG, did you hear that? You're really popular now. And you have great skills, and you're highly appreciated, STRONG. So, you can just stay in the background and there might be times when you want to come forward and help in another way. But right now, you can just stay in the background. And that's fantastic. And all those parts can appreciate and care for each other. And Sophia, how are you feeling now?

Sophia:

Good.

Emmerson:

And with RELAXED there, and RELAXED doing her thing, you can just allow your eyes to open so that we can talk about it and go on with the day.

(Sophia opens her eyes.)

Thank you, Gordon.

Emmerson:

Hopefully that feels a bit balanced. And that's all we can ever ask for in life is to have our parts balanced to handle life in the best way that our vision allows.

Sophia:

I didn't realize that's where my feelings of being overwhelmed came from.

Emmerson:

It's amazing, isn't it? It's really interesting.

Sophia:

But I loved, I loved, I loved RELAXED. I was that cloth in the sun. It was just beautiful. And, and I just felt everything go. It's all good.

(RELAXED was a part that was found earlier in the session. She had been relaxing in the sun, and was able to offer her skills.)

Sue: Can't sleep in fear of making mistakes at work

Presenting concern: Sue presented with the issue of thinking too much when she went to bed. This thinking was keeping her from being able to go to sleep.

Diagnosis

Emmerson:

Tell me what I need to know.

Sue:

All through the night, and nearly every waking moment, I'm going over and over information, I'm going online, I'm trying to find everything I can to make sure that I'm actually doing the best I can for people who I'm working with. And it's just, at times it's waking me up, because, and then my mind is going over and over and over. Have I checked everything; have I've done everything?

Emmerson:

Do you have a fear that you might not do it well enough?

Sue:

There probably, there might be a little bit of fear that I'm not covering every aspect, like legality wise for myself as well. Because it's very unclear at the moment.

Emmerson:

So, your concern is that you might mess it up in some way?

Sue:

That I'm not giving it the fullest. Don't think I'll mess it up, because I'm very stringent with what I do, but I think it's I'm wanting to cover all bases and to do the best I can and give all the information I can to people and making sure I'm giving the correct, you know, details.

Emmerson:

I'm wondering if this is a fear of letting somebody down, a fear of not being good enough, or confusion.

> *(Sue is aware of the different Resource Therapy pathologies. She originally thought her state was Vaded with Confusion, but it is looking more like Vaded with Rejection, as she has a fear of not being good enough in her work.)*

Sue:

Yeah, I was hoping it was confusion to help.

Emmerson:

We can work with whatever it is.

Sue:

Yeah. Yeah.

Emmerson:

It sounds to me like it might be a fear of not being prepared, not being good enough. Being in trouble in some way if you mess up, legally. Does that sound accurate?

Sue:

Yeah, it probably is. When you speak of it like that.

Getting the right state into the Conscious

Appendix 1: Therapy Transcripts

Emmerson:

When have you felt this the most?

Sue:

In the middle of the night.

Emmerson:

And when you feel it in the middle of the night, it keeps you awake? What happens?

Sue:

It wakes me up.

Emmerson:

Wakes you up?

Sue:

Yes.

Emmerson:

Okay. So, is it dark when you get awakened or is there light in the room?

Sue:

No, it's dark.

Emmerson:

It's dark. Okay. Did it happen last night or the night before or when did it happen?

Sue:

Maybe a week ago.

Emmerson:

Okay. Just allow your eyes to close, so you can really focus in on that. It's maybe a week ago, and you have been awakened from sleep, and you're feeling some anxiety?

Sue:

Yes.

Emmerson:

Are your eyes still closed, there in your bed, or are they opened?

Sue:

No, my eyes are open. And there's just my mind racing, wanting to get as much information in my head as possible and have clarity about the information.

Emmerson:

And it's like, I really need to get this information so I'm more prepared.

Sue:

Yes, yes.

Bridging

Emmerson:

And that racing mind, that anxiety. What adjectives can you put with that anxiety that you're experiencing?

Sue:

Now, I would say fear.

Appendix 1: Therapy Transcripts

Emmerson:

Is that in your chest?

Sue:

Yes, as you're saying that, it is right central in the chest here. (she points)

Holding the state in the Conscious

Emmerson:

And that fear in the chest. That, "Will I be good enough," fear in the chest. It seemed like you indicated it's quite a big area.

Sue:

Yes. (She makes a big circular movement around her chest.)

Emmerson:

Like a basketball?

Sue:

Yeah.

Emmerson:

And is that sort of, like gaseous or electric, or heavy? Or what's it like inside that big fear area?

Sue:

Probably more gaseous but it's a really deep, deep, heavy gaseous.

Emmerson:

It wouldn't be very comfortable standing in that?

Sue:

No. Not too much.

Emmerson:

No, it's heavy, and would you say dark?

Sue:

Yes. It's heavy, and not so dark on the edges, but really dark on the inside.

Emmerson:

In the middle. It's worse in the middle?

Sue:

Yeah.

Emmerson:

And it's sort of scary in that middle.

Sue:

Yes.

Getting the age

Emmerson:

And, if you're in that middle area, just sitting above it, letting your child's feet dangle in that heavy gaseous, fear, I may be in trouble here, area, just letting your feet dangle. Do your feet move easily in that, or not?

Sue:

Yes, yep. They're moving relatively easily.

Appendix 1: Therapy Transcripts

Emmerson:

And if those are child's feet, notice about how old are they?

Sue:

About seven.

Funneling into the ISE

Emmerson:

About seven. And being about seven, right now. Having this fear, having this heavy gaseous fear racing. Am I in trouble? Am I going to let somebody down? Am I good enough? Does it feel like you're more inside a building or outside in the open air?

(By continuing to repeat the feelings of the state, as illustrated in the shaded comments, the state is held in the Conscious, otherwise another state can take over the Conscious and prevent Bridging.)

Sue:

Outside.

Emmerson:

And are you ALONE or is someone else there?

Sue:

Nobody's there.

Emmerson:

Is it daylight or dark?

Sue:

Dark.

Emmerson:

Where are you?

Sue:

In the backyard, at home. I'm locked out.

Emmerson:

Are you going to be in trouble?

Sue:

I am already in trouble.

Emmerson:

What can I call you there? In trouble?

Sue:

SCARED.

Emmerson:

What's that?

Sue:

I'm SCARED. My name is SCARED.

Emmerson:

SCARED, thank you for talking with me. It's pretty scary, not knowing how much trouble you're in, isn't it?

SCARED:

Yes!

Emmerson:

SCARED, who might you be in the most trouble with, Mom or Dad?

SCARED:

Dad.

Expression

Emmerson:

Okay, SCARED. I've got a secret for you, SCARED. This really isn't happening right now. So, we can do anything we want. So even though he's not really here, let's have your Dad right in front of you. And I want you to tell him how scared you are, and how you feel.

(Frequently using the name of the part helps hold it in the Conscious, it lets it know you are aware of it and are talking directly to it.)

SCARED:

I'm just feeling so scared out here on my own alone. It's cold. It's dark.

Emmerson:

Are you scared of your Dad, SCARED?

SCARED:

I'm scared that I'm going to be left out here alone all this time.

Emmerson:

Tell him that.

SCARED:

I'm just scared. You can leave me out here, on my own, all the time, all overnight.

Emmerson:

Yeah.

SCARED:

Somebody might come and take me away.

Emmerson:

SCARED, I can understand that.

Introject Speak

Emmerson:

Dad, your little girl just said that she's really scared out here. She's afraid you're going to leave her out here, Dad. Dad, what do you have to say?

Dad:

Oh, you shouldn't have done what you did.

Emmerson:

Are you punishing her, Dad?

Dad:

Yes.

Emmerson:

So, you feel this is an appropriate punishment for a seven-year-old, Dad?

Dad:

Yes, she'll learn the lesson.

Appendix 1: Therapy Transcripts

Emmerson:

Thank you for talking with me. I really appreciate you talking with me. I appreciate your honesty. I hope in the future, you become more empathetic and learn how to communicate better with people. But right now, I just want to say thank you for talking with me.

> *(The conversation with the rejecting person does not need to be long. The purpose is merely to enable the Vaded State to feel the rejecting person's inability to give unconditional love, so the Vaded State can understand it is not her fault, as it is the fault of the other person at that time. There is no need to villainize the other person, just to help the state see it was not the fault of the child.)*

Affirming the feelings of the state

Emmerson:

SCARED, wow, I can see why you're scared. Your Dad scares me. Every, every child deserves to be protected and know they're loved. And to think of their parents as people who can take care of them and keep them safe, SCARED, and your Dad may be a great guy, but right now he's being silly. And I want to make sure you get what every child should have, SCARED. I want to make sure that you have a sense of safety and love and appreciation.

> *(These comments confirm the child's right to feel upset, and they place the responsibility on the adult. This moves the feeling from, "There is something wrong with me", to "I did not get what every child should get." This is a huge shift.)*

Removal

Emmerson:

In the meantime, SCARED. Do you want your Dad in this space, or not? This is your space. It's not a real space. You can have it cleared of him, or you can let him stay here, whatever you want. What would you like, SCARED?

SCARED:

Yeah, he can go. He can go.

Emmerson:

Okay let's just, Swoosh, the space is just clear now.

Relief

Emmerson:

Now. Sue, if there was a seven-year-old girl who was outside and really wanting to feel safe and loved and appreciated. Somebody you know and love, Sue, what would you do?

> *(Here I call the client by name and ask her how she would help a child like the Vaded State. The part of her that answers this question is the part that wants to help and is able to.)*

Sue:

I'd go up to them and I'd kneel down beside them and I'd give them a big hug. And just tell them that I'll stay here.

Emmerson:

That's fantastic. What can I call you, part?

CARE:

CARE.

Emmerson:

CARE, thank you for being here. CARE, the more you do the more powerful you become, and you can do many things at once. So, you can always be here with SCARED. I'd like for you to go to scared now. Right where she is. Put your arm around her. Send her love to every cell and fiber and let her feel your presence and your understanding and your knowing, and just let that love sink in her.

Emmerson:

SCARED, how does that feel?

SCARED:

It feels really good. I've got her here with me.

Emmerson:

That's really good. And I'm sorry, SCARED, that it's taken so long for you to get this love and understanding. Every child should have this and you're always going to have it SCARED. SCARED, is it okay with you if you give CARE a bit of a hug? That will make her feel good too.

SCARED:

Yeah. (smiling broadly)

Emmerson:

You can do that. And you can have, since this is your space, you can have lots of light, if you like.

SCARED:

Yeah, I want light.

Emmerson:

You can have light; you can have warmth. You can have couches, if you want you can have anything, this is your space, but you've always got CARE there with you. You've been really brave. You're feeling much better now, aren't you?

SCARED:

Yes.

New name for the resolved state

Emmerson:

What would you like to be called now?

PLAYFUL:

PLAYFUL

Permission for another state to act in the future

Emmerson:

PLAYFUL, that's fantastic, PLAYFUL. From now on, I'll call you PLAYFUL. That's a great name. And PLAYFUL, maybe when the adult wants to play, you could help her enjoy that. But if there's any kind of mature adult things, another part might be better for that. And you can just stay down there with CARE. So, I'll come back to you in a moment PLAYFUL.

Find Resource

Emmerson:

Sue, when you are preparing and thinking about doing your work in the workplace, how would you like to feel and how would you like to act?

> *(This is the Find Resource Action. Sue needs to find her best state to be out in the future, rather than a childhood state, even one that has been resolved.)*

Sue:

Very knowledgeable. Very, I suppose, precise, directive, so I can direct people and know my stuff really well.

Appendix 1: Therapy Transcripts

Emmerson:

So, you want to feel on top of it. And would you say calm and focused?

Sue:

Yes, focused, Yeah and calm and be good too. Yeah.

Emmerson:

Okay, and tell me when you do feel focused and calm and professional.

Sue:

When I'm doing my classes, and I'm with couples, and I'm giving all the information, and I know how to give it to them.

Emmerson:

Okay, You're with those couples now. How does that feel?

Sue:

Great. (Said with strength)

(Because of the strong smile, I can see she is in a strong, mature state, so I am ready to just get a name for that state and ask it for help.)

Emmerson:

That's' good. What can I call you part, with couples?

KNOWLEDGEABLE:

KNOWLEDGEABLE.

Emmerson:

KNOWLEDGEABLE, thank you, for being here. You're a wonderful part of Sue, KNOWLEDGEABLE. Sue needs your expertise even more than you've been helping her and you've been helping her quite a lot, already. But you're probably the best part for this, KNOWLEDGEABLE. When she's doing work in her workplace. Would you be happy to make sure that she knows what she needs to know and feels focused and clear and can help other people feel calm? Would you be happy to help Sue in that time, KNOWLEDGEABLE?

KNOWLEDGEABLE:

Yes.

Emmerson:

Fantastic. Thank you. Thank you Knowledgeable.

Young state thanks future acting state

Emmerson:

PLAYFUL, right down there with CARE. You're such a wonderful little part PLAYFUL. Would you like to say thank you to KNOWLEDGEABLE for taking care of that stuff up there on the adult side, so you can stay there with CARE and enjoy playing?

PLAYFUL:

Thank you so much, KNOWLEDGEABLE.

Emmerson:

Thank you PLAYFUL. KNOWLEDGEABLE, did you hear that? You're a hero. You're stepping in with your focus, your maturity, your ability to take the information that's available and use it in a wise way. Thank you very much. Thank you for your help.

> *(Now we are ready for the Imagery Check Action to see how the parts can work together.)*

Imagery Check

Emmerson:

Sue, let's go back, you're in your bed, it's night. It's been a long day, how are you feeling?

Sue:

Exhausted.

Emmerson:

It's a nice time to sleep, isn't it? You've got the part there that says this is my time, I'd like to take this time and just go into Slumberland.

Sue:

Yeah.

Emmerson:

And does that feel like you've got permission for that?

Sue:

There's a little twinge, I might miss something, but there's a general feeling of, yeah, this is what I need.

Emmerson:

Fantastic, and that twinge that I might miss something, I just want to say to you, part, make sure you get some time before bed or after. You're a wonderful part and that rest part really is going to prepare the body for you to do a better job. So, you can appreciate that rest part. Thank you to all the parts and you can settle in where you belong. And as you settle in, you can just allow your eyes to open.

(This was me ending the session when I was out of time. The twinge part was probably just related to the habit of thinking about how to do better at this time, and without being energized by a Vaded State it will most likely quickly subside, but I don't know that. Had I had more time, I would have spoken directly with that part to see if it needed anything. When you don't have time to go further you can just allow clients to give you further feedback later.)

Ally (1st Bridge): I think I'm really bad

Presenting concern: Ally could not get out of her head the thought that she was a bad person. She also carried a fear that she was always going to do something bad.

Emmerson:

Okay, Ally, what are you ready to change today?

Ally:

I'm ready to change a recurring thought or idea that I'm bad, or I'm going to do something bad. And the anxiety that comes with that.

Getting the right state into the Conscious

Emmerson:

When does this happen?

Ally:

It particularly happens in relationships, I say the wrong thing and it's going to be bad. Like that word "bad" kind of feels really prominent with it. It's like …

Emmerson:

What feeling do you get with that? I'm going to be in trouble or what feeling?

Ally:

Yeah, like I'm going to be in deep shit.

Emmerson:

Okay, can you give me an example of when this happens?

Ally:

So, just a really small little example that kind of brought my awareness to it recently was I screenshot a conversation. I was having a conversation with somebody, and I screenshot a photo of them and and then I sent it to them, and I said, "I don't know if this is really bad, but I didn't get your consent to take this little screenshot." Like it's such a silly little thing, but my thing is, oh my god, this is so bad. Like I didn't get their consent, and they might be really angry at me. So, then I go into like, I can delete it. Maybe it was a really silly thing. Yeah, so it's bad but maybe it is bad.

Emmerson:

Where are you when this happens?

Ally:

I'm like, I could be anywhere but in that particular situation I think I was at work. I think I was just in my car going to work.

Emmerson:

So, you're in your car, using your phone?

Ally:

No, no, I'm like at work sitting in the car. About to walk into work. No, no, no, no, I would never do that. Like I'm like...

Emmerson:

I was bringing it up more for you. Okay, so you're parked.

Ally:

Uh-huh.

Emmerson:

And you're at work and you haven't gotten out of the car yet to go in? Is that right?

Appendix 1: Therapy Transcripts

Ally:

Yeah.

Emmerson:

And you've taken the screenshot. How are you feeling?

Ally:

Well, at the moment when I did it, I thought it was fun.

Emmerson:

Yeah.

Ally:

Like this is a cute conversation. I'll, I'll screenshot there.

Emmerson:

Lead me through what happens.

Ally:

Then, I get a wave of like terror.

> *(This feeling of terror is when the Vaded State comes into the Conscious with its unresolved feelings.)*

Emmerson:

Allow your eyes to close. Now, when does this wave of terror come?

> *(Ally is now telling about the point where the emotion starts. I want to make sure this state is in the Conscious so I will be able to bridge. This is the Vivify Specific Action.)*

Ally:

When I realized that I've done something that's potentially bad.

342

Emmerson:

Oh my god, I've done something potentially bad.

Ally:

Uh-huh.

Emmerson:

And are you looking at the screenshot while you're experiencing this wave?

Ally:

Yeah.

Bridging

Emmerson:

What are you feeling?

Ally:

Like prickly.

Emmerson:

Where?

Ally:

In my chest.

Holding the state in the Conscious

Emmerson:

And I might be in real trouble here. How big is the area in your chest?

Appendix 1: Therapy Transcripts

Ally:

Like a soccer ball.

Emmerson:

And that, I might be in real trouble here, I've done something, maybe bad. In that soccer ball, if you're on the inside of that, what's it like in there?

Ally:

Black.

Emmerson:

Black. It's not fun at all.

Ally:

And I can still feel my head as well. I feel my brain breaking.

Emmerson:

I could be in trouble here.

Ally:

Yeah.

Emmerson:

And is that black in that soccer ball area, is it darker in the middle or the same all the way across the soccer ball area? In the chest?

Ally:

It's probably darker in the middle.

Getting the age

Emmerson:

In that darkest place in the middle area, where it's really bad, like terror. I could be in trouble here. If you're sitting on the edge of that, in that really scary area letting your feet dangle in that terror black area, I could be in so much trouble. Look at those feet and tell me how big they are, dangling down in that terror black stuff. It's really scary.

Ally:

Five.

Funneling into the ISE

Emmerson:

You're doing really well, being about five, I might be in real trouble here. Are you inside a building or outside a building?

Ally:

Inside.

Emmerson:

Inside. Are you alone or with someone else?

Ally:

Dad is there.

Emmerson:

You don't have to go in any detail. What do you want to say? Is your dad angry at you?

(Anytime I think there could be some content that might be hard to share I say, "You don't have to go into any detail." Details are not important. Empowerment is. RT is not a voyeuristic therapy.)

Ally:

Yeah.

Appendix 1: Therapy Transcripts

Emmerson:

I've got a secret for you. What can I call you? Can I call you BAD or what can I call you? UPSET? SCARED?

> *(I will accept a negative name for a Vaded State because it can reflect how it feels at the time. When it feels better later a negative name can be changed to a positive name, that better reflects the more positive feeling. The change in name seems to help the client feel the transition.)*

Ally:

Um, probably SCARED.

Expression

Emmerson:

SCARED. Thank you for talking with me. SCARED, I've got a secret for you. This isn't really happening now. So right now, SCARED, you can say to your Dad, anything you want. As a matter of fact, let's shrink him down to where he's just two centimeters tall. One inch tall. Just, Swoosh, tiny little Dad's has a squeaky little voice and still has the same stupid expression. But please, SCARED don't step on him because I want you to be able to tell him how you feel. SCARED, tell Dad how you feel.

> *(Shrinking the provoking Introject and asking the Vaded State to be careful not to step on him is a good way to help the state to feel more power. Had I told her she had more power than her Dad, she likely would not have believed that, but she believes she has to be careful not to step on him.)*

Ally:

You're really terrifying. You scare me, Dad. Don't, you shouldn't scare me like this. You're a lot bigger than I am, normally. And I want to be a good girl. And you make me feel like I'm bad.

Introject Speak

Emmerson:

What's the expression on Dad's face? That little, tiny face?

Dad:

Angry.

Emmerson:

Dad. Dad, thank you for talking with me. Dad, your little girl's just five years old. You're scaring her, Dad. She's told you you're scaring her. What's going on with you, Dad? Are you having trouble living in this life? What's going on with you, Dad?

Dad:

Yeah, yeah. I've got a lot going on.

Emmerson:

Are you feeling out of control in your life? Do you want to make sure you're the boss?

Dad:

Yeah, you need to be in control.

Emmerson:

Is this the way you were raised, Dad?

Dad:

Yeah.

Appendix 1: Therapy Transcripts

Emmerson:

Dad, there's a better way. I hope you learn it. But I want to thank you for being honest with me. And I hope you soften up and learn the value of connection and love and relationship later on. I don't know if you will. But thank you, Dad.

> *(Our purpose is not to villainize a parent. Our purpose is to demonstrate to the Vaded State that it was the parent who was not able to show unconditional love at the time. It is not the responsibility of a child to be lovable.)*

Affirming the feelings of the state

Emmerson:

SCARED, SCARED, I can understand why you'd be SCARED. I'd be scared, too. This guy doesn't know how to be soft and loving and connected and gentle and encouraging. I'm sorry, SCARED that this is something you've had to go through. I want to make sure you get what every child should have. Every child should feel safe and loved and protected and encouraged by parents. And I'm sorry that that's not your experience right now, SCARED.

Relief

Emmerson:

Ally, if there's a little girl and she's feeling really scared and afraid she's done something bad, and you know it's really her father that's out of control. Ally, how would you help that little girl?

Ally:

I would take her away from it. And talk to her and teach, teach her she didn't do anything bad, or teach her what's okay and what's not okay and be calm about it.

Emmerson:

Would you be kind, and would you give her a hug?

Ally:

Uh-huh.

Emmerson:

Would you give her love?

Ally:

Yeah.

Emmerson:

What can I call you, part?

Ally:

KINDNESS.

Emmerson:

KINDNESS, beautiful. KINDNESS, thank you for being here. KINDNESS, I would like for you to go to SCARED right there where she is on the inside, and take her someplace away, and give her a hug and love and let her know that you're going to instruct her in a very kind and loving way and that kids and adults do things right and they do things wrong and it's just all to learn, and that she can be loved no matter what. If she does it right, she's loved if she does it wrong, she's loved. And just let that love flow from you, KINDNESS, to every cell and fiber of SCARED, and let her feel very, very safe. And very, very, very connected.

(Here I have heard how KINDNESS will help, and I am asking KINDNESS to go to SCARED and help in that way. She has already told me this is how she would help, so what I am asking of her is exactly what

349

> *she has already confirmed she would like to do. When I am saying these things SCARED can hear them too.)*

Emmerson:

SCARED, how does that feel?

SCARED:

Yeah, it feels really calm.

Emmerson:

That's fantastic. Is it okay with you, SCARED, to give KINDNESS a bit of a hug, also?

> *(This question makes SCARED a participator, deepens the positive feeling, and improves self-image with the state becoming a giver.)*

SCARED:

Yeah.

Removal

Emmerson:

That's fantastic. That makes her feel good, too. And so, do you want your Dad in this space? Or do you want him out of this space? He can be someplace else, or he can be here.

> *(This is the Removal Action. It does not matter how it is answered. Having the choice is empowering to the state.)*

SCARED:

No, he can go.

Emmerson:

That's fine. Swoosh, let's just have you and KINDNESS and you can have lots of light there, if you want. You can have anything you want there. And this is your space now and you're safe and you're loved, and everything is nice with the right amount of light. You can play; you can do whatever you want. And you can get a hug from KINDNESS anytime you want. And you can give KINDNESS a hug anytime you want.

New name for the resolved state

Emmerson:

What would you like to be called now? LOVED, or something else? SAFE?

SAFE:

Calling me SAFE is good.

Emmerson:

SAFE. Fantastic. From now on I'll call you SAFE. And SAFE, you've always got KINDNESS there. And do you want light there too?

SAFE:

Uh-huh.

Emmerson:

You can have beautiful light. And anything you want there you can have, because this is your space. What do you like to do SAFE when you're having fun?

SAFE:

Play.

Permission for another state to act in the future

Emmerson:

That's fantastic. You know, it's fun for a child to play. So, if this adult gets a chance to play, you might help her enjoy playing. But other times, it is okay with you if more mature parts take care of the outside and you can stay down there with KINDNESS.

SAFE:

Yeah.

Emmerson:

You're a really special, sensitive part. And that's wonderful, and you can help this adult feel nice things. But there's always a better adult part to take care of the hard things on the outside. That's not your role. You're, you're a wonderful child.

Find Resource

Emmerson:

And, Ally, let's go back to how would you like to respond, Ally, if you took a picture, a screenshot and you were concerned whether this other person would think that was okay or not? How would you like to act? And how would you like to feel?

> *(This is the start of the Find Resource Action to find Ally's best adult part to help her in the future. Notice, I am calling the client by name. I am speaking to the mosaic of the client so any part can respond. The name of the person is the mosaic of all parts.)*

Ally:

I would just like to still probably take the same caution. But not being so terrified, just calm about it.

Emmerson:

I understand, you want to just check it out with the other person.

Ally:

Yeah.

Emmerson:

Oh, by the way, I took this, I just want to make sure that …

Ally:

Yeah.

Emmerson:

That sounds very mature and like good communication. When are you mature with good communication?

Ally:

When I'm teaching.

Emmerson:

When you're teaching, fantastic. I'd like you to be teaching now. Who is in front of you?

> *(I want to make sure to get the teaching part into the Conscious so I can line it up to be helpful in the future. It is always important to talk with a part directly. A part might volunteer to help, but if it does not really want to help, it might not be available in the future.)*

Ally:

My students.

Appendix 1: Therapy Transcripts

Emmerson:

Your students are there. You're very mature. You've got good communication. What can I call you?

CONFIDENT:

CONFIDENT.

Emmerson:

CONFIDENT, would you be willing to help Ally at other times too? Like for example, if she takes a screenshot and she needs to communicate with someone? You're a mature part and you can check it out. Would you be willing to be helpful to Ally, CONFIDENT?

CONFIDENT:

Yeah.

Young state thanks future acting state

Emmerson:

Fantastic. SAFE, would you like to say thank you to CONFIDENT for being there to help?

SAFE:

Thanks, CONFIDENT.

Emmerson:

And you don't have to do that now that CONFIDENT is going to take care of it. You can stay down there with KINDNESS.

Imagery Check

Emmerson:

CONFIDENT, you're sitting in the car. Ally has been communicating with a friend. She's taken a screenshot. CONFIDENT, you're aware that maybe I should check this out with my friend. How do you want to handle this, CONFIDENT?

> *(This is the Imagery Check Action where the client is taken back to the original problem image, after the Vaded State has been resolved and with the mature state in the Conscious to help. This will show either that the work has been done, or more work is needed. It will also give practice and confidence to the client.)*

CONFIDENT:

I'll just ask, I'll just say, oh, I would share it and say I took a screenshot. Would you like it, or would you like me to delete it?

Emmerson:

Fantastic. That sounds very good, CONFIDENT. You're not only CONFIDENT, but you're also wise. So, thank you for that.

Emmerson:

Ally, how does that feel to you?

Ally:

Yeah, fine.

Emmerson:

Fantastic.

Ally (2nd Bridge): Upset about being mean to another kid

Getting the right state into the Conscious

Presenting concern: Ally originally presented with the thought that she was bad. After working with one state, we continued to work with a second state that added to this feeling.

Ally:

I have a little thought going on. Is that bad? Like, is it bad? Did I do a really bad thing? Taking it?

(This shows that all the work is not done. That is a value of doing the Imagery Check. It is better than to future project into a new situation, because the client has already lived through this event and the Imagery Check can see if there is still a fragile state feeling upset. If a second Bridging is needed it tends to happen very quickly.)

Bridging

Emmerson:

And, that little thought, is it bad? Where do you feel that in your body?

Ally:

My head.

Emmerson:

In your head? And what's it feel like in your head?

Holding the state in the Conscious

(The state is held in the Conscious by continuing to repeat the core feelings. These are denoted in the shaded comments.)

Ally:

Like swirly?

Emmerson:

Like what?

Ally:

Like swirly.

Getting the age

Emmerson:

Swirly. And, how old does that feel? How old is this swirly part?

> *(Because it is the second Bridging in the session, I was able to ask more quickly how old she felt, without having her to dangle her feet in the area and see what they look like.)*

Ally:

Maybe about 10.

Funneling into the ISE

Emmerson:

And being about 10, feeling did I do a bad thing, am I good enough? Am I guilty, being about 10? Are you inside or outside?

Ally:

Outside?

Emmerson:

And what's happening?

Appendix 1: Therapy Transcripts

Ally:

There's like, another kid there. And I was mean to them.

Emmerson:

And what can I call you? TEN, or what can I call you?

Ally:

TEN.

Expression

Emmerson:

TEN, you were mean to that other kid. What do you want to say to the other kid?

TEN:

That I'm really sorry.

Emmerson:

Just go ahead and say it to that other kid. You're doing a really good thing.

TEN:

Yeah, okay, I'm really sorry. (said with tears)

Introject Speak

Emmerson:

Kid, she said she is sorry. How does it make you feel?

Kid:

Yeah, good.

Emmerson:

You want to thank her for telling you that she's sorry.

Kid:

Thank you.

Emmerson:

What do you think about her, Kid? Do you like her or not?

Kid:

Yeah.

Emmerson:

Do you look up to her?

(I picked up that the kid looks up to her from the tone in her voice. It is more important to hear emotion than content.)

Kid:

Yeah.

Emmerson:

Thank you, Kid.

Emmerson:

TEN:

Did you know that that other kid looks up to you?

TEN:

Yeah.

Affirming the feelings of the state

Emmerson:

I was proud of you. That was a very nice thing for you to say to her, that you're sorry. How are you feeling now, TEN?

TEN:

Relieved.

> *(No Removal step is needed here, as the other kid is not now causing the Vaded State to feel uneasy. There was also no need to look for a new name for the state because TEN is quite a nice name already.)*

Emmerson:

TEN, there is another part I want to introduce you to in a moment.

Find Resource

Emmerson:

Ally, when you are in a mood, where you want to know if something's right or wrong, when you are rising above yourself to get sort of the spiritual answer, of correct or not, non-selfish and pure. What can I call you part?

> *(Most people can connect with a part of themselves that has a high moral character, and this part is sometimes useful in therapy.)*

Ally:

WISDOM.

Emmerson:

WISDOM, thank you for being there. WISDOM, I was talking to a really nice little part, TEN, and TEN sometimes needs some guidance. WISDOM, I wonder if you would mind being there for TEN for guidance, if TEN has a question about something?

WISDOM:

(Shakes head yes.)

Emmerson:

And you can do all the stuff you do on top of this, you can do many things at once, WISDOM. So just go to TEN and let TEN know that anytime TEN's got an ethical concern, you're there for TEN, and you're very wise, and you've sort of plugged into the higher level of consciousness.

> *(It is better to not refer to parts as he or she, as they can identify as either. The name of the part can just be used, as above. You can ask a part about its gender, but it really does not matter. Sometimes one part will refer to another part as he or she.)*

Permission for another state to act in the future

Emmerson:

TEN, how does that feel having that asset that you don't have to worry about what's right and wrong, you can ask WISDOM.

TEN:

Really good. Relief.

Emmerson:

You don't have too much stuff to worry about. That's nice having WISDOM there, isn't it?

TEN:

Yeah.

Appendix 1: Therapy Transcripts

Emmerson:

And TEN, is that okay with you, if it's the big parts on the outside that handle things and if CONFIDENT handles things, and you can stay there with WISDOM.

TEN:

Yeah.

Young state thanks future acting state

Emmerson:

Fantastic. Would you like to say thank you to CONFIDENT for doing that?

TEN:

Yeah.

Emmerson:

Thank you. SAFE, you want to say thank you to CONFIDENT again too, don't you SAFE?

SAFE:

Yeah. Thank you, CONFIDENT.

Emmerson:

CONFIDENT, did you hear that? You're really appreciated.

CONFIDENT:

(Nods yes.)

Emmerson:

Fantastic. And, and how are the parts feeling now?

Ally:

Yeah, good. Rested.

Imagery Check

Emmerson:

So, CONFIDENT, you're in the car and you have the phone.

CONFIDENT:

(Nods in approval.)

Emmerson:

You want to punch those buttons in to send that message?

CONFIDENT:

(Nods in approval.)

Emmerson:

That feels like the right thing to do, doesn't it?

CONFIDENT:

Yeah.

Emmerson:

How are you feeling Ally?

Ally:

Yeah, good. …

Emmerson:

As all that settles in, you can just allow your eyes to open.

Appendix 1: Therapy Transcripts

Emmerson:

You went through something there, didn't you? Do you have a tissue?

(That's a bad thing about the internet. What I normally do if a client has her eyes closed, I will just say to the client, I'm going to lay a tissue on your hand. I do not touch a client. I don't think it's appropriate to do that. I just say I'm going to lay a tissue on your hand. And I'll lay a tissue on their hand and let them pick it up with their other hand. If their eyes are open, I just hand them a tissue. Some therapists say it's okay to cry. That takes them out of it. You don't want to take them out of it. You just want to give them a tissue. But I couldn't do that because she was on the net.)

Ally:

Thank you for the offer.

Emmerson:

Thank you for volunteering. Is there anything you want to say about that session?

Ally:

No, I just, that I've been carrying that little 10-year-old story for a really long time, feeling really guilty and shameful about it.

Appendix 2: Resource Therapy Actions

Table 11: RT Actions

Core Actions	Description
1. Diagnosis	Identifying the **Resource Pathology**, determining which state needs intervention.
2. Vivify Specific	Bringing any state into conscious awareness for therapy.
3. Bridging	Moving from the **Vaded feeling** to the **Initial Sensitizing Event (ISE*)** where the issue originated.
4. Expression	The **Vaded State** expresses itself to the feared or rejecting **Introject**.
5. Introject Speak	The client speaks as the rejecting **Introject**, voicing its perspective.
6. Removal	The image of the feared or rejecting **Introject** is removed from the **ISE**.
7. Relief	The **Vaded State** receives loving support and a new **positive name**.

Appendix 2: Resource Therapy Actions

Core Actions	Description
8. Find Resource	A mature **Resource State** is found to respond to the situation in a healthier way.
9. Changing Chairs Introject Action	The client physically **changes chairs** while engaging in a dialogue with an **Introject**.
10. Retro State Negotiation	A **Retro State** is negotiated with for a preferred behavior.
11. Conflicted State Negotiation	Two Conflicted States **negotiate understanding** and work together.
12. Imagery Check	The client revisits the original scene to **assess emotional change** and confirm resolution.

Supplemental Actions

(Optional) Complimentary Resource Actions	These supportive techniques can be used whenever helpful but are not required Actions for any particular pathology.
13. Resistance Alliancing	Moving a **resistant state** into a **helping state** to support therapy.
14. The Separation Sieve	A metaphorical exercise to help the client **choose to let go** of something holding them back.
15. Anchoring	Establishing an **anchor** to help the client access a **preferred state** when needed.

Definitions:

- *ISE (Initial Sensitizing Event, Boswell, 1987). The event linked to the onset of a problem or reaction.
- **Introject: An internalized representation of a person or their traits that influence one's psychological state.

See Table 12 to view the Treatment Actions for each diagnostic category. Obviously to understand treatment protocols more in-depth information is required, but the reader can gain a clearer understanding of the RT process.

Table 12: RT Actions for each Diagnosis

Diagnosis ⇓ by Action →	1	2	3	4	5	6	7	8	9	10	11	12
Vaded with Fear	✓	✓	✓	✓		✓	✓	✓				✓
Vaded with Rejection	✓	✓	✓	✓	✓	✓	✓	✓				✓
Vaded with Confusion	✓	✓							✓			✓
Vaded with Disappointment	✓	✓						✓		✓		✓
Retro Original	✓	✓						✓		✓		✓
Retro Avoiding	✓	✓	✓	✓	✓	✓	✓	✓		✓		✓
Conflicted States	✓	✓									✓	✓
Dissonant State	✓	✓						✓				✓

Appendix 3: Pathologies linked to Vaded with Fear

Table 13: Vaded with Fear Pathologies

Pathology	Relation to "Vaded with Fear" in Resource Therapy
Abreactions	Sudden, intense emotional releases often triggered by unresolved **fear-based trauma**.
Acute Stress Disorder	Fear response to recent trauma; **Vaded with Fear** state holds the distress.
Addictions	Fear-driven coping mechanism to escape **underlying anxiety or trauma**.
Aggression to Others	A defensive response from a **Vaded with Fear** state trying to protect itself.
Aggression to Self	Self-harm to avoid fears, shame, or self-rejection.
Agoraphobia	Fear-driven avoidance of places perceived as unsafe, linked to a **Vaded with Fear** state.
Adjustment Disorder	Struggles with life changes fueled by **fear of uncertainty or failure**.

Appendix 3: Pathologies linked to Vaded with Fear

Pathology	Relation to "Vaded with Fear" in Resource Therapy
Anger as Protection for a Fragile State	Anger is used as a defense against deeper, underlying fear.
Anxiety Disorders	Fear-based states create excessive worry, avoidance, and panic.
Antisocial Personality Disorder	Fear may underlie **impulsive and defensive** behaviors as a survival mechanism.
Body Dysmorphic Disorder	Fear of judgment and rejection due to perceived physical flaws.
Borderline Personality Disorder	Intense **fear of abandonment** drives emotional instability and impulsivity.
Business Phobia	Fear of failure and rejection in professional settings.
Claustrophobia	Fear of being trapped, linked to past **Vaded with Fear** experiences.
Compulsive Shopping	A coping strategy to suppress underlying **fear-based anxiety**.
Conversion Disorder	Physical symptoms emerge from suppressed fear and emotional trauma.
Crisis Reaction	Fear response to sudden, overwhelming events.

Pathology	Relation to "Vaded with Fear" in Resource Therapy
Delayed Ejaculation	Fear of performance, intimacy, or rejection affecting physical response.
Depersonalization/ Derealization Disorder	Dissociation as an escape from overwhelming **fear or anxiety**.
Dissociative Identity Disorder (DID)	Multiple states form as a defense against **severe fear or trauma**.
Dissociative Amnesia	Fear-based repression of traumatic memories.
Dissociative Convulsions	Physical symptoms arise from repressed **fear or distress**.
Elimination Disorders	Fear and stress-related loss of bodily control.
Enuresis	Fear-related bedwetting, often linked to childhood trauma.
Encopresis	Unconscious fear-based loss of bowel control.
Erectile Disorder	Performance anxiety driven by **fear of failure or inadequacy**.
Excoriation Disorder (Skin Picking)	Compulsive behavior used to cope with **fear-driven anxiety**.

Appendix 3: Pathologies linked to Vaded with Fear

Pathology	Relation to "Vaded with Fear" in Resource Therapy
Female Orgasmic Disorder	Fear of intimacy, control, or past trauma affecting sexual function.
Female Sexual Interest/Arousal Disorder	Fear or past trauma linked to **emotional or physical intimacy**.
Fetishistic Disorder	A way to manage **underlying fear, anxiety, or emotional wounds**.
Frustration in Coping Ability	Feeling incapable, stemming from a deep **Vaded with Fear** state.
Generalized Anxiety Disorder	Persistent, excessive worry controlled by a **fear-driven state**.
Hoarding Disorder	Fear of **loss, instability, or lack of control**.
Inability to be Alone	Fear of abandonment or being left unprotected.
Insomnia Disorder	Fear-based intrusive thoughts preventing restful sleep.
Nightmare Disorder	Unprocessed fear and trauma resurfacing in dreams.
Nightmares	Fear states replaying past traumatic experiences.

Pathology	Relation to "Vaded with Fear" in Resource Therapy
Obsessive-Compulsive Disorder (OCD)	Intrusive thoughts and compulsions based on **irrational fear**.
Panic Attacks	Intense episodes of fear and physical distress.
Paraphilic Disorders	Sexual behaviors may develop as an escape from **fear or trauma**.
Pathological Gambling	A coping mechanism to suppress **fear of failure or emotional distress**.
Pavor Nocturnus (Night Terrors)	Fear-based sleep disturbances linked to past trauma.
Pedophilic Disorder	Fear-driven, maladaptive coping or defense mechanism.
Personality Disorder: Antisocial	Fear of vulnerability results in **defensive, aggressive behaviors**.
Personality Disorder: Borderline (EUPD)	Fear of abandonment leads to emotional instability and impulsivity.
Personality Disorder: Impulsive	Impulsivity may stem from avoiding **fear-based emotions**.

Appendix 3: Pathologies linked to Vaded with Fear

Pathology	Relation to "Vaded with Fear" in Resource Therapy
Personality Disorder: Obsessive-Compulsive	Fear of imperfection, disorder, or losing control.
Personality Disorder: Paranoid	Fear of betrayal, harm, or deception by others.
Personality Disorder: Schizoid	Social withdrawal due to **deep-rooted fear of connection**.
Pica	Fear-based coping through non-nutritive eating behaviors.
Psychomotor Agitation	Restlessness due to excessive **fear-driven stress**.
Post-Traumatic Stress Disorder (PTSD)	Trauma-induced **Vaded with Fear** states causing flashbacks, anxiety, and avoidance.
Pyromania	Fire-setting may be an outlet for suppressed **fear-based distress**.
Rage as Protection for a Fragile State	Anger shields against deeper **fear-based** emotional pain.
Rumination Disorder (Eating Disorder)	A compulsive, fear-driven focus on past distressing events.

Pathology	Relation to "Vaded with Fear" in Resource Therapy
Selective Mutism	Fear of speaking due to social anxiety or trauma.
Self-Harming Behavior	A way to manage overwhelming **fear-based emotional pain**.
Sexual Sadism Disorder	Control over others may stem from a **fear-based need for power**.
Sleep Disturbance	Anxiety due to **fear-based stress or trauma**.
Sleep-Wake Disorder	Fear-related disturbances in sleep regulation.
Social Phobia	Fear of rejection, or failure in social settings.
Somatic Symptom and Related Disorder	Fear manifests as physical symptoms without medical explanation.
Specific Phobia	**Intense, irrational fear** of objects or situations.
Suicidality	Fear of continued emotional pain, hopelessness, and isolation.
Transvestic Disorder	A coping mechanism for managing underlying **fear or anxiety**.
Trauma and Stressor-	Fear states stuck in past traumatic events.

Appendix 3: Pathologies linked to Vaded with Fear

Pathology	Relation to "Vaded with Fear" in Resource Therapy
Related Disorders	
Trichotillomania (Hair Pulling Disorder)	Fear-based compulsion to relieve stress.
Voyeuristic Disorder	A way to manage **fear of direct intimacy or connection**.
Withdrawal	Fear of interaction, vulnerability, or failure.
Workaholism	Fear of inadequacy or failure, leading to compulsive overworking.

Appendix 4: Pathologies linked to Vaded with Rejection

Table 14: Vaded with Rejection Pathologies

Pathology	Relation to "Vaded with Rejection" in Resource Therapy
Acute Stress Disorder	Intense stress response due to rejection-based trauma or abandonment.
Addictions	Substance or behavioral addiction as an escape from **deep-seated feelings of rejection**.
Aggression to Others	A defensive reaction to prevent further **rejection or perceived humiliation**.
Adjustment Disorder	Difficulty adapting due to fear of **not being accepted** in a new situation.
Anger as Protection for a Fragile State	Anger masks deep feelings of **unworthiness and rejection**.
Anorexia Nervosa	Fear of rejection tied to **body image, control, and perfectionism**.

Appendix 4: Pathologies linked to Vaded with Rejection

Pathology	Relation to "Vaded with Rejection" in Resource Therapy
Antisocial Personality Disorder	Rejection fuels distrust, **detachment from emotional connection**, and disregard for others.
Anxiety Disorders	Anxiety linked to **fear of social rejection, criticism, or failure**.
Avoidant/Restrictive Food Intake Disorder	Food avoidance driven by **fear of being judged or controlled**.
Binge-Eating Disorder	Overeating as a coping mechanism for **feeling unloved or unwanted**.
Body Dysmorphic Disorder	Obsession over perceived flaws due to **fear of rejection based on appearance**.
Borderline Personality Disorder	Extreme **fear of abandonment** leading to emotional instability and impulsivity.
Bulimia Nervosa	Cyclical behavior driven by **shame and fear of rejection regarding body image**.
Business Phobia	Fear of **failing and being rejected in professional settings**.

Pathology	Relation to "Vaded with Rejection" in Resource Therapy
Compulsive Shopping	Seeking validation through possessions to compensate for **low self-worth**.
Conversion Disorder	Emotional distress from rejection **manifesting as physical symptoms**.
Delayed Ejaculation	Performance anxiety tied to **fears of inadequacy or rejection**.
Depersonalization/Derealization Disorder	Disconnecting from reality as a response to **intense rejection trauma**.
Disruptive, Impulse Control, and Conduct Disorders	Acting out due to **feeling unwanted or rejected by authority figures**.
Elimination Disorders	Fear-based bodily reactions linked to **early experiences of shame and rejection**.
Enuresis	Bedwetting tied to **early-life feelings of rejection and insecurity**.

Appendix 4: Pathologies linked to Vaded with Rejection

Pathology	Relation to "Vaded with Rejection" in Resource Therapy
Encopresis	Loss of bowel control as a reaction to **shame and rejection-related stress**.
Erectile Disorder	Anxiety from **fear of sexual inadequacy and rejection by a partner**.
Excoriation Disorder	Skin-picking as a response to **internalized shame and rejection**.
Exhibitionistic Disorder	Seeking **attention and validation** to counter feelings of rejection.
Feeding and Eating Disorders	Relationship with food shaped by **early-life rejection experiences**.
Feeling Unlovable	A core experience of **Vaded with Rejection**, leading to emotional distress.
Feelings of Ineptitude	Rooted in childhood rejection, leading to **self-doubt and low confidence**.
Female Orgasmic Disorder	Fear of rejection or emotional disconnection affecting sexual response.

Pathology	Relation to "Vaded with Rejection" in Resource Therapy
Female Sexual Interest/Arousal Disorder	Suppressed sexuality due to past **rejection or emotional wounds**.
Fetishistic Disorder	Sexual focus on objects as a **detachment from fear of rejection in relationships**.
Gender Dysphoria	Deep distress over **rejection of one's gender identity** by society or family.
Histrionic Personality Disorder	Excessive need for attention to compensate for **rejection wounds**.
Hoarding Disorder	Accumulation of objects as **a barrier against emotional rejection**.
Inability to be Alone	Fear of **abandonment and rejection**, needing constant external validation.
Inability to be Real Self	Suppressing true identity due to **fear of rejection**.
Insomnia Disorder	Racing thoughts about **past rejection or future fears** preventing sleep.

Appendix 4: Pathologies linked to Vaded with Rejection

Pathology	Relation to "Vaded with Rejection" in Resource Therapy
Kleptomania	Stealing as a **self-soothing behavior** tied to feelings of unworthiness.
Low Self-Worth	A defining trait of **Vaded with Rejection**, influencing behavior and emotions.
Male Hypoactive Sexual Desire Disorder	Sexual avoidance due to **fear of rejection or past emotional wounds**.
Narcissism	Overcompensation for deep-seated **fears of rejection and inadequacy**.
Narcissistic Personality Disorder	Inflated self-image as a defense against **internalized rejection wounds**.
Nightmare Disorder	Dreams processing **trauma or rejection-related fears**.
Obsessive-Compulsive Disorder (OCD)	Rituals to control outcomes and avoid **feeling rejected or imperfect**.
Over-Competitiveness	Fear of failure and **rejection drives extreme achievement behaviors**.

Pathology	Relation to "Vaded with Rejection" in Resource Therapy
Paraphilic Disorders	Seeking **control and acceptance** through non-traditional sexual behaviors.
Pathological Gambling	Risk-taking as an escape from **feelings of rejection and worthlessness**.
Pedophilic Disorder	Unresolved rejection issues influencing inappropriate coping mechanisms.
Personality Disorder: Antisocial	Emotional detachment due to **fear of rejection and betrayal**.
Personality Disorder: Avoidant	Extreme social withdrawal due to **fear of rejection and criticism**.
Personality Disorder: Borderline (EUPD)	Intense emotional responses linked to **abandonment fears**.
Personality Disorder: Impulsive	Impulsive actions fueled by **a need for validation**.
Personality Disorder: Narcissistic	Defense mechanism against **deep-seated rejection wounds**.

Appendix 4: Pathologies linked to Vaded with Rejection

Pathology	Relation to "Vaded with Rejection" in Resource Therapy
Personality Disorder: Obsessive-Compulsive	Hyper-control to avoid **rejection through imperfection.**
Personality Disorder: Paranoid	Mistrust and defensiveness due to **early-life rejection experiences.**
Pica	Eating non-food items as a self-soothing **response to rejection-based stress.**
Premature Ejaculation	Performance anxiety tied to **fears of rejection or inadequacy.**
Psychomotor Agitation	Restlessness due to **internalized rejection stress.**
Pyromania	Fire-setting as **an outlet for rejection-based frustration.**
Rage as Protection for a Fragile State	Anger shields **deeper feelings of rejection and emotional pain.**
Relationship Blame	Blaming others due to **fear of personal rejection or inadequacy.**
Rumination Disorder (Eating Disorder)	Overthinking past rejection experiences, fueling emotional distress.

Pathology	Relation to "Vaded with Rejection" in Resource Therapy
Selective Mutism	Fear of speaking due to **rejection anxiety in social settings**.
Self-Harming Behavior	Physical pain as an escape from **emotional rejection pain**.
Sexual Masochism Disorder	Seeking control over rejection through **pain or humiliation**.
Sexual Sadism Disorder	Exerting control to **counter feelings of past rejection**.
Sleep Disturbance	Fear of rejection leads to **rumination and disrupted sleep**.
Social Phobia	Deep-rooted fear of **social rejection and criticism**.
Somatic Symptom and Related Disorder	Physical symptoms manifest from **emotional rejection wounds**.
Specific Phobia	Fear linked to rejection-based **trauma or self-worth issues**.
Suicidality	Deep despair from **chronic feelings of rejection and unworthiness**.

Appendix 4: Pathologies linked to Vaded with Rejection

Pathology	Relation to "Vaded with Rejection" in Resource Therapy
Transvestic Disorder	Coping with rejection-related identity struggles.
Trauma and Stressor-Related Disorders	Rejection trauma fuels **stress and emotional pain**.
Trichotillomania	Hair-pulling as a **self-soothing response to rejection stress**.
Voyeuristic Disorder	Watching others instead of engaging due to **fear of direct rejection**.
Withdrawal	Social isolation due to **fear of further rejection**.
Workaholism	Overworking to **gain validation and avoid feelings of rejection**.

Appendix 5: Pathologies by Diagnoses

VWF:	Vaded with Fear	VWR:	Vaded with Rejection
VWC:	Vaded with Confusion	VWD:	Vaded with Disappointment
RO:	Retro Original	RA:	Retro Avoiding
C:	Conflicted	D:	Dissonant
O:	Organic		

Table 15: RT Diagnoses by Pathologies

DSM-Diagnosis/ Presenting concern	RT-Diagnosis	When Retro Avoiding: Underlying Vaded State
Abreactions	• VWF	
Acute stress disorder	• VWF / VWR	
Addictions	• RA	VWF/VWR
Aggression to others	• RA (or sociopathic or psychopathic)	VWF/VWR
Aggression to self	• RA	VWF
Agoraphobia	• VWF	

Appendix 5: Pathologies by Diagnoses

DSM-Diagnosis/ Presenting concern	RT-Diagnosis	When Retro Avoiding: Underlying Vaded State
Adjustment disorder	• VWF/VWR	
Anger as protection for a fragile state	• RA	VWR/VWF
Anorexia Nervosa	• RA	VWR
Antisocial personality disorder	• RA	VWR/VWF
Anxiety disorders	• VWF/VWR/VWC	
Avoidant personality disorder	• RA	VWR
Avoidant/ restrictive food intake disorder	• RA	VWR
Below par performance	• D	
Binge-eating disorder	• RA	VWR
Blame	• VWC	
Body dysmorphic disorder	• RA	VWF/VWR
Borderline personality disorder (EUPD)	• VWF/VWR/RA	VWF/VWR
Bulimia Nervosa	• RA	VWR
Business phobia	• VWF/VWR	
Chronic fatigue	• C	

DSM-Diagnosis/ Presenting concern	RT-Diagnosis	When Retro Avoiding: Underlying Vaded State
Claustrophobia	• VWF	
Cognitive dissonance	• C	
Complicated bereavement	• VWC/VWD	
Compulsive Shopping	• RA	VWR / rarely: VWF
Confusion over the breakdown of a relationship	• VWC	
Conversion Disorder	• VWF/VWR/O	
Crisis reaction	• VWF	
Delayed Ejaculation	• VWF/VWR/VWC/VWD	
Dependant personality disorder	• RO	
Depersonalization/ Derealization Disorder	• VWF/VWR/O	
Depression	• VWD/O	
DID	• RA/C	VWF
Difficulties to decide something	• C	

Appendix 5: Pathologies by Diagnoses

DSM-Diagnosis/ Presenting concern	RT-Diagnosis	When Retro Avoiding: Underlying Vaded State
Disruptive, impulse control and conduct disorders	• VWR	
Dissociative Amnesia	• VWF	
Dissociative convulsions	• RA	VWF
Elimination disorders	• RA	VWF/VWR
Enuresis	• VWF/VWR/O	
Encopresis	• VWF/VWR/O	
Erectile disorder	• VWF/VWR/VWC/VWD	
Excoriation disorder	• RA	VWF/VWR
Exhibitionistic disorder	• RA	VWR
Existential Fear	• VWC	
Feeding and eating disorders	• RA	VWR
Feeling unlovable	• VWR	
Feelings of ineptitude	• VWR/D	
Female orgasmic disorder	• VWF/VWR/VWC/VWD	
Female sexual interest / arousal disorder	• VWF/VWR/VWC/VWD	

DSM-Diagnosis/ Presenting concern	RT-Diagnosis	When Retro Avoiding: Underlying Vaded State
Fetishistic disorder	• RA/O	VWF/VWR
Frustration in coping ability	• D	
Gender dysphoria	• VWR/O	
Generalized anxiety disorder	• VWF	
Guilt	• VWC	
Histrionic personality disorder	• RO/RA/O	VWR
Hoarding disorder	• RA	VWF/VWR
Hypersomnolence disorder	• O	
Impulsive personality disorder	• RA	VWF/VWR
Inability to be alone	• VWF/VWR	
Inability to be real self	• VWR/D	
Insomnia disorder	• VWF/VWR/VWC/C/O	
Kleptomania	• RO/RA	VWF/VWR
Low self-worth	• VWR	

Appendix 5: Pathologies by Diagnoses

DSM-Diagnosis/ Presenting concern	RT-Diagnosis	When Retro Avoiding: Underlying Vaded State
Male hypoactive sexual desire disorder	• VWF/VWR/VWD/O	
Narcissism	• RA	VWR
Narcissistic personality disorder	• RA	VWR
Narcolepsy	• O	
Nightmare disorder	• VWF/VWR	
Nightmares	• VWF	
Obsessive compulsive personality disorder	• RA	VWF/VWR
OCD	• RA	VWF/VWR
Over-competitiveness	• VWR	
Panic attacks	• VWF	
Paranoid personality disorder	• VWF/VWR	
Paraphilic disorder	• RA/O	VWF/VWR
Passive-aggressive behaviour	• RO	
Pathological gambling	• RA	VWF/VWR
Pavor Nocturnus	• VWF	
Podophilic disorder	• VWF/VWR/O	

DSM-Diagnosis/ Presenting concern	RT-Diagnosis	When Retro Avoiding: Underlying Vaded State
Personality disorder: Antisocial	• RA/O	VWF/VWR
Personality disorder: Avoidant	• RA	VWR
Personality disorder: Borderline (EUPD)	• VWF/VWR/RA	VWF/VWR
Personality disorder: Dependant	• RO	
Personality disorder: Histrionic	• RO/RA/O	VWR
Personality disorder: Impulsive	• RA	VWF/VWR
Personality disorder: Narcissistic	• RA	VWR
Personality disorder: Obsessive compulsive	• RA	VWF/VWR
Personality disorder: Paranoid	• VWF/VWR	
Personality disorder: Schizoid	• RA	VWF
Personality disorder: Schizotypal	• O	
Pica	• VWF/VWR/RA	VWF/VWR

Appendix 5: Pathologies by Diagnoses

DSM-Diagnosis/ Presenting concern	RT-Diagnosis	When Retro Avoiding: Underlying Vaded State
Pouting	• RO	
Premature ejaculation	• VWR/O	
Procrastination	• C	
Prolonged and intense feelings of loss	• VWD	
Prolonged and intense confusion of loss	• VWC	
Psychomotor agitation	• RA	VWF/VWR
PTSD	• VWF	
Pyromania	• RA	VWF/VWR
Rage as a tantrum response	• RO	
Rage as protection for a fragile state	• RA	VWF/VWR
Relationship blame	• VWR/VWC/VWD	
Rumination	• VWC	
Rumination disorder (Eating disorder)	• VWF/VWR/VWD/O	
Schizoid personality disorder	• RA	VWF
Schizotypal personality disorder	• O	

DSM-Diagnosis/ Presenting concern	RT-Diagnosis	When Retro Avoiding: Underlying Vaded State
Selective Mutism	• VWF/VWR	
Self-harming behaviour	• RA	VWF / rarely: VWR
Sexual masochism disorder	• VWR	
Sexual sadism disorder	• VWF/VWR	
Sleep disturbance	• VWF/VWR/VWC/C	
Sleep-wake disorder	• VWF	
Social phobia	• VWF/VWR	
Somatic symptom and related disorder	• RA	VWF/VWR
Specific phobia	• VWF/VWR	
Sporting slumps	• D	
Suicidality	• VWF/VWR/VWD VWC (guilt)/ RA (escape)	VWF/VWR
Transvestic disorder	• O/VWF/VWR	
Trauma and stressor related disorders	• VWF/VWR	
Trichotillomania	• RA	VWF/VWR

Appendix 5: Pathologies by Diagnoses

DSM-Diagnosis/ Presenting concern	RT-Diagnosis	When Retro Avoiding: Underlying Vaded State
Voyeuristic disorder	• VWF/VWR/O	
Withdrawal	• VWF/VWR/VWD/RO	
Workaholism	• RA	VWF/VWR
Writers block	• D	

Glossary

Changing Chairs Introject Action:

This is a Resource Therapy activity designed to assist patients to hold less confusion in relation to an Introject. The patient is instructed to imagine the essence of an Introject in an empty chair, to say everything that they would like to say to that Introject, then to move into that chair and speak as the Introject back to the patient, expressing how what was just said made the Introject feel. It often results in a cathartic sense of understanding.

Conscious:

The Conscious is held by the Resource State that is currently aware and behaving. When a different Resource State takes over the Conscious, sense of self, emotions, behavior and abilities, change. The Conscious awareness may change from intellectual and reflective to reactive and emotional with a change of Resource State.

Conflicted States:

Resources in a conflicted condition are in a level of conflict with another Resource to the extent that the individual experiences psychological distress. While it is common and appropriate that Resources hold different opinions (I would really like the car, and there's no way I can afford a new car) Conflicted States achieve a level of conflict that becomes stressful to the patient.

Dissonant State:

A Resource State that is in the Conscious at the wrong time.

Glossary

Resource State:

A personality part that was created by the repetition of returning over and over again to a coping skill. It is a physiological part of the nervous system created by axon and dendrite growth and trained synaptic firings. Each Resource manifests the traits of the coping skills that formed it. Each will have its own level of emotion, intellect, and abilities. Whenever a person is Conscious there is a Resource holding the Conscious.

Resource Personality Theory:

A theory that assumes that personality is composed of separate parts, called Resources. Resource therapists assume that the most direct way to promote change is to work specifically with the Resource that is troubled, rather than with an intellectual state that can easily talk about the problem.

Imagery Check:

At the beginning of the intervention the Vivify Specific Action is used to locate the Resource that requires change. Following the intervention, the Imagery Check is used to return to this initial image to test the effectiveness of the intervention, to give the patient practice, and to give the patient confidence that the intervention has been effective. If the Imagery Check reveals no change, there is an indication that more therapeutic work is required relating to the issue.

Intellectual Memory:

An Intellectual Memory is one that when recalling an occurrence, the emotional experience is not relived. Intellectual memories may be held by Surface States that were not holding the Conscious during the original event. Sensory Experience Memories differ from Intellectual memories in that the recalling process includes the emotional experience of the original event.

Intellectual Protector States:

These are protector states that come to the Conscious to protect the personality from the emotional feelings of Vaded States. During therapy Intellectual Protector States may attempt to block the therapist from Bridging to the ISE where a resolution is needed. The patient intellectualizes, rather than feels. The Intellectual Protector State normally dislikes the Vaded State, seeing it as a state that gets in the way.

Initial Sensitizing Event:

This is a difficult and emotional event that has overwhelmed a Normal Resource, causing it to become a Vaded State. Later, when this Vaded State comes to the Conscious it brings with it the same negative emotional feelings that it experienced during the Initial Sensitizing Event.

Introject:

A Resource's internalized impression of another person, an animal, or something inanimate. Most Introjects are experienced as emotionally positive, but Vaded States hold Introjects from which they have experienced negative emotion. Introjects have only the power given them by the Resource States that hold them.

Normal States:

Resources in the Normal condition exhibit psychological health. They function well both externally and within the personality. They are not conflicted with other states, and they do not hold psychological distress.

Protector States:

Therapeutic resistance is caused by protector states. These are states that attempt to protect fragile Vaded States from coming to the Conscious where the personality would experience the overwhelming emotions they feel. Behavioural examples of Protector States coming into the Conscious include anger, withdrawal, intellectualizing, and perseveration. Protector States merely deflect attention, while Retro Avoiding States conduct unwanted behavior to save the personality from the negative feelings of Vaded States.

Glossary

Retro Avoiding States:

Retro States that learn to hold the Conscious to avoid the experience of a Vaded State. In problem-gambling, the state that gambles is a Retro Avoiding State. It has learned to protect the patient from a painful vaded emotion-filled state by filling the Consciousness with gambling activity. Other Resources will dislike this gambling Resource, but the Retro State believes its role in saving the patient from the negative emotions of the Vaded State is more important than the disapproval it endures. Other examples of Retro Avoiding States include the states that cause a client to feel numb, states that act out OCD behavior, self-harming states, and states that are involved with eating disorder activities. These states will hold a strong compulsion to maintain their "helping" behavior as long as the emotional state they protect the patient from remains vaded.

Retro Original States:

These are states that have learned a functional coping skill in childhood that is no longer wanted by the patient. Much antisocial behavior is a result of Retro Original States and examples include passive aggressive behavior and rage. These Retro States will continue to see their role as important, until they can be negotiated with to take on an altered or lesser role.

Retro States:

Resources that, when conscious, act in ways that other Resources (and usually other people) find problematic. There are two types of Retro States, Retro Original States and Retro Avoiding States. Antisocial behavior, gambling, OCD behavior, and eating disorder behavior are examples of Retro States assuming the Conscious.

Sensory Experience Memory:

A Sensory Experience Memory is one that, when experienced, the person emotionally re-experiences the original event. A Sensory Experience Memory is most normally experienced only closer in time to the event. For example, immediately after experiencing something emotional, good or bad, it is common to relive the emotional experience during recall.

Sensory Experience Memories may only be experienced in the longer term when the Resource State that had the original experience is holding the Conscious.

States Vaded with Confusion:

Following an Initial Sensitizing Event, this Resource is left with a fundamental and profound level of confusion, and its response to this lack of ability to understand is a profoundly uncomfortable unknowing. While Resources Vaded with Fear, Rejection, or Disappointment hold a distinctly negative emotion, Resources Vaded with Confusion exhibit anxiety about what is not known to a level that is problematic to the patient. These states are often characterised by rumination.

States Vaded with Disappointment:

This Resource takes on an overwhelming feeling of disappointment because of the gulf between what was desired or expected in life and the perceived reality. It is not the magnitude of what has happened that vades this Resource, it is the interpretation of what has happened that vades the state. These states cause psychological depression.

States Vaded with Fear:

Resources Vaded with Fear are carrying internal fear everywhere they go and when they come to the Conscious, they bring it to the surface with them. Resources Vaded with Fear prevent clients from feeling free to live their lives in a way that they choose, and they are the root of many psychological disturbances.

States Vaded with Rejection:

Resources Vaded with Rejection feel unlovable. This feeling of not being good enough drives the client, when it comes to the Conscious, to experience emotions of disempowerment, and they sometimes create a need to be perfect, as expressed in over competitiveness, out-of-control purchasing, and eating disorders.

Glossary

Surface Resources:

Surface Resources, as opposed to Underlying Resources, are those that are observing the Conscious State. They will have a memory of what they have observed, and they may communicate with the Conscious State when they are surface. A Surface State can assume the Conscious position, or it can sink to an underlying position.

The Separation Sieve:

The Separation Sieve is a metaphoric Action that enables the client an opportunity to experiment with letting something go, without first having to commit to it. With eyes closed, the client is asked to imagine being in a giant sieve where the client can slip through, while temporarily leaving what may not be wanted. The key is to tell the client that this is just an experiment, and everything can return to normal, if that is what the client chooses. If the client likes the feeling of no longer keeping what is in the sieve (e.g. anger), then it can be swooshed away.

Underlying Resources:

Underlying Resources, as opposed to Surface Resources, are dissociated from the Conscious. While a Surface State can become an Underlying State at any time, some Underlying States rarely come to the surface. Most childhood states are Underlying Resources, with memories not readily available to Surface States. Vaded States are most commonly Underlying States, which occasionally come to the Conscious harbouring feelings of angst.

Vaded Avoided States:

Vaded States are problematic for a client in two ways, they can be Vaded Conscious States or Vaded Avoided States. Vaded Avoided States do not hold the Conscious, but when they come near or temporarily into the Conscious a 'helping state' (a Retro Avoiding State) uses an addictive behavior to force the Vaded State out of the Conscious, saving the patient from having to re-experience the overwhelmingly bad feelings of the Vaded State.

Vaded Conscious States:

Vaded States are problematic for a patient in two ways; they can be Vaded Conscious States or Vaded Avoided States. Vaded Conscious States come into and hold the Conscious, causing the patient to feel emotional and out-of-control while they do. When they come to the surface they bring with them their overwhelming negative emotions, and this is what the client experiences when they are in the Conscious.

Vaded States:

Resources that were in a Normal Condition prior to experiencing an Initial Sensitizing Event that, because there was no form of crisis intervention, left them feeling chronically overwhelmed with the negative emotions. These Resources, while in a Vaded Condition, are the cause of much pathology.

Vivify Specific:

This refers to vivifying a specific instance when a Resource has been in the Conscious, to bring it back into the Conscious during therapy for the purpose of intervention. Some clients attempt to give the therapist general times a Resource has been out, and this presentation will not bring the desired Resource into the Conscious. The Vivify Specific Action requires gaining very specific detail relating to a time the state has been conscious. During this process present tense language is used and the client's eyes are closed.

Bibliography

Arif, A. (2014). Resource Therapy: Ego State Therapy of Gordon Emmerson. Jakarta, Indonesia. Media Space. ISBN 978-6-0271131-9-0. https://bukukita.com/Psikologi-dan-Pengembangan-Diri/Psikologi/131387-Resource-Therapy-:-Ego-State-Therapy-of-Gordon-Emmerson.html

Berne, E. (1957). Ego states in Psychotherapy. American Journal of Psychotherapy, 11, 293 -309. Transactional analysis in psychotherapy: A systematic individual and social psychiatry. New York: Grove Press.

Blakemore, C., and Price, D. J. (1987), "The organization and post-natal development of area 18 of the cat's visual cortex", Journal of Physiology, 384, pp. 293–309.

Boswell, Louis K. (1987). The Initial Sensitizing Event of emotional disorders. Medical Hypnoanalysis Journal, 2(4), Dec, pp. 155-160.

Bryck, Richard L.; Fisher, Philip A. (2011). Training the brain:

Practical applications of neural plasticity from the intersection of cognitive neuroscience, developmental psychology, and prevention science. American Psychologist, Jul 25.

Buisseret, Pierre, Gary-Bobo, Elyane, and Imbert, Michel (1982)."Plasticity in the kitten's visual cortex:

Effects of the suppression of visual experience upon the orientational properties of visual cortical cells", Developmental Brain Research, 4 (4), pp. 417–26.

de Graaf, Theo K., & van der Molen, Gjalt M. (1996). A Personal Sensitization Factor (PSF) mediating between life events and post-traumatic psychiatric or psychosomatic disease in adult life. The European Journal of Psychiatry, 10:3, Jul-Sep. 137-148.

Bibliography

Emmerson, G. J. (1999). What lies within: Ego states and other internal personifications. Australian Journal of Clinical Hypnotherapy & Hypnosis, 20(1), pp. 13-22.

Emmerson, G. J. (2003, 2007, 2010). Ego state therapy. Carmarthen, Wales: Crown House Publishing

Emmerson, G. J. (2006). Advanced skills and interventions in therapeutic counseling. Carmarthen, Wales: Crown House Publishing

Emmerson, G. J. (2011). Ego state personality theory. Australian Journal of Clinical Hypnotherapy and Hypnosis, 33(2), pp. 5-23.

Emmerson, G. J. (2012). Healthy Parts Happy Self. Charleston, SC, CreateSpace.

Emmerson, G. J. (2013). Ego State Conditions. Australian Journal of Clinical Hypnotherapy and Hypnosis, 35(1), 2013. pp. 5-27.

Emmerson, G. J. (2014). Resource Therapy. Blackwood Victoria, Australia: Old Golden Point Press.

Emmerson, G. J. (2015). Learn Resource Therapy. Blackwood Victoria, Australia: Old Golden Point Press. ISBN 978-0-9924995-3-2.

Emmerson, G. J. (2017). Sensory experience memory in Resource Therapy. International Journal of Clinical and Experimental Hypnosis, 65(1), 120–131. Doi: 10.1080/00207144.2017.1246882

Federn, P. (1952). Ego psychology and the psychosis. London: Image Publishers.

Guntrip, H. (1961). Personality structure and human interaction. London: Hogarth.

Hebb, D.O. (1949). *The Organization of Behavior.* New York: Wiley & Sons.

Holopainen, Debbi; Emmerson, Gordon J. (2002). Ego state therapy and the treatment of depression. Australian Journal of Clinical Hypnotherapy & Hypnosis, Vol 23(2), pp. 89-99.

Jacobson, E. (1964). The self and the object world. New York: International University Press.

Kernberg, O. (1976). Object relations theory and clinical psychoanalysis. New York: Jasonc Aronson.

Levin, Berry. (2010). Interaction of perinatal and pre-pubertal factors with genetic predisposition in the development of neural pathways involved in the regulation of energy homeostasis. Brain Research, Sep2010, Vol. 1350, p. 10-17

Lynch, T. (2019). The Bella Journey Children's Books on Resource Parts. Wickham NSW, Australia. https://www.tracylynch.com.au/books

Mackey, Edward F. (2009). Age regression: A case study. Annals of the American Psychotherapy Assn. 12(4), Winter, 46-49.

Muir, Darwin W., Dalhousie, U., and Mitchell, Donald E. (1973), "Visual resolution and experience: Acuity deficits in cats following early selective visual deprivation", Science. 180 (4084), pp. 420–2.

Nalendra, A. (2024). Resource Therapy in Action. Bandung, Indonesia. Alguskha Nalendra & Associates. https://www.alguskha.com/book-urt/

Nalendra, A. (2024). Understanding Resource Therapy. Bandung, Indonesia. Alguskha Nalendra & Associates. https://www.alguskha.com/book-urt/

Nalendra, A. (2020). Performance in the 5th Dimension: A comprehensive Big Book in Applying Resource Therapy for Performance Treatment. Bandung, Indonesia. https://www.alguskha.com/book-pit5d/

Opperman, M. C., (2007). The creation and manifestation of reality through the re-enactment of subconscious conclusions and decisions. Dissertation Abstracts International: Section B: The Sciences and Engineering, 68:5-B, 3406.

Ritzman, Thomas A., (1992). Importance of identifying the initial sensitizing event. Medical Hypnoanalysis Journal, 7(3), Sep. pp. 98-104.

Schrott, L. M. (1997), "Effect of training and environment on brain morphology and behavior", ActaPaediatrica, 422, pp. 45–7.

Bibliography

Wark, Robert C., and Peck, Carol K. (1982), "Behavioral consequences of early visual exposure to contours of a single orientation", Developmental Brain Research, 5 (2), pp. 218–21.

Watkins, J. G. (1978). The therapeutic self. New York: Human Sciences.

Watkins, J. G. & Watkins, H. H. (1997). Ego states: Theory and therapy. New York: W. W. Norton & Co.

Wilkinson, Frances, and McGill, U. (1995), "Orientation, density and size as cues to texture segmentation in kittens", Vision Research, 35 (17), pp. 2463–78.

Winnicott, D. W. (1965). The maturational process and the facilitation environment. New York: International Universities Press.

Weiss, E. (1950). Principles of psychodynamics. New York: Grune & Stratton.

Index

Index

About the authors

Dr Gordon Emmerson is the author of the books 'Ego State Therapy' (2003, 2007, 2010), 'Advanced Techniques in Therapeutic Counseling (2006), Healthy Parts Happy Self (2012), and Resource Therapy (2014). He developed Resource Personality Theory and Therapy and has developed techniques for working with many psychological conditions. Dr Emmerson has published numerous refereed articles and has conducted and published experimental clinical research . Dr Emmerson has conducted workshops in Australia, South Africa, Germany, the UK, New Zealand, the US, and the Middle East. He makes keynote conference and convention addresses on his therapeutic approaches.

Further information can be found at http://www.resourcetherapy.com.

Christiane Essing is a member of the board of Resource Therapy International as Director of Training Resources and Executive Director for the German-speaking area. She is co-founder of the Resource Therapy Center Germany (Ressourcen-Therapie-Zentrum Deutschland) and is giving national and international Clinical and Advanced Trainings. Christiane is also engaged in establishing and supervising the first RT conducted childrens home.

After having encountered Resource Therapy on a congress in 2015, she has devoted her professional life to spreading this immensely effective therapy form in the world. In her private practice in Bavaria, Germany she is working with children, adolescents and adults.

Further information can be found at http://www.resourcetherapy.com. and at https://www.ressourcen-therapie-zentrum-deutschland.de